P9-EDX-311

Self-Directed IRAs: Building Retirement Wealth Through Alternative Investing

Richard Desich, Sr.

Foreword and Introduction by:
John Bowens,
Equity University National Education Specialist

Copyright © 2015 Equity University

All rights reserved.

ISBN-13: 978-0692346532 (Equity University)

Editor-in-chief: Keith Blazek

Table of Contents

Disclaimer   iii

How Do I Access the Bonus Resources Found Throughout the Book?   iv

Foreword: From Humble Beginnings, an Industry Leader Emerges   vii

       by John Bowens

Introduction: A Retirement Reality   xiii

       by John Bowens

1   Who Is This Book For?   pg 1

2   The ROI Beyond the ROI: Self-Directed IRAs Impacting Lives Across America   pg 11

3   The Upside to Alternatives   pg 35

4   Understanding IRAs – Types of Accounts   pg 45

5   How Self-Directed Accounts Can Offer Diversity with the Most Power   pg 63

6   Toolbox of Options – What Makes Sense for You?   pg 75

7   It's Time to Start Self-Directed Investing! – Understanding the Process   pg 83

8   Investing in Rehab Properties   pg 91

9   Investing in Rental Properties   pg 103

10   Investing in Foreclosures   pg 113

11   Investing in Commercial Real Estate   pg 121

12   Investing in Tax Liens   pg 129

13   Investing in Raw Land   pg 137

14   Investing in Notes, Mortgages and Deeds of Trust   pg 147

15	Investing in Probate	pg 155
16	Investing in Real Estate Options	pg 161
17	Investing in Precious Metals	pg 167
18	Investing in Private Equity, LLCs and REITs	pg 175
19	Not Enough Money Yet? – How to Get Started Anyway	pg 181
20	What You Need to Know – Rules, Regulations and Prohibited Transactions	pg 195
21	Importance of Due Diligence and Your Support Team	pg 203
22	Check Before You Invest – Identifying and Preventing Fraud and Scams	pg 211
23	It's Time to Cash In! – Taking Distributions	pg 225
24	Building and Keeping Wealth for Generations to Come	pg 231
25	Getting Started – Selecting a Custodian	pg 241
26	Time to Take Control of Your Financial Future	pg 247
	Contact Us for More Information	pg 251
	About the Author	pg 252
	Available Resources	pg 253
	Footnotes/References	pg 265

Disclaimer

This material is presented with the understanding that <u>neither Equity Trust Company nor Equity University (jointly referred to as "Equity"), its representatives, officers, and affiliates provide planning, investing, tax, or legal advice.</u>

Questions relevant to your specific tax, investment, accounting, legal, estate or planning needs should be addressed to practicing members of those professions only after fully disclosing all relevant and material facts regarding your specific situation. <u>Equity does not endorse any speaker, presenter or any printed materials belonging to any third party and provided herein.</u>

The information, ideas, and suggestions contained herein have been developed from sources, including publications and research, that are considered and believed to be reliable, <u>but cannot be guaranteed insofar as they apply to any particular taxpayer or individual desiring to establish an asset protection, estate planning, investment, retirement, education or tax plan. We strongly recommend that you engage the assistance of a competent, qualified professional before implementing any ideas presented in the material.</u>

Equity and its representatives specifically <u>disclaim any liability, loss, or risk, personal or otherwise, incurred as a direct or indirect consequence of the use or application of any of the techniques or contents presented in this material.</u>

Equity, its affiliates, representatives, or officers <u>do not provide any legal or tax advice.</u> We provide education on topics related to Self-Directed Retirement Accounts, and recommend that you work with a financial professional to determine whether an investment product, plan, or idea is right for you.

How Do I Access the Bonus Resources Found Throughout the Book?

We've packed this book with bonus education and resources to maximize your time with us and to help provide a more complete understanding on the topics we will discuss. The bonus resources are conveniently hosted within one customized user account that you can access at any time.

To set up your free user account you will need your name, email address, and a password of your choosing. Once you set up your account you will be able to log in at any time to download the educational bonus resources.

Get Started Today:

https://uz966.infusionsoft.com/app/page/ebook-resources

Richard Desich, Sr.

Foreword: From Humble Beginnings, an Industry Leader Emerges

by John Bowens, Equity University National Education Specialist

Equity Trust Company is a leading custodian of self-directed retirement accounts with over 130,000 clients in all 50 states and $12 billion of retirement plan assets under administration. Despite its successful growth over the last four decades, Equity Trust Company came from humble beginnings and is still a family-owned-and-operated Company.

Richard Desich, Sr., the Founder and Chairman of the Board, grew up two blocks away from a steel mill in Lorain, Ohio. The value of hard work and education was instilled in him from an early age. After serving four years in the United States Armed Forces, Mr. Desich attended night classes until he graduated from college.

After putting himself through school he quickly rose through the ranks and become one of the top financial advisors at a brokerage company. Mr. Desich experienced stock market volatility firsthand and yearned for another solution.

Just like you, he would not accept the status quo and was searching for a way to diversify his portfolio.

He had been exposed to real estate as a youth because his grandparents (who raised him) operated a small rental unit on their property and he remembered the steady residual income they received from the unit. With his mind racing with ideas and opportunity he asked himself, "Why couldn't I invest in real estate like I invest in stocks and bonds?"

At this point in 1974, Mr. Desich had already established his own brokerage firm called Mid-Ohio Securities. He knew he was on to something – but investing in real estate with your IRA…was this even legal?

He wanted to take advantage of the power of compounding interest within a tax-advantaged retirement account, but was still skeptical. It sounded good on paper but, like you, he wasn't sure if it was real.

Since IRAs were fairly new at this time, Mr. Desich sought out one of the top ERISA attorneys in the country. (An ERISA attorney is someone who specializes in the tax laws as it relates to retirement investing.)

He took a leap of faith and spent thousands of dollars to learn that the Internal Revenue Code in fact permits non-traditional investments in an IRA.

He saw how powerful this strategy could (and would) become, but like many of you, still had his doubts. He was skeptical. Why had he never heard of this? Why wasn't anyone doing it? Even his trusted CPA hadn't heard of the concept.

In his research Mr. Desich learned that most brokerage firms didn't offer alternative investing options (within or outside an IRA). He learned that the banks didn't offer it either.

So now it made sense. He understood that it was legal and possible, but he needed to know what he was allowed to invest in with his IRA.

His ERISA attorney told him that a self-directed IRA is no different than any other IRA with another financial company. The only difference is that you can choose the types of investments that are suitable for you. He was able to choose to diversify his portfolio into assets such as real estate, precious metals, tax liens, and all types of other options rather than relying on only the stocks, mutual funds, and other traditional assets offered by most custodians.

As he continued to research, his ERISA attorney told him that he would need a custodian to invest with a self-directed IRA.

He eventually found one that was a bank trust department and was shocked at the price they were going to charge. How could he grow his retirement savings and build wealth with such a high cost?

Well as I'm sure you're learning, Mr. Desich wasn't about to let something like cost hold him back from an opportunity he believed in. He decided to take the bull by the horns and petitioned the IRS until he was able to turn his brokerage company into its very own passive custodian!

Finally after years of research, hard work, and hundreds of thousands of dollars in attorney and research fees, he knew he could move forward with his idea. In 1983 he received IRS approval for Mid-Ohio Securities to become a passive custodian for self-directed IRAs.

This approval was necessary to facilitate self-directed investments, including the Company's very first one – an investment in a local pharmacy in Lorain, Ohio.

In 1984 Mr. Desich and a group of 22 investors purchased the Ohio drug store. Each investor put in $6,000, and over the next 19 years the investors each made nearly $200,000 through the triple-net-lease investment. The returns far-outpaced what they were currently receiving with their traditional investments and, soon after, other clients approached him to help them learn how to diversify into alternative assets as well. From that moment, an industry leader was born.

Mr. Desich has a passion for education and has made it his mission, and the Company's mission, to educate investors around the country about the power of self-directed IRAs. Mr. Desich had the foresight to see the tremendous potential in the self-directed IRA market and has fought to better educate investors so they have the opportunity to tap into this potential as well. Mr. Desich believed everyone should be able to take advantage of these investments, not just the wealthy.

By 1996 his Company was servicing investors in all 50 states. In 2003, Equity Trust Company was created and obtained a trust charter from the South Dakota Division of Banking. Equity Trust Company purchased the IRA assets from Mid-Ohio Securities, Inc., allowing Mid-Ohio to continue as a brokerage firm, with Equity Trust serving as a passive custodian.

He traveled the country on speaking engagements and founded Retirement Education Group in 2001, now d.b.a. Equity University, to help accomplish this mission.

To this day, Equity Trust Company is still a family-owned Company, and is now run by Mr. Desich's son, Jeffrey Desich, who became CEO in 2008.

Mr. Desich's Company began in an old funeral home with only four employees. The "family feel" has remained intact as the Company has blossomed over the last four decades to over 400 employees with locations in Cleveland, Ohio, Sioux Falls, South Dakota, and Denver, Colorado.

Equity Trust now proudly serves over 130,000 clients and completes tens of thousands of transactions per year, as directed by our clients.

Mr. Desich has been one step ahead of the markets from the beginning. He is considered a pre-eminent authority on IRAs, and specializes in real estate as well as oil and gas. Mr. Desich has been a Board member for Lorain County Community College for over 35 years and is the longest serving Board member for any school in the state of Ohio. As successful as he has been in his career, Mr. Desich has never forgotten his passion for education and his humble beginnings.

As you can see, Equity Trust was founded by an investor like you – someone looking for another, and a better, way to invest for retirement and build wealth. Ever since the humble inception of the Company it has been the Company's mission to educate people around the country and to bring the same opportunities that were identified 40 years ago to the forefront of the industry.

Video: The Equity Trust Difference

For more information about how Equity Trust got started and to hear from the Desich family regarding the Equity Trust difference, please watch this 6-minute video. Set up or log in to your user account to watch it here:

https://equityuniversity.customerhub.net/equity-trust

Introduction: A Retirement Reality

by John Bowens, Equity University National Education Specialist

For some, retirement seems far away – like a distant ship on the horizon that you know you'll have to board, but with plenty of time to figure things out before it arrives. After all, there are still decades of work left before retirement is even an option, right?

For others, the ship is cruising into harbor like a speed boat with no sign of slowing down and no clear instructions on how to board the ship safely. Either way, retirement is something that everyone should be concerned with, regardless of where you are personally or financially as you read this book.

Unfortunately most people don't spend enough time thinking about retirement, let alone consistently planning for it. In fact, I recently read an article that reported the average Americans spend almost as much time planning for a two-week vacation as they do planning for their retirement, which may last as long as 20 or 30 years.

I want you to stop for a second and think about that.

Think of the last vacation you went on, and then think of the amount of time you spent planning it. How does it compare to the amount of time you've spent planning and investing for your retirement? For you and your family's financial future?

Considering that your retirement will (hopefully) last much longer than two weeks, an increased focus on retirement planning is critical for American workers, regardless of how confident they may currently feel in their preparations.

Your retirement should be the best (and longest) vacation you ever have! But for that to be possible you need to start planning, and revisiting your plan consistently, from now until it's time to retire.

The retirement reality is that most individuals will work 40 to 50 years, and the money they set aside during those working years will need to fund a retirement for an additional 20 or 30 years as life expectancy rates have continued to improve. The benefit of living longer is you should have the great joy of being able to spend your retirement years doing the things you love most: pursuing hobbies, relaxing, traveling, visiting family, and spending your hard-earned time as you wish.

But in order to enjoy the benefit of increased life expectancy, you must first set aside enough money during your working years to pay for the value of that time. Too often I've heard horror stories of individuals outliving their retirement savings or having to stress and scramble to make ends meet when they should be relaxing and enjoying the fruits of their labor. A lack of preparation can result in a retirement lifestyle that falls short of what you had hoped and dreamed.

What Do You Want Your Retirement To Look Like?

Whether retirement is 40 years away or 5 years away, you should have a vision of how you would like to be living. For some, it is sipping martinis by the ocean with a loved one, listening to the waves as they lap at the shore, and days consisting of long walks on the beach and leisurely strolls through a local farmers market. Perhaps your ideal retirement includes time fishing for local trout or playing golf at a different course each week.

Maybe you imagine yourself having more adventure and doing all the things you never had a chance to do while you were working. Perhaps retirement means zip-lining through a rain forest in Costa Rica, whitewater rafting down the Colorado River, or hang-gliding in the Outer Banks of North Carolina. It could include visiting exotic places like Morocco, the Egyptian Pyramids, or the ice hotels in the northern reaches of the Netherlands.

Whatever your perfect retirement is, most Americans don't imagine themselves only living on a $1,300 monthly Social Security check, moving in with their children, or selling their home to move into a small apartment to make ends meet. Yet for millions of Americans, lack of planning results in this unfortunate reality.

How to Get There?

The difference between those who live out their retirement dreams and those who must settle for a life of struggle is simple: planning. Those who plan and prepare for retirement have the opportunity to make their retirement dreams a reality. Those who simply go with the flow and never employ a well-thought-out retirement strategy often end up working longer and living on less.

The first step to getting to your goal is to envision what your ideal retirement looks like, and write it down. Share it with your loved ones and remind yourself every day of the long-term goals you are working toward. It will remind you what you're working, sacrificing, and saving for and will keep you focused on what is most important. You'll begin to understand and appreciate that downsizing a vacation or foregoing the latest gadget today will help you reach your ultimate goals of tomorrow.

Once you have set a few of your retirement lifestyle goals, try to put a number on what it will take financially to make these goals a reality. The easiest way to do this is in terms of what you are currently making. Do you need 100 percent of your income, 90, 80 or 70 percent?

Do a little bit of dreaming. How much will it cost to live, to travel, or participate in the hobbies that are part of your retirement goal?

As you continue this exercise you'll move from lifestyle and extracurricular wishes to essential needs and fixed daily income goals. This can be difficult at first because throughout our working years, income and spending are paired together. We typically budget according to what we make and then try to keep our spending below our income.

When most people think about their retirement savings, it is difficult to translate a lump-sum total into spending needs. Although later in this book we'll demonstrate how certain self-directed IRA investments have the potential to produce income as well.

So how do you begin to prepare for that reality? It can be difficult to shift your thinking to consider the cost of living years in the future, but a simple way to think about it is in terms of a daily cup of coffee.

Let's say you are 55 and every weekend you look forward to walking to your local coffee shop, purchasing a large cup of coffee, and catching up with friends. As you picture your ideal retirement, at the age of 65, you imagine doing this every day. How much will that cost?

Let's assume that today your coffee costs $1.95 per cup. For simplicity's sake, let's remove inflation from the equation and assume the price of your cup will not change. That means:

- Each year of coffee will cost $711.75.

- Ten years of coffee will cost $7,117.50.

- If your retirement lasts 30 years, you will eventually spend $21,352.50.

If you're thinking that's an expensive cup of coffee, don't worry, you won't need all $21,000 at once. But you will need to determine the lump-sum total required to support $21,000 worth of coffee over 30 years.

This example should help to demonstrate the exercise of determining your retirement income needs and a shift in how you think about retirement income – in terms of a cost to the balance of your portfolio that must be planned and accounted for.

Calculators: Retirement Income and Distributions

Interactive calculations, dynamic graphs and fully customizable reports are just a few of the features that make our calculators stand out!

Retirement Income – Use this calculator to determine how much monthly income your retirement savings may provide in your retirement. Your annual savings, expected rate of return and your current age all have an impact on your retirement's monthly income. View the full report to see a year-by-year break down of your retirement savings:

https://www.trustetc.com/resources/tools/calculators/retirement-income

How long will my savings last? – Use this calculator to see how long your retirement savings will last. This is based on your retirement savings and your inflation-adjusted withdrawals:

https://www.trustetc.com/resources/tools/calculators/retirement-distribution

---

As we'll discuss in a few moments, there are other factors to consider outside of personal goals and spending estimates. Macroeconomic factors such as the health of the economy, taxation, healthcare costs, education costs, decisions of the government, and market volatility, for example, must also be considered.

Armed with this information, you can begin to create the basic framework of what you want your retirement to look like and how much it is likely to cost. As you continue reading and begin to learn about the various opportunities and investment options, write down what you like or are interested in learning more about and consider if it can help you reach the retirement you deserve.

Retirement Reality

Now that you have envisioned your perfect retirement, and considered what it may take to get there, let's take a moment for a reality check.

The majority of retirement plans are underfunded. Most Americans do not have enough money saved and are not on pace to be able to enjoy their retirement years as they could have with proper planning.

Let's take a closer look at some frightening statistics that will hopefully motivate you to take the planning process seriously so you remain the exception, rather than the rule.

According to the U.S. Census Bureau, if you take 100 people at the start of their working careers and follow them for 40 years until they reach retirement age you will find that statistically: three will still be working, 29 will be dead, 63 will be dependent on Social Security, friends, relatives or charity, four will be financially secure, and only one will be considered wealthy[1]. The goal of this book is to help you get to be one of those five, to be one of the 5 percent of people who will attain their dreams of retirement, and on their own terms. And ultimately, the goal is to improve those numbers and help every American improve their financial future.

---

[1] Statistics Brain. (2015, September 8). Retirement Statistics. 2015 Statistic Brain Research Institute, publishing as Statistic Brain. Retrieved from http://www.statisticbrain.com/retirement-statistics/

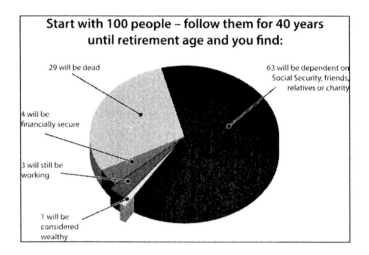

Additionally, according to Statistics Brain, the following statistics relate to the average American at retirement[1]:

- $42,797 is the average amount saved for Americans at the age of 50.

- In order to provide a $3,000 monthly income in retirement for 30 years, assuming 6% annualized return and 2% annual inflation erosion during the course of retirement, you would need to save $636,450.

- 80% of Americans ages 30 to 54 are not confident they will have enough saved for retirement.

- 36% of Americans over 65 live 100% dependent on Social Security income

- From July 2014 to July 2015, the average Social Security benefactor received approximately $16,244, or about $1,354 per month[2].

- 38% of Americans have zero money saved.

- Only 4% of Americans will have enough money saved by the age of 65 to live comfortably.

---

[2] United States Social Security Administration. (July 2015). Benefits awarded – time series for all benefit types. Retrieved from http://www.ssa.gov/cgi-bin/awards.cgi

- 63% of retirees are dependent on friends, relatives, charities, and Social Security to provide their retirement needs.

These statistics are presented not as a scare tactic, but to demonstrate the need for planning. Benjamin Franklin famously said, "If you fail to plan, you are planning to fail." A lack of planning can result in the frightening statistics we just covered. To position yourself above these numbers, be a part of that successful 5 percent, and establish a meaningful retirement for you and your loved ones, a commitment and focus on retirement planning is absolutely essential.

Yet it takes more than establishing a plan and saving money. Aaron DeHoog, the financial publisher of *Newsmax*, said, "The biggest retirement mistake people make (besides not saving at all) is they stick their money in the bank.[3]"

He said this because *saving* money is much different than *investing* money. Savers tend to be very conservative, and often place their money in products that do not keep up with inflation. If inflation averages 3 percent, and you have money in a CD earning 2 percent, you are losing money every year whether you realize it or not. Add the tax burden placed on your income and the situation is even worse.

Many Americans believe that they will have enough in Social Security to support their retirement. But as we covered, the average Social Security benefactor is only receiving about $16,000 per year. Is that enough to fulfill the retirement dreams you have? What plan do you have in place that Social Security will supplement? It's not the other way around anymore.

And what's frightening is that you've been paying into this fund your entire working career with the hopes it would be there for you when you retire. But with 6,100 Americans turning 65 every day[1], there is a terrible strain on the one safety net that was supposed to help support retirees. The safety net that *over one-third of all retirees completely*

---

[3] Moneynews. (2014, October 29). 5 Shocking Retirement Facts. Retrieved from http://www.moneynews.com/MKTNews/Retirement-Financial-Crisis/2013/07/08/id/513815/

rely on for their income is already overstretched and continually deteriorating.

According to the 2014 Annual Report by the Social Security and Medicare Boards of Trustees, the Social Security's cash expenses have exceeded its cash receipts every year since 2010 and the negative cash flow for 2013 was about $55 billion. They went on to project that the Social Security Administration's reserves will be fully depleted in less than 20 years, by 2033. At this point the tax revenue will only be enough to pay about three-quarters of scheduled benefits.[4]

The Board of Trustees also projects Medicare will deplete in 2030, at this time the dedicated revenues will only be enough to pay 86 percent of the costs.[5]

If you're the government and you're trying to shore up Social Security there are basically two things you can do: Raise your revenue (and if you're the government, you raise your revenue by raising taxes) or reduce benefits.

Those are the two things the government can do. Which brings me back to the original purpose of this book – what can you do?

A self-directed IRA is a vehicle that can be used to help combat some of the challenges we've touched on so far, and others we'll review shortly.

State of the Economy

Part of understanding your retirement needs includes determining what you can control, and what you cannot. There are many factors that will impact your retirement that are out of your control. A few of these factors include the overall health of the economy, tax rates, healthcare costs, educational costs, and stock market fluctuations. While these socioeconomic factors may seem to be completely outside your control, this book will show you ways to position

---

[4] DeSilver, D. (2013, October 16). 5 Facts About Social Security. Retrieved from http://www.pewresearch.org/fact-tank/2013/10/16/5-facts-about-social-security/
[5] Social Security and Medicare Boards of Trustees. (2015). A Summary of the 2015 Annual Reports. Retrieved from http://www.ssa.gov/oact/trsum/

yourself favorably against them and take back control of your financial future.

Taxes have a direct relationship with government spending. The more services the government offers to its citizens, the higher taxes must be. Taxes can pay for education, roads, police and fire services, governmental assistance programs, healthcare, and many other social initiatives.

Over the last decade the government has begun to offer more and more services at the expense of the taxpayers. Another element that impacts taxes is government waste. Spending money we do not have, taking on more debt, and drafting policies we can ill afford has become an increasing problem within our political system and resulted in increasing tax rates. Take one look at the running calculator of our nation's debt at http://www.usdebtclock.org/ and you will no longer need convinced that taxes are likely on the rise.

As of August 2015, the National Debt was more than $18 trillion. Each citizen's share of this debt, *your* share of this debt, is more than $57,000. Even bleaker, the average amount of debt *per taxpayer* is more than $154,000.[6]

Furthermore, as seen on the U.S. Debt Clock and according to the Congressional Budget Office, our federal spending has increased 108 percent since 2000.[6]

Each year, tax laws change, only adding to the challenge of taxes. In fact, according to the National Taxpayer Advocate Annual Report to Congress there were approximately 4,430 changes to the tax code from 2001 through 2010, an average of more than one per day, including an estimated 579 changes in 2010 alone![7]

---

[6] US Debt Clock. (2015). Retrieved from http://www.usdebtclock.org/
[7] Internal Revenue Service. (2014, October 31). National Taxpayer Advocate Delivers Annual Report to Congress; Focuses on IRS Funding and Taxpayer Rights. Retrieved from http://www.irs.gov/uac/National-Taxpayer-Advocate-Delivers-Annual-Report-to-Congress;-Focuses-on-IRS-Funding-and-Taxpayer-Rights

The primary benefit of self-directed IRAs is the potential tax savings. Depending on the account type, you can either reduce your taxable income and defer the taxes until withdrawal or you can pay tax on the contribution and benefit from tax-free growth for the remainder of your life.

Inflation is the impact of price increases on the cost of living and therefore, decreased purchasing power. Investors must consider whether the returns on their investments will outpace the general rate of inflation.

It is important to consider inflation as you evaluate an investment opportunity, particularly for long-term investments. Both inflation and taxes require your investments to perform better to keep pace with the higher cost of living and the taxes that must be paid.

Healthcare costs have continued to rise and are a major component of retired life. Therefore, it is important that you factor in the cost of healthcare as you plan for retirement.

According to the *HealthView Services* 2015 Retirement Health Care Costs Data Report[8], "the average lifetime retirement health care premium costs for a 65-year-old healthy couple retiring this year and covered by Medicare Parts B, D, and a supplemental insurance policy will be $266,589," assuming the Medicare subscribers paid Medicare taxes while employed and are not subject to Medicare Part A premiums.

The report continues, "If we were to include the couple's total health care (dental, vision, co-pays, and all out-of-pockets), their costs would rise to $394,954. For a 55-year-old couple retiring in 10 years, total lifetime health care costs would be $463,849."[8]

While the rising cost of healthcare is one we cannot directly control, we must factor it into our retirement as a significant expense for retirees, and one that is often overlooked in the planning stages. Later in the book we'll explain the self-directed Health Savings Account

---

[8] HealthView Services Financial. (2015). 2015 Retirement Health Care Costs Data Report. Retrieved from
https://www.hvsfinancial.com/PublicFiles/Data_Release.pdf

and how it can help combat the rising cost of healthcare with tax-free savings.

Education costs are also rising significantly every year. The competitive job market has increased the importance of obtaining an advanced education and it has been said that today's bachelor's degree is equivalent to yesterday's high school diploma and is almost seen as a requirement now. College is not just for 19- and 20-year-olds anymore either. More and more Americans are returning to school to remain competitive in the job market. This increased demand is putting a strain on the educational system and resulting in higher than usual annual increases. In fact, according to InflationData.com the rate of inflation of college education has increased to over three and a half times the inflation rate of the consumer price index, and the trend is continuing[9]. College is only growing more expensive, and at a faster rate. Whether it is for you, your children or your grandchildren, proper planning is critical.

When it comes to managing expenses during retirement years, most people do not consider student loans to be among the items they must account for. Yet, many seniors are finding themselves with debt from student loans – their children's, grandchildren's or even their own.

A Government Accountability Office report says 706,000 senior citizen households carry student debt.[10] As their healthcare needs come with great frequency and cost, many people are realizing they can't manage those expenses in addition to paying back education loans.

Don't wait until you find yourself in a situation like this. We'll discuss the Coverdell Education Savings Account (CESA) and how it can help you save for educational expenses.

---

[9] Wadsworth, G. H. (2012, June 14). Sky Rocketing College Costs. Retrieved from http://inflationdata.com/Inflation/Inflation_Articles/Education_Inflation.asp
[10] Herships, S. (2014, September 16). Rising numbers of seniors are paying off student loans. Retrieved from http://www.marketplace.org/topics/wealth-poverty/rising-numbers-seniors-are-paying-student-loans

Stock market fluctuations have been a reality within the stock market as long as it has been in existence. This volatility has been known to wipe out a decade's worth of growth in a matter of days when the market adjusts. These adjustments are analyzed by professionals in the industry, but are very unpredictable. At any given time professional analysts will be split on who predicts the markets will rise, and who predicts they will fall. When analysts who make a living studying the markets cannot agree on the direction, how are consumers supposed to fare?

The following graphs demonstrate the volatility of the markets.

The first compares the S&P 500 with its trailing 12-month earnings per share (EPS) value. The two series were adjusted for inflation using the headline CPI number.[11]

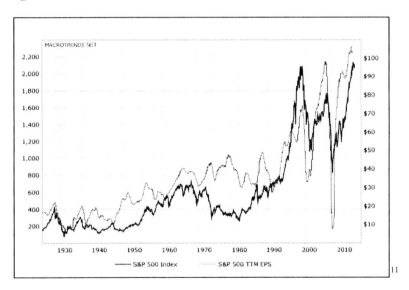

11

[11] Shiller, R. & Standard and Poors. (2015). S&P Earnings History. MacroTrends. Retrieved from http://www.macrotrends.net/1324/s-p-500-earnings-history

The bar chart below depicts the Dow Jones Industrial Average total yearly return for close to 60 years.[12]

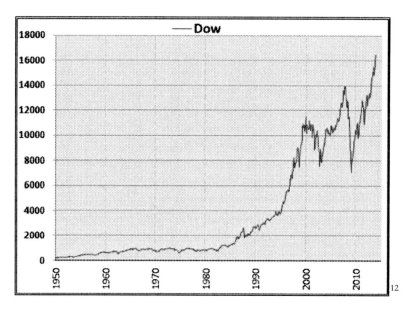

As you can see, despite the volatility of the stock market it has still demonstrated positive gains over time. Looking back, it can be easy to presume money left in the markets will continue to build in value until it is time to retire.

Yet, how can you predict where the market cycle will be when you are in need of your hard-earned funds? What happens if you are set to retire or request a withdrawal of income at a time when the graph trends downward? How can you be sure the portfolio balance you have today will still be there at the exact time you need it or in the year you decide to retire?

Conclusion

When considering the state of the economy it becomes clear why everyone must diligently prepare for retirement. Identifying which

---

[12] Schaeffer's Investment Research. (2013, December 30). History Suggests Dow's Bull Run Still Has Legs. Retrieved from
http://www.forbes.com/sites/greatspeculations/2013/12/30/history-suggests-dows-bull-run-still-has-legs/

factors you can control, learning the tools available to do so, and preparing for factors outside of your control are ways to make your retirement dreams a reality. It's time to look at retirement differently than you have in the past, to be open to new ideas and strategies and to plan the road that you must take to reach financial freedom and become one of the 5 percent with a success story.

Over the course of this book we will present various opportunities and investment options, will showcase how real life investors and successful clients have been utilizing them to build wealth for retirement, and will explain the rules and investing process in a simple manner.

As you continue reading, take your time and write down the concepts that you like and would like to implement. There will be a lot of new information and multiple concepts you've likely never been exposed to, so it may feel overwhelming at times.

But hang in there.

This book is about how everyday investors like you can overcome these obstacles. It's about how investors across the country have looked at their current situation and the economic landscape that lies ahead, and decided to take control. This book is about how the 2 percent of investors currently utilizing self-directed IRAs have the opportunity to not only overcome these obstacles, but thrive in retirement.

Richard Desich, Sr.

Chapter 1: Who Is This Book For?

The short answer is this book is for everyone! The great thing about self-directed IRAs is that you do not have to be a financial analyst or investment guru to take advantage of the opportunity. In fact, throughout this entire book we will share how average Americans have self-directed their retirement to success. We will share how self-directed IRA investing is possible for anyone who is willing to try, regardless of age, investment experience, or portfolio balance. We'll even show you how children as young as 10 years old have gotten started with self-directed IRAs!

The long answer however, is that self-directed IRAs, the topic of this book, are only for those who are willing to break away from the mold of traditional investments and put in the time and effort required to find success.

Let me say that again because this is important. While this book is for anyone, and the goal is to help you understand the concept, investing with self-directed IRAs isn't. And it's okay if it isn't for you.

As the author Mark Caine once said, "The first step toward success is taken when you refuse to be a captive of the environment in which you first find yourself."

It's important to remember that anything worthwhile in life requires effort. But as you'll find out as we continue, self-directed investing is not as intimidating as it may sound at first.

There is only a 5-percent rate of financially secure retirees for a reason: most are unwilling to fully commit to their retirement success. If you wish to have a successful retirement, and/or you are dissatisfied with the current performance of your investments, this book is for you. If you are just getting started and don't know which direction to turn, this book is for you. If you've delayed saving for retirement and are worried you're not prepared, this book is for you.

It is easy to exclude yourself from something that really might be the best thing for you because you are unfamiliar with the concept or are afraid you will make a bad choice. I say to you, hang in there. Finish the book and then decide.

As with all new things, there is a learning curve associated with self-directed IRAs.

But you don't need to start out with complex commercial real estate projects or innovative loan structures. You start with what you know and use that as the building blocks to identify the strategies that will help you succeed. This book is meant to help you discover the possibilities, evaluate your current circumstances, and help you learn the appropriate steps that lead to successful self-directed IRA investing.

So let me be completely upfront with you about why we're here, and it's best to start with what we're NOT going to do.

We are not here to:

- Sell you investments

- Become your financial advisor or

- Act as your tax professional

And finally, we are NOT here to offer any type of get-rich-quick information.

2

What we *are* here to do is to provide great quality education in hopes that you will prosper with your investments and refer friends, family, and colleagues to our education and services.

Our goal is for you to become successful. *Your success is our success.*

We want you to start off by learning from the information and case studies we share in this book and then be able to give us another great success story that we can share with others.

Common Concerns

I am a very conservative investor so alternative investments aren't for me. When you think of alternative investing it is easy to think high risk. Yet that may not be the case. According to Investopedia[13], an alternative investment is "An investment that is not one of the three traditional asset types (stocks, bonds and cash)."

So, in a nutshell, alternative investments are non-Wall Street investments. The "alternative" label was given to this asset class because it is different than the traditional investment options such as stocks and bonds. Unfortunately, when people hear the word "alternative" they often think it means an unconventional asset that is difficult to understand. People have been investing in these so-called "alternatives" (like real estate and physical gold) for thousands of years, but the "alternative" label has kept this group of assets relatively under the radar for retirement accounts.

That leaves a lot of room to find an investment that is considered "alternative." Very likely, some will fall within your comfort level. Every investment has certain risks and there is no investment that is perfect for everyone. The key to smart investing is to understand the risks associated with a particular investment and to evaluate ways to mitigate those risks in your favor. Then, after performing your research and due diligence you can feel comfortable investing with a good understanding of the opportunity.

---

[13] Alternative Investment. (n.d.). In Investopedia Dictionary online. Retrieved from http://www.investopedia.com/terms/a/alternative_investment.asp

By doing so, conservative investors can often find alternative investments that can strengthen their portfolio and enable strong and diversified returns.

As you get older there is the tendency to avoid risk out of fear – fear that you will lose your hard-earned savings and fall years behind schedule with less time to recoup the losses. If this sounds like you, focusing on alternative investments that involve things you know and understand may actually reduce your fear and uncertainty. You can move forward with an investment you understand and are passionate about.

My firm was recently contacted by a client named Jim during our Self-Directed Investor of the Year contest. Jim is from Ohio and had an account with us for a number of years, but never started investing with his self-directed IRA because he didn't think he had enough money saved to get into real estate. I'll let Jim explain from here.

> "In January of 2014 I located a small, vacant three bedroom fixer-upper house in Bedford, Ohio – a Cleveland suburb. I negotiated the price down from $40,000 to $20,000, all cash. I used an option agreement with a $100 deposit that would come from my Equity Trust Roth IRA.

> When the property closed, the title company sent my profit directly to my account at Equity Trust. For my $100 investment, I made a modest $1,900 tax-free back into my Roth for a 1,900-percent ROI in 6 months.

> This WAS the deal of the year for me because, although I have had a Roth IRA at Equity Trust for nearly seven years, I had never invested in real estate with it. I am a retired police officer and have only a very small amount of money in my IRA.

> The structure of using an option with a small option consideration (like a down payment) meant that the most I could lose was only $100. And, because it was an assignable option contract, I could sell it and let someone else actually purchase the property.

This is what I did – so I had no rehab costs, no tenants to deal with, no closing costs, and the title company handled the entire transaction with the simple paperwork that I used (which was only two pages – the Option & the Assignment).

I got the entire $1,900 that I sold my option for, and because I am over 59½ and have had my Roth IRA for more than five years, my entire profit is tax-free even if I took it out the next day!

I have since optioned two more properties through my Equity Trust Roth IRA. I learned you don't need much money to get started, you can work to eliminate risk, your investment profits are tax-free, and $1,900 is the smallest return I will ever get investing this way now that my account has grown! What's not to love? You CAN teach an old dog new tricks!"

This is a powerful message because it demonstrates the power self-directed IRAs can have on your financial future. Jim, like many Americans, did not have much saved for retirement and did not know where to turn. He clearly liked the idea of self-directed IRAs, opening an account seven years before making his first investment, but never thought it was possible for him.

His story proves that with patience, a commitment to learning and improving as an investor and a slight leap of faith – you can turn your retirement around, regardless of the amount of money you start with or how close you are to retirement age.

I started too late. While it is certainly true that time is your most powerful ally when it comes to compound interest, starting behind schedule is no reason to feel helpless. Starting today is the most important thing. No one can turn back time and reset the clock to start earlier, and if I said "you should have started earlier" it wouldn't be helpful.

The good news is that starting today will put you ahead of the game, regardless of what today is. The longer you wait, the more difficult your challenge.

If you are behind schedule you may have to find more creative ways to reach your goals. You may have to adjust your expectations so that you have more realistic goals and you may also be required to make more sacrifices today to reach your goals for tomorrow.

In any event, starting now is the key. Whether you are 20, 40 or even 60, if you choose to ignore the challenge of retirement you will likely wind up living below your expectations and may even become one of the unfortunate statistics we shared earlier – relying on friends, family, or Social Security. By committing to an investment plan, you allow yourself to imagine a different life. You allow yourself the opportunity to achieve your goals (even if it is a modified version).

Today is the day to take control of your finances.

Only you can do that.

Here is an example: Patty was in her 50s when her husband had a mild heart attack. This was the reality check that she needed as she pondered her financial situation without her husband's income. They, like many Americans, had a bare minimum in savings. Patty, like many others who are self-employed, had invested everything in her business and virtually nothing in her own retirement. After her husband's heart attack Patty decided she would start paying herself first. After setting up a retirement account and automatically putting money in the account each month she soon realized she barely noticed a difference in her income or lifestyle while still growing her retirement account balance.

Excited about this found money, Patty began looking at ways she could use her tax-advantaged savings. Through her business experience she had a good understanding of accounting, receivables and the lending process. Building on what she already understood, Patty was able to create an investment strategy that has offered double-digit returns for over a decade. She decided to lend her self-directed IRA money to various real estate investors in her network who needed funding for their projects in exchange for an agreed-upon rate of return as interest on the loan.

While she regrets waiting until a traumatic event shook her into action, Patty is grateful there were investment opportunities that enabled her to build adequate savings on her way to retirement.

I don't have enough money for an investment. One common misconception about self-directed IRA investing is that you need a lot of money to invest in alternatives. The good news is that there are a variety of alternative investment opportunities that do not require a large amount of money to get started. While buying a $200,000 property requires a lot of funds, and good financing, there are many options that only require a few hundred dollars to get started.

A few options, many of which will be covered more extensively later in the book, include mobile homes, tax liens, lending within your IRA, financing investments, real estate options, and land contracts. Each of these investments have the potential to provide a high upside and, with a little research, can help you grow your investments much faster than traditional stocks, bonds and CDs generally allow.

Here is an example: Brad attended a seminar hosted by Equity University and after learning about the tax advantages IRAs had to offer, decided to open an account. He did not know what to invest in since he had a very limited amount of cash and virtually no alternative investing experience. Brad decided he wanted to investigate tax liens. After studying this strategy and performing his due diligence, he was ready to invest. Brad identified a property he was interested in because it was on a busy street near a major hospital. In his research he discovered close to 15,000 cars drove by the property each day, so he knew if he was patient a buyer interested in the heavily trafficked location would eventually surface. At the tax lien sale his Roth IRA was able to purchase the tax lien certificate on a half acre of land for $823.71.

Brad held the property in his Roth IRA for two years and needed approximately $5,000 of additional funding from his account to clear title to the property (paying for attorney fees and other administrative costs). At that time a medical office developer approached him and paid $97,500 for the same half-acre lot, netting Brad approximately $90,000 back into his Roth IRA, tax-free.

As this example demonstrates, Brad only needed around $6,000 to get started with his self-directed IRA investing and grow his portfolio in his very first deal. This book will expose you to a variety of ways to capitalize on small-dollar investments as you get started and prove that "I don't have enough money to get started" is not a valid excuse for a committed self-directed IRA investor.

Webinar: Small-Dollar Opportunities for Self-Directed IRA Investors

In this bonus webinar you will discover 4 alternative investment options that don't require large lump sums of money to get started. Equity University's National Education Specialist, John Bowens, breaks down small-dollar opportunities such as mobile homes, real estate options, land contracts and tax liens. Set up or log in to your user account to watch it now:

https://equityuniversity.customerhub.net/small-dollar

I don't currently have an IRA or retirement account. Fortunately, investment accounts can be started at any time and do not require large contributions to get started. The best way to begin is to open an account and arrange for automatic drafts to be deposited in the account each month, or each paycheck. This will allow the funds to accumulate until you are ready to invest. During the time money is in the account it will gain interest, but the true gains will come from finding investments that will grow the account well beyond the interest accrued.

You may have money tucked away that you have forgotten about. If you worked for a former employer that had a 401(k), 403(b), Thrift Savings Plan, pension, or other retirement account, you can typically convert or rollover that account into an IRA.

I don't have an investment in mind. The best way to get started is by opening an account before you have an investment in mind. If you will make monthly contributions to the account it will motivate you to identify an investment that can get the ball rolling.

Many investments happen quickly and the account needs to be in place for you to take advantage of an opportunity when it presents itself. Investments such as foreclosures, tax liens, or even private lending opportunities can materialize within a day to 10 days. It may take up to two to four weeks to roll over a 401(k) or IRA into a self-directed IRA and you could miss your opportunity by waiting until you have a deal in mind before opening your account.

The other advantage to opening an account right away is that the funds will accumulate while you research and learn about your options. Then when you identify an investment, you will be able to capitalize on the opportunity immediately.

Remember Jim from a few moments ago? He had an account with us for seven years before he learned enough and felt comfortable pulling the trigger on his first investment. Had he not already opened and funded his Roth IRA, he may have missed the opportunity to earn a 1,900-percent ROI on his first deal and would never have gotten started on the path to his other profitable investments.

Moving Forward

Saving can become a virtuous cycle. When people start saving for retirement, they begin to take control of their lives. And once they feel that pull of empowerment, they realize they can in large part determine their own future for themselves.

Essentially, that's what this book is about. We're here to help prove to you that it's possible. We're here to showcase how our own clients, most of which were just like you, have used the power of self-directed IRAs to take control of their financial futures and decided to determine their own retirement realities.

Richard Desich, Sr.

Chapter 2: The ROI Beyond the ROI – Self-Directed IRAs Impacting Lives Across America

The majority of this book is devoted to exposing you to all the options available in your retirement, not just the traditional ones you are likely familiar with.

Our mission and goal is to provide education that can serve as the catalyst for wider participation in government sponsored retirement plans for every American, not just the wealthy. As we discussed in the Introduction, the reality of America's financial climate is that a majority of Americans are not positioned for a comfortable retirement, and we want to change that. We want to tell the middle-class success stories of our clients and prove that profitable investing is not exclusive to the elite and wealthy.

We know that when it comes to financial planning and retirement investing, there is not a one-size-fits-all solution – nor should there be. But everyone deserves the same opportunities.

The question is – will you take the opportunities when they are presented? You may not have been aware of self-directed IRAs before, but after reading this book, will you take action?

A study of high-net-worth individuals by Morgan Stanley uncovered that 77 percent of millionaires owned real estate in their portfolios.[14]

Including real estate and other alternative investments in your retirement portfolio should not be exclusive to millionaires. Successful investing, especially as it pertains to self-directed IRAs, is not just for savvy and experienced investors. In fact, as you'll learn, self-directed IRAs are a critical tool made available by the federal government for everyone to use and have helped countless Americans from all walks of life take control and build a more secure and prosperous retirement.

We want to make every option known so that anyone can further diversify their retirement holdings and participate in the democratization of capital, regardless of income or social status.

The Democratization of Capital

What is the democratization of capital? It sounds like a buzzword you'd find in politics, but what I mean is important. The democratization of capital provides the opportunity for everyone to be able to raise, lend or borrow money in pursuit of their passions and to be in control of their own investment selections.

In recent decades there has been a gradual shift in control of capital from institutions to the markets. It is a historic shift that has "democratized" capital by making it more broadly available. The idea behind the democratization of capital is that no one should be denied the right to participate in economic society or to aspire to business ownership rather than just a job.

---

[14] Morgan Stanley Wealth Management. (2014, February 6). Millionaire Investors Name Real Estate as Most Popular Alternative Asset Class by Wide Margin. Retrieved from http://www.morganstanley.com/about-us-articles/404f321a-29ad-438c-afab-ff18ceb302ac.html

America is built upon the ideas of democracy, capitalism, and the entrepreneurial spirit. If an entrepreneur is looking to launch a start-up company, the democratization of capital (and self-directed IRAs as a source of capital) no longer limits the investor to the traditional lending institutions. The entrepreneur can open the opportunity to the democracy at large and other investors can invest in the new start-up, providing the start-up with the much-needed capital and the investors another avenue to potentially grow their wealth.

You can see the democratization of capital working today. Online crowdfunding platforms have helped fund anything from innovative technology start-ups, charity fundraisers, children's medical expenses, or even something as trivial as a college student's spring break.

One exciting aspect of the democratization of capital is what people have decided to do with it to make a difference in their own financial future. Even more powerful is what we've seen our clients do to impact the communities in which they live. As we'll discuss, self-directed IRAs are an unheralded but important component of the U.S. economy.

You see, this book is NOT just about money and making profits. Although if that is all you get out of this book, you can certainly still benefit.

As promised, we'll educate you on the opportunities available, how the investment process works, and the rules that need to be followed. And we'll share how hundreds of thousands of our clients have used self-directed IRA investing to take control of their financial futures with greater diversification and control of their returns.

But, as you continue reading and learning, I want you to notice the big picture. Self-directed IRAs can be used toward a greater good that goes beyond making money and personal gain.

In fact, several themes will begin to emerge from the fabric of the self-directed investment stories:

- You'll learn how self-directed IRA investors are helping Americans get back to work by investing in small businesses, creating jobs, and stimulating the local economies in which they invest.

- You'll see how self-directed IRA investors have helped in the housing recovery and have expanded the opportunity of home ownership to many who had been spurned by traditional standards. You'll see how self-directed IRA investments have revitalized American neighborhoods across the country and left a lasting legacy in the communities.

- You'll discover how self-directed IRA investors are impacting their communities by investing money back into America's infrastructure, providing much-needed funding for schools, roads, bridges, and more.

Most importantly, you'll learn how these same opportunities and successes are available to you, and how they are available to you right now. If you're not working towards an enjoyable and prosperous retirement, what are you working for?

Let's see what self-directed IRA investors look like in action and how they've used their IRA money to make a difference in their retirement, their communities and beyond.

Creating Jobs, Stimulating Local Economies and Jumpstarting Small Businesses Across America

As you'll discover when we tackle the self-directed IRA rules and investment process, self-directed IRA investments require the investor to remain at arms-length throughout the entire investment process. Quite simply, the work must be completed by a third party in order to take advantage of the tax benefits the account provides.

Thus, by its very nature, a self-directed IRA investment creates a job opportunity on nearly every investment.

When you purchase a piece of real estate with your self-directed IRA with the intent to rehab and resell the property for a profit, your self-directed IRA must pay the roofers to install a new roof, it must pay the contractors to install new appliances and floors, and it must pay the painters to change the interior of the home.

While creating jobs isn't the primary goal for the average investor, it demonstrates the greater good and deeper importance of the self-directed IRA industry as a whole.

Long-Distance Rehab Success

Equity Trust's 2014 Self-Directed Investor of the Year Award Winner, Arnold from Michigan, is a perfect example of this concept. Arnold used his research skills, real estate knowledge, and the internet to buy, rehab, and earn income from a rental property in Hilton Head, South Carolina without ever stepping foot on the property. (As we share Arnold's story of success, watch out for the impact his investment made on the community of Hilton Head, even from over 1,200 miles away.)

Arnold grew up on the eastern seaboard and considers anywhere from Florida to Maine as his target market. He routinely scours the internet for investment opportunities and considers it one of his greatest tools. Research on the internet enables him to conduct his due diligence in areas where he doesn't live, analyze the market and location, and identify team members who can help make the investment happen. (Notice how Arnold was able to use the internet to find and vet his investment. Often, identifying an opportunity isn't as complex as many believe.)

During one of his routine internet searches Arnold came across a property in Hilton Head that was on the auction block for the third time in the last 60 days. He had vacationed there with his family several times in the past so he understood the area enough to know that this was an opportunity worth investigating.

After researching further, he connected with a real estate agent located in Hilton Head named Joan. Armed with his own extensive internet research and a trusted local real estate agent, Arnold felt confident bidding on the property. He was able to win the auction for less than the maximum bid he and Joan had decided on and purchased the property with his self-directed IRA.

After Arnold's IRA purchased the property Joan was able to enter the home, send Arnold pictures, and help him determine what was needed in the rehab. He then hired local contractors or department store employees to measure what was needed for each aspect of the project. "Most of them didn't even realize I didn't live in South Carolina," he recalls.

Here's a rundown of his rehab process:

1) Local contacts in Hilton Head measured out what he needed for each aspect of the rehab and provided the details to Arnold. They did this for new carpet, kitchen cabinets, paint, granite countertops, bathrooms, and more.

2) Arnold visited a nearby national department store in Michigan to get installation quotes for the provided measurements and to see the materials firsthand before ordering the supplies. Once finalized, he then ordered the supplies from the same department store chain in Hilton Head and paid local contractors in Hilton Head to install what he selected.

3) Payment for the supplies and work came from Arnold's self-directed IRA, per IRS guidelines.

After two months of long-distance management, Arnold took a trip to Hilton Head to check on his investment. "By the time I arrived more than 60 days after purchase, 95 percent of the work was done," he says. All that remained were some finishing touches, appliances, and furniture.

Arnold originally planned to break even on rent with the hopes of appreciation. Monthly rental income around $800-$900 would break even, but he discovered in his internet research that he could raise the rent significantly and stay within the market averages.

Now, he has a tenant with a three-year lease paying $1,250 a month, netting Arnold an approximate 33 percent return on investment (ROI) per year, tax-deferred back into his IRA. Additionally, during our interview with Arnold we learned he was faced with a tough decision, but it was a good problem to have. Rental prices in the area had increased to $1,800 – $2,100 per month and with the improvements and appreciation he estimated he is now sitting on $40,000 of added value in the property.

He is currently deciding between holding the property, possibly raising his rent, and keeping the cash flow or selling the property and cashing out on the appreciation and value he's added to the home. Either way, his investment has been a success.

A side effect of his own personal financial success (and we've found this is often the case for our clients) is that neighbors of his investment property have since contacted Arnold and thanked him for rehabbing an eyesore, filling the unit, and increasing the value of their neighborhood.

Furthermore, did you notice the local jobs that were created from Arnold's investment? His rehab project employed a local real estate agent, local contractors, and even improved the value of a local neighborhood.

Building Veterans

Another Equity Trust client, Roger from Maryland, has used his self-directed IRA to "give life to a ministry in a town, Brunswick, which has had trouble growing – not so much for a great financial return."

Roger's friend Bob had a dream to help Veterans, especially those returning from Iraq and Afghanistan who are having difficulty returning back to civilian life. Many of the Veterans struggle with post-traumatic stress disorder (PTSD), much like Bob did when he returned from Vietnam. Bob's dream was to create a ministry called *Building Veterans* to provide spiritual guidance and skills training, such as carpentry and construction, as both therapy and as a way to help the Veterans find meaningful and gainful employment.

Bob is a pastor and Vietnam veteran who is retired with his wife and had limited funds to start his dream on his own. They were hoping to purchase a bank-owned property in Brunswick, Maryland and make it the very first building for the *Building Veterans* ministry. Bob thought he had a local bank lined up to finance the property, but they backed out last minute.

"If I wasn't able to step in and use my self-directed IRA funds as the initial financer for the house, the whole thing would have fallen through," recalls Roger. "If they had to go to a hard money lender, those terms are pretty onerous and would have been around 15 to 20 percent."

Roger was able to step in and finance the property with a loan from his self-directed IRA for $100,000. He received 6-percent interest tax-deferred back into his account, about which he comments, "in general the ROI isn't great, but the real purpose of the loan was to support the *Building Veterans* ministry."

The real ROI is that the organization now supports 10 veterans and is already looking for another house in Brunswick as the ministry continues to grow. Those 10 veterans are now getting support, guidance, and employment opportunities. Thanks to Roger's self-directed IRA the ministry now has the financial support to continue making a real impact on the lives of the courageous men and women returning from overseas.

Is there a more fulfilling 6-percent return than on one whose slogan is "*Building Veterans*: Building Communities Builds People, Building People Builds Communities"?

Plus, a 6-percent return on a retirement portfolio isn't too bad when you look at the industry averages returning on some traditional investment options. Were it not for Roger's self-directed IRA and the democratization of capital, this important ministry may never have gotten off the ground.

Self-Directed Small Business Success

As mentioned earlier, one of the beneficiaries of the "democratization of capital" is small business. Small businesses (most often defined as those having fewer than 500 employees) are a vital component of the American economy – representing almost half of the country's GDP and generating almost two-thirds of all new jobs.[15]

Unfortunately, a myriad of recent regulatory developments and the consolidation among banks has left fewer, and larger, lending institutions for small businesses to turn towards. According to the Small Business Administration, there was $580 billion of outstanding loan balances at the close of 2013. Furthermore, a recent report released by the Federal Reserve Bank found that more than 50 percent of small businesses reported they were unable to get the capital for which they applied.[16]

Enter self-directed IRA capital.

Matt, an Equity Trust client from Pennsylvania, has been investing in the stock market from a very young age. Yet despite some success, he wasn't thrilled with this investment strategy. "I was putting trust and money into people who weren't doing such a great job," he says.

A few years ago he discovered self-directed IRAs, opened an account, and transferred his retirement savings. He wasn't sure what direction he wanted to take, but he took an interest in buying and selling homes.

Matt's investing started going in a slightly different direction after he began scanning local classified ads. He came across a local used-car dealer who was seeking funding to repave his parking lot. He met with the dealer and worked out a private lending agreement with him.

---

[15] U.S. Small Business Administration Office of Advocacy. (2014, March). Frequently Asked Questions about Small Business. Retrieved from https://www.sba.gov/sites/default/files/FAQ_March_2014_0.pdf

[16] Harmon, K. (2015, June 15). Invest Local. The Huffington Post. Retrieved from http://www.huffingtonpost.com/kevin-harmon/invest-local_b_7586582.html

That wasn't the end of Matt's dealings with the car dealership. Through his IRA, he has since provided floor-plan financing to this dealer and other non-franchise dealership owners in the area. The loan was structured as a one-year, interest-only note with monthly interest payments. The car dealer was required to provide car titles as collateral to secure the loan.

Every time the dealer sells a car, instead of paying down the line (since the funds are in an IRA, he doesn't need the principal payments) the dealer pays a title exchange fee of $250 and sends a new title to secure the line. The more cars the dealer sells, the better the returns can be for Matt's IRA. The model can be tweaked depending on what type of cars (expensive vs. inexpensive) the dealer sells. The principal value of the investment remains the same until the loan is due or the dealer pays it off.

The model works better with low-priced cars, remarks Matt, adding the returns from the loans have remained around 30-35 percent per year.

Here's a breakdown of one of his loans:

$15,000 loan

10% interest → $1,500/year

22 cars sold x $250 title exchange fee → $5,500

$5500 + $1500 = $7,000 yearly income

$7000/$15000 = 46.66%

This type of investment can be ideal for investors without a lot of capital. Many car dealers can buy two to three cars at wholesale pricing for $5,000, Matt recalls.

On top of that, the returns can be perpetual. "As long as the dealer keeps selling cars, the IRA continues to prosper," he says. "Anyone can do this type of deal; most people know at least one small car dealer that would love to add cars to their inventory."

The beauty of this type of private lending is that the need could exist in any industry.

"For new people who are just getting into self-directed investing, there are a ton of opportunities to do stuff like this," Matt says. "It doesn't have to be cars. There are probably safer or better deals out there, but I happen to be comfortable with the dealers I'm working with."

Self-directed IRA investment flexibility has enabled a few of our clients to grow their retirement wealth while also filling a need they identified in industries such as medical technology (repairing and leasing X-ray and other machines), musical instruments (renting for music lessons), and transportation and logistics (investing in FedEx delivery routes or financing new trucks for a shipping company).

Matt suggests looking around the neighborhood for owners of smaller businesses who might need some capital to get up and running or make some improvements. Consider all of the people you know. Consider all of the businesses you frequent or come in contact with. Do you see a need for funding anywhere?

"Dealing with banks and lenders can be such a pain in the butt; small business owners would do back flips to pay someone 10-12 percent interest if they didn't have to go through the process of qualifying for a traditional loan," he says.

This example again demonstrates the democratization of capital at work. It's an example of how self-directed IRAs can help position investors like Matt to profit in their retirement investing beyond the stock market, while also providing much-needed funding to small businesses in their communities.

It also demonstrates the outside-the-box thinking that can lead to investing success. Matt initially wanted to invest in real estate but realized there were other opportunities to grow his self-directed IRA while still having control of his retirement funds. He found a void in the marketplace and used his tax-advantaged money to fill it.

Sometimes investment opportunities are less about what you need to learn and more about finding ways to help.

Aiding in the Housing Recovery, Providing Affordable Housing to Those in Need and a ROI on People instead of Property

When the real estate bubble burst in the subprime mortgage meltdown of 2008, real estate values across the country plummeted. Millions of families were either foreclosed upon and forced out of their homes or went underwater on their mortgage and tried to hang on as long as they could.

Since, the housing recovery has been a slow and arduous climb back.

One of the primary driving forces behind the housing recovery is from investors who were either incentivized by the unfortunate circumstances (i.e. ability to purchase foreclosed homes for pennies on the dollar) or those who have found a way to make the most out of a difficult situation.

Specifically, self-directed IRA investors have contributed to the nation's housing recovery by investing their tax-advantaged retirement dollars into alternative assets such as real estate with the hopes of generating a profit on a rehab or steady cash flow from a rental. Real estate is one of the most popular asset classes for self-directed IRA investments because it is a tangible asset outside the stock market and has the potential for large returns.

Each time one of our clients purchases a piece of real estate in his or her IRA and then improves the property and either sells it for a profit or fills the home with a tenant, the client is doing more than earning a prosperous return in his or her retirement portfolio – though if that's all that was accomplished it would certainly still be worth it! Each improvement, each vacant lot that is filled, and each rental agreement contributes to the nation's housing recovery and provides a home to a family in need.

Hurricane Katrina Rehab

Take for example a couple who used their Roth IRAs to fund a rehab property in Hurricane Katrina ravaged New Orleans, helped a friend and their community, and earned a 35-percent ROI in the process.

Wayne and his wife Alicia have been utilizing the power of self-directed retirement accounts to invest in alternatives since 2003. After Hurricane Katrina devastated New Orleans, the recovery was slow and painful for countless families. Wayne was approached by his friend Shawn because Shawn had a plan to purchase one of the "flooded and gutted" homes in their city and resell it. This not only turned out to be a lucrative investment, but it helped get the community back on its feet.

Shawn needed $106,000 in additional funding to purchase, renovate, and carry title to the property. Lucky for Shawn, Wayne and Alicia were able to lend the money from a combination of their Roth IRAs in a 75/25 split between the two. (As you can see, it's possible to partner multiple accounts to fund an investment.)

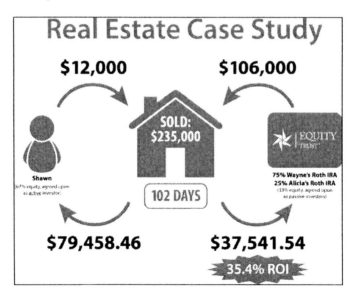

When the house resold for $235,000 and was split according to the agreement the friends had reached, Wayne and his wife could deposit approximately $38,000 of tax-free money into their retirement accounts for a 35-percent ROI! The trio was so excited by this return that they began planning to rehab two more homes in the area, not only helping to change the community for the better but their retirement future as well.

A Helping Hand

Another Equity Trust client, Tom from Illinois, is using his self-directed IRA to help various families from his church get their feet back on the ground with an affordable housing solution. The term "win-win" is thrown around too often, but Tom's investment approach has remained focused on a win-win situation for both his tenants and his retirement.

Tom is retired and works part time for his church and said he considers many of those in his church to be brothers and sisters.

"My brothers and sisters have experienced job loss and a loss of assets, including the loss of their homes. I use my Equity Trust self-directed IRA to help provide good shelter at lower-than-market costs for these families while making a strong, but low-risk, return," he says.

Tom has used a lease-option strategy for his self-directed IRA real estate investments with the goal the tenants will purchase the home at the conclusion of their three-year lease. He involves the family in his investment process from the very beginning, never losing sight that there are people (other than himself) involved in his retirement investment.

Tom explains, "I first meet with the family to discuss their needs, their work situation, and sit down with them to work on their budget. We come to an agreement as to what they can safely afford and then decide when to move forward."

He works with a real estate agent in the area who has helped him set up search criteria for the properties he is looking for and says he focuses primarily on distressed properties to allow for higher equity growth. Part of Tom's model is that the family helps to improve the property while they live there so he attempts to match their skill set with any improvements needed on the home.

Tom then allows the potential renters to select their own home from a list of options provided by his real estate agent. This is important for his goal to have the tenant purchase the home after the three-year lease, but also because he wants the families he is helping to enjoy where they live. Tom visits the home they select and determines whether or not he approves of the purchase. This is important because as Tom puts it, "though the intent is to sell them the home in three years, I don't want to have a home dropped in my lap that I wouldn't want to own as a simple rental."

Tom also factors rehab costs, any costs associated with his self-directed account, and other costs before he determines his potential for return. He tries to keep 9.6 percent as the minimum return on his investments (primarily through rent), but can recoup more if he profits on the sale of the home as well.

Another part of the agreement is that the renters must set aside "forced savings" to be used as a down payment at the conclusion of the three-year lease so the family can more easily purchase the home from Tom's IRA. If the family elects not to purchase, his IRA keeps the down payment as part of his investment's return. The down payment and the ability to select the home of their choosing help to bolster the level of commitment of his tenants, increasing the likelihood he can sell the property back to them when the lease expires.

Let's let Tom explain how one of his families is doing:

> "I am currently doing a three-year lease (with the option to buy) for a family of seven – a friend of mine, his wife, and their five young kids. They were renting outright for more than I am charging for rent, in addition to the savings I'm helping them set aside for the purchase in three years. We agreed on the work that needed to be done to the home and my IRA will pay as the work is completed. I budgeted $15,000 for rehab work and added that to the base of the investment when I was calculating my return. I still plan to

make more than 9.6 percent per year over the next three years, plus any profit on the sale of the home when the lease expires."

The word of Tom's win-win investment properties has begun to spread and he now has a list of people waiting on a potential opportunity, allowing him to be more selective when choosing tenants. He's even using the IRA funds from the sale of his first "win-win home" to help two other families get back on their feet.

A solid, steady 9.6 percent ROI is ideal for the retired Tom, but the ROI goes beyond the money he's received tax-deferred back into his IRA. "They had financial troubles a few years back and this is helping them get back on their feet," he recalls.

Self-directed IRA investors can provide a unique and much-needed funding source for families in need. The ripple effect of self-directed IRA investments go beyond the ROI for the individual investor, but extend to all those who are positively impacted by the investment itself.

Save the Family Home

One of my favorite client success stories is a powerful example of what self-directed IRA investing is all about. It centers around one of our clients, Rex from Illinois, and how he used his retirement funds to help a family stay in their home after living there for 40 years.

Rex has been investing his Equity Trust self-directed IRA into distressed single-family homes in the rural Northern Illinois area for over 10 years. In April 2014 he came across a home that had been foreclosed upon and was for sale by an online auction company.

After reviewing some information on the property he decided to drive by to take a look. It was obvious the home was occupied so he decided to knock on the door. As he stood on the porch he noticed a lovely plaque mounted that displayed the family's name. "It was sad looking at the proud plaque knowing this family home was in trouble," Rex recalls.

No one was home during his first visit so he left his business card and received a call from the homeowner, Lily, the following day. Lily was in her late 60s and, although her husband had passed away several years ago, they had lived in the 100-year-old home for over 40 years.

Like many families across the country, Lily had encountered some unforeseen challenges and, though she still worked, the home had gone into foreclosure and needed too many repairs. She intended to move to a smaller rental property nearby after the foreclosure process completed.

Rex was enamored with the home and informed Lily that he intended to bid on her property. Rex's IRA won the online bid and he called Lily to inform her that he was the new owner. Lily expected to move in three weeks but Rex assured her that there was no rush, and she could stay another month without rent while the investment closed.

Enter Katie, Lily's daughter. Katie had moved back to Illinois three months prior and was determined to rebuild her life back in Illinois. Rex saw this as an opportunity to help the family stay in the home while also benefitting his IRA. Here's the deal Rex and Katie put together to save the family home:

- Katie met with a "friendly" home lender in town who is very good at credit challenges. He put a Credit Improvement Plan together for Katie and she is expected to qualify for a home loan.

- Rex signed Katie up with a Rent-to-Own (RTO) Agreement at $650 per month and agreed to update the roof and furnace.

Rex likes to see his rent-to-own customers pitch in with some kind of improvement to the home, so Katie agreed to put up a new porch railing. She provided the labor and Rex's IRA bought the materials. She left with what Rex described as a "new appreciation for the building process" and a brand new porch railing. Another part of Katie's credit improvement plan was paying off any personal debt. Rex's IRA funded a $3,600 payoff of a past collection and some medical bills so Katie could qualify for financing in order to purchase the home from Rex's IRA. Once approved for the home loan, Katie would purchase the home for $20,000 under market value from Rex's IRA.

Here's a breakdown of the full deal:

- Rex's IRA is receiving $650 per month rent per the RTO agreement

- A $540 monthly payment from the small loan of $3,600 to pay off the collection and medical expenses at a 15% return

- $1,500 down payment from Katie

- Home sale to Katie for a $20,000-plus profit at closing

Here is the one-year breakdown of income and expenses for only the home owned by his IRA. It does not include the small loan for a 15-percent return to be received over the next two-plus years.

$30,000 Purchase price at auction

+ $17,000 Rehab costs and property taxes for one year

= **$47,000 Total investment**

$7,800 Rent received at $650 per month

+ $69,900 Sales price to family

= **$77,700 Total income to IRA**

$77,700 total return

– $47,000 total investment

=$30,700 Total net profit to IRA (65-percent ROR projected at a 12 month holding period if needed.)

This story embodies what self-directed IRA investing is all about. Not only was Rex able to diversify his retirement portfolio into real assets with an exciting 65 percent and 15 percent ROI, respectively, but he was able to use his IRA capital to make a positive impact on a family in need.

As Rex concluded in our interview, "Katie (the new homeowner) mentioned she thought many times this would never happen with all the borrower home loan hurdles and recent changes in her life, but today the family owns their home again. After perhaps 300-plus home transactions in my career THIS is my most fulfilling. What a fun day! Thanks to Equity Trust for providing the platform and education for me which helped this transaction occur."

There are people on each end of most every self-directed IRA investment and it is people who are benefitting from the transactions. An IRA or a 401(k) is simply a vehicle to be used to save and invest for retirement. The powerful and uplifting side of the story is the lives that have been impacted by the opportunity self-directed IRAs provide – the investor receiving the much-needed growth in their portfolio, the contractors and local economies that benefit from the investment, and – as is often the case for real estate – the families that are given an opportunity to live and start anew in a self-directed IRA property.

Helping to Rebuild America: Investing in Infrastructure, Education and the Public Good

Taxes are not the most popular topic, but they are necessary to fund governmental programs and services. While the majority of this book is dedicated to teaching you various tactics and techniques that allow you to invest your retirement savings without taxation, our country would be in a dire situation if it were not for tax revenue.

Roads, bridges, damns, public school systems, and public transportation are all byproducts of tax revenue. As county, municipality, state, and federal governments collect taxes from their citizens, they use the tax revenue to fund the various projects and services that the public relies on.

Unfortunately, many public programs are underfunded, specifically the infrastructure of this country. Bridges need to be repaired, roads need to be repaved, and school buildings need to be upgraded – but for many local governments the tax revenue does not meet the demand.

Again, self-directed IRA capital has been able to help fill this void.

Tax liens and tax deeds are two popular alternative investment options among self-directed IRA investors. We'll discuss the topic further in a later chapter, but essentially when a county or municipality has not been paid property taxes on a piece of real estate (it could be land or a building), it eventually places a lien on the property. The lien is then auctioned off to potential investors, many of whom are using their tax-advantaged retirement dollars, so that the county or municipality may cash in and collect some revenue they are owed in property taxes.

We'll discuss the investing side of tax liens later in the book, but I want to draw attention to the mechanism at work here. In addition to investors being able to make a profit (more on that later) and diversify a portfolio by investing in tax liens within their retirement accounts, self-directed IRA capital directly impacts the ability for the country's infrastructure and public services to continue and improve by repaying the much-needed delinquent tax revenue.

As you're discovering, there is more than meets the eye on each self-directed IRA investment and the impact goes well beyond the profit made by the individual investor.

A New School

For instance, Roger from Missouri used his self-directed IRA capital to help a new multi-purpose facility and school in North Kansas City get off the ground. Roger's wife is on the board of the school district and the board put an offer on a piece of land in the area that was owned by a nearby church. They had a limited amount of time to close the deal, with one problem – they didn't have the money.

At this time Roger began to scramble to find a way to fund the $300,000 closing costs. "I knew self-directed IRAs existed, but didn't know a lot about them. It was a real eye-opener from that point of view."

He consulted with various financial advisors, banks, and insurance brokers and Equity Trust kept coming up in the conversation. "I had a considerable amount of money in various funds that I could access," he recalls. Roger spoke with an Equity Trust Senior Account Executive who explained the rules and investing process and then sent him some materials so he could have his attorney review it as well. "You guys were very helpful," he said. "I'm glad I went through you first. Self-directed is the better way to go."

With his newly established self-directed IRA, Roger was able to loan $300,000 to the organization with a promissory note that was secured by the land they were closing on. Roger's loan enabled the deal to close in time, initiate a capital campaign to raise money for the facilities, and hire a Development Director for the project.

"The partnership between parents, civic leaders, and private education provides a desired opportunity for over 300 kids. The capital campaign is going great; they've already raised $2.4 million and are hoping to break ground in the fall of 2015."

The land that Roger's IRA helped acquire will soon house a gymnasium, theater group, a brand new school, and various facilities the entire community can use. This is the real ROI on his investment.

As Roger describes his three-to-five-year promissory note you will notice the return he received goes beyond the profit: "The return monetarily was 5 percent per year, but the difference it made in the attitude of the administration, faculty, and most importantly the children and their parents is not measurable."

Were it not for Roger's ability to invest his retirement funds into the raw land the organization needed, 300 children would still be searching for a brand new facility.

Not only can investors self-direct their savings into alternative investments such as real estate, promissory notes, and tax liens, but an entire town isn't out of the realm of possibilities when investors join a self-directed IRA custodian such as Equity Trust.

An Entire Self-Directed Town

One of our clients, John, is turning a town with a troubled past into a resort and tourist destination in northern California with the help of his self-directed IRA. That's right; John is investing his self-directed IRA into an entire town.

It all started with lakefront property that John owned in his IRA. He and his wife decided to offload the parcel of land in exchange for something with more income potential and worked with his partner to strike a deal with a corporation that owned an entire town. At the time the town of Keddie, California was under the corporation's ownership but John discovered in his research that the corporation was primarily interested in owning lakefront property to build cabins.

John worked with his partner (another Equity Trust client) to strike a deal with the corporation and traded his lakefront property for the town of Keddie. John and his wife's IRA now have a 50-percent stake in the 40-acre with a mere population of 66 people (according to the 2010 U.S. Census).

John's IRA investment has breathed new life into the town of Keddie and several former residents have responded well to John and his partner's pitches for help with the rejuvenation effort. Many have offered to pitch in by either volunteering to mow the grass or lending their construction expertise. The investors have also brought in skilled workers to renovate the town and have made a deal that includes reduced cabin rental in exchange for their volunteer work.

"One nice part of my project is that the final rehab supports hiring over 60 laborers, which will virtually eliminate unemployment in the local community," John says. In addition to renovating and updating the town's cabins for rental, the town's 24-room hotel is being converted into 12 bridal suites and the town's other lodge will either remain as a hotel or be transformed into a convention center.

The investors are also working on reopening the town's lone restaurant and adding actual train cars to it as a sort of homage to the town's beginnings. A restaurateur from Sacramento has donated about $250,000 worth of items from eateries he's closed, including everything from appliances to fixtures.

In addition, a wedding chapel, gift shop, theater and coffee shop are in the works. Away from the town center, an amphitheater is being planned for concerts and old movie screenings.

"It's a fun project, and as you know, it's all IRA money, so it has to build on itself," John explains. "I can't put anything into it. So that's what it's doing. The people we put into the town are working on it; they're building it themselves. From the rent that they pay us, we buy materials they need to continue the rehab. So it's working on itself; it's building itself up."

That last sentence is worth highlighting again. Self-directed IRAs and the investors who utilize them embody the middle class success story that is so important to the American economy – working on itself and building itself up.

Whether it's a house or a town, John is building his nest egg on his terms and keeping every cent he makes. What he's doing in Keddie is nothing short of remarkable and would not have been possible without the ability to self-direct his retirement into this unique investment opportunity.

As we've shared, self-directed IRA capital has far-reaching consequences beyond the ROI for the individual investor's retirement balance. Self-directed IRAs are a tremendous vehicle to grow your personal wealth, and the majority of this book will show you how it's possible, but as you continue reading I want you to keep in mind the ripple effect in the communities and the macro benefits that are also made possible through the use of self-directed IRAs.

Richard Desich, Sr.

Chapter 3: The Upside to Alternative Investments

Investments are often broadly defined by two general categories: traditional investments and alternative investments. Traditional investments include CDs, stocks, bonds, and other similar investment strategies. These types of investments are typically purchased through banks and financial brokers.

The stock market began in 1792 and is one of the most important sources for companies to raise money. The stock market allows businesses to be publicly traded and raise additional financial capital for expansion by selling shares of ownership of the company in a public market. Today, companies continue to raise capital through Initial Public Offerings (IPOs).

Self-directed IRAs haven't received much attention until recently because most custodians who offer IRAs (banks and brokerage firms) don't offer true self-directing at their firms. Large banks and brokerage firms primarily allow stock-related investments because of the ease of management and ability to charge management fees.

The media does not frequently discuss alternative investments because there is not a single source to point to in order to gauge the success or failure of these investments. For example, the stock market uses indexes like the S&P 500 or the Dow Jones Industrial

Average (DOW) to gauge the success or failure of the markets as a whole. They can gauge the risk of bonds through standardized rating systems and provide a point of evaluation for both brokers and investors.

Alternative investments provide a wide range of opportunities that cannot easily be indexed in a single, uniform manner. This additional layer of complexity reduces media coverage for alternative investments and can intimidate investors who turn away great alternative investment opportunities out of concern of the unknown. However, alternative investments can be as simple to understand as the markets. These same marketing challenges that have prevented alternative investments from going mainstream can be the same reason there is opportunity for investors like you.

Unsure of Investing in Alternatives to the Market? We Can Help...

Often, lack of knowledge or experience with alternative investments is a roadblock to using self-directed IRAs. Don't let this happen to you.

With more than 30 years of alternative investing experience, educating investors and providing extraordinary service is a cornerstone of Equity Trust's mission. We are focused on making everyone feel comfortable through the self-directed IRA investing process no matter their experience level.

Every client has exclusive access to:

- Comprehensive education offerings that reveal real investment success stories for every level of investor.

- Training webinars that share real case studies and explain the self-directed IRA investment process and rules.

- Experienced staff to walk you through each transaction.

Plus, our industry-first online account management, client community and educational tool – myEQUITY – is available to help investors become more educated. Over 40,000 clients discuss ideas and experiences in the forums and take part in the monthly "Ask the Expert" question-and-answer forums with guest educators.

Why Warren Buffett said He Would Buy "A Couple Hundred Thousand" Single Family Homes if He Could

When Warren Buffett speaks, people listen. A recent CNBC article[17] reported that, if it were practical to do so, (imagine fixing one hundred thousand leaky faucets) he would purchase a few hundred thousand homes. Buffett even felt that if you can purchase homes at low rates and hold those for long periods of time, this strategy could be better than stocks.

Let's discuss five reasons why alternative investments are becoming more popular with each passing year.

1) **Potential for higher rates of return.** With CDs and fixed-rate investments barely paying a 1 or 2 percent return, investors are looking for better ways to invest their money. Inflation has remained around 3 percent, while fixed investments have plummeted. This has ordinarily conservative investors asking themselves, what other options are available?

   These conservative investors are looking to keep their low-risk profiles in check, while increasing their rate of return. There are many investment prospects that have the potential to maintain lower risk while still providing strong returns that cannot be achieved through bank products like long-term CDs or bonds.

   Those investors who have been heavily invested in the stock and bond markets have grown weary of losing 10 years' worth of gains in the blink of an eye due to market fluctuations. The average return of the S&P 500 from 2001 to 2010 was around 3.5 percent, but included wild fluctuations such as an average loss of 36.6 percent in 2008 and an

---

[17] Crippen, A. (2012, February 27). Warren Buffett on CNBC: I'd Buy Up 'A Couple Hundred Thousand' Single-Family Homes If I Could. Retrieved from http://www.cnbc.com/id/46538421

average gain of 26 percent in 2009.[18] Although long-term returns of the stock market have always trended upward and the market has rebounded and done well more recently, investors rarely know when the next crash will occur. Many in or nearing retirement are searching for other ways to invest their money. Alternative investments provide a wide range of opportunity for those with a little time and a higher risk tolerance to add diversification, and potentially better returns, to their portfolios.

Consider John from Indiana, who after losing close to 50 percent of his IRA in the catastrophic stock market collapse in 1987 known as Black Friday, decided he wasn't about to place his future in the hands of unknown factors again:

> "With all the things going on in the stock market, which you have absolutely no control over, at least with property I'm able to control my investment and be hands-on," John said. "If something bad happens, it's my doing – not Greece, or Japan, or an earthquake."

John's confidence only grew when he purchased a tax lien for $5,000 as his first alternative investment, and ended up selling a deed to the property for $20,000 later that same year. From there he has gone on to make several other successful investments and recalls, "When I think about how many years it would take me to make contributions to an IRA equivalent to what my deals have added into my account…it's just mind boggling."

2) **Invest in what you know.** Alternative investments provide a channel to invest in products or industries you know and understand. Knowledge about an investment substantially reduces risk because the investor understands the intricacies of the industry. This aspect of alternative investments may

---

[18] New York University Leonard N. Stern School of Business. (2014, January 5). Annual Returns on Stock, T. Bonds and T. Bills: 1928 – Current [Data file]. Retrieved from http://pages.stern.nyu.edu/~adamodar/New_Home_Page/datafile/histretSP.html

give investors a greater sense of confidence and control with their investment decisions.

Turning hobbies into investments has been a profitable investment strategy for some. Do you understand a lot about music, or theater? There are opportunities to invest in these industries. What about real estate? Most are at least familiar with real estate from your own experience either purchasing or renting their own homes. Rehabbing homes, property rentals, raw land, tax liens, and even commercial property are potential avenues for tax-advantaged growth in a self-directed IRA.

Even if you do not have experience in alternative investments, many of our clients have researched and learned about a particular industry or investment type and have been able to succeed.

Knowledge is power and this has never been truer. We live in the information age and investors have more access to information than ever before through the Internet, networking opportunities, educational events, and more. Consider the expertise that you've gained through employment, volunteering, or hobbies you've pursued in your lifetime and keep these in mind as the various investment classes are discussed. There are options that can capitalize on your wide range of experience, and that of people you trust, to help make smart investment decisions and grow your retirement savings.

3) **Better control over investments.** When an investor puts money in the stock or bond market, he or she has no control and no input over how the investment performs. They put the money in and hope that advisors, money managers, and executive leadership will make good choices that will bring positive results.

By selecting areas you understand it is possible to more clearly understand the risks you face. Many investors reference the comfort they feel by being able to drive by their investment property or walk through a rehabbed house before making a final decision on their investment. This level of comfort is what attracts a wide range of investors.

Imagine being able to complete research on potential investments, and then the ability to choose where your money will be directed. Maybe it's a foreclosure that is priced well below market value or a private equity position in an industry you know intimately.

Brian, a music teacher from Arizona, used his passion and knowledge for music to help students in his community, and grow his retirement as well. Brian teaches music and kept noticing the same problem when he spoke with other music teachers in the area. Students were interested in learning a particular instrument, but weren't interested enough to want to purchase the expensive piece of equipment for a "test run." Brian realized his self-directed IRA could help. He decided to purchase music equipment with his self-directed IRA, which in turn is rented to children in the community who wish to take music lessons. The proceeds return to Brian's IRA without being taxed and grow tax-deferred.

Brian understood musical instruments and knew a good value when he saw it. He was able to use his self-directed IRA to invest in an "alternative" asset, but one he knew and understood.

When you know what to look for and use your knowledge and imagination, the self-directed IRA investment opportunities are virtually endless.

4) **Better diversification.** Alternative investments allow investors to choose a variety of assets that are in independent industries. You can have some money that is liquid, some in mid-range investments that might tie up your funds for three to five years, and then longer-term investments which might have a horizon of 10 years or longer. This layering provides the opportunity to access funds when they are needed, with the upside potential longer-term options afford.

It is also possible for investors to invest in a range of industries which might include real estate, gold, tax liens, lending and more. There are possibilities for very conservative investors as well as for those seeking a more aggressive portfolio position.

5) **Clearer time horizon.** One important note about most alternative investments is they require a full level of commitment. This is why investing in industries you understand is important. For example, if you are investing in tax liens you may have to wait for two or three years before cashing in the investment. Real estate may require time to improve the property or find a tenant before you can turn a profit. Depending on the strategy, however, you can plan for a shorter turnaround. Lending options can be structured for shorter or longer time periods depending on the specific opportunity.

This level of flexibility gives you the ability to choose a timeframe that best works for your needs. Staggering investments over various time horizons may provide a reduction in risk and can leave funds available when additional opportunities arise.

In our society of instant gratification, waiting can be a challenge. Understanding the time horizon of the investment will provide a greater chance of success and can be factored into your portfolio planning. The best part is that, depending on the type of alternative investment, the time horizon can often be understood upfront. It is difficult to time the markets when investing in stocks or other traditional investments and one never knows when the markets will be up or when they will be down. This can make it more difficult to plan your cash flow and other retirement needs. This uncertainty often results in investors moving to more conservative positions earlier than is necessary.

Who Invests in Alternative Investments?

McKinsey & Company, a global consulting firm established in 1926, and a trusted advisor of over two-thirds of Fortune 1000 companies, released a report titled *The Mainstreaming of Alternative Investments: Fueling the Next Wave of Growth in Asset Management in 2012*. The report detailed that over the last half decade, the amount of alternative assets under management more than doubled and the 14 percent compounded annual growth rate far outpaced that of traditional investments.[19] It was estimated that by the time you are reading this book, as much as 25 percent of their portfolios will be allocated for alternative investments.[19]

So what's the secret that the world's largest investors know? And how can a regular investor like you, with retirement dreams in mind, take advantage? This book is committed to pulling back the curtain to this strategy and empowering everyday investors.

Given that the main source of investment advice is the very banks and brokers that offer traditional investments, the question quickly arises as to who is benefitting from alternative investments?

In October 2013, *MarketWatch* published an article that described how the Harvard and Yale endowment funds have gained an average of 11.3 percent and 12.5 percent respectively, for the fiscal year ending June 30, 2013.[20] These returns are not an anomaly. Yale has averaged 11 percent each year since 2007, when the market collapsed, while the S&P 500 had a 7.1-percent gain over the same time period.[20]

In 1987, Yale changed its investment strategy to include alternative investments and its funds have not had a negative year since. A few

---

[19] Erzan, O., MacAlpine, K., & Szmolyan, N. (2012, June). The Mainstreaming of Alternative Investments: Fueling the Next Wave of Growth in Asset Management. Retrieved from
http://www.mckinsey.com/insights/financial_services/how_alternative_investments_are_going_mainstream

[20] Vardy, N. A. (2013, October 15). How to invest like Harvard and Yale. Retrieved from http://www.marketwatch.com/story/how-to-invest-like-harvard-and-yale-2013-10-15?page=1

years after Yale shifted its investment funds, Harvard followed suit and veered from its traditional investment portfolio of a 65/35 stock to bond split and gained similar returns as a result. The institution's investment strategy now includes investing in real estate, private equity, forests and farmland.[20] This strategy has drawn the attention of other endowment funds, which are utilizing similar strategies and investing in alternative assets.

While it is easy to understand how large endowment funds can take advantage of a large network of resources in order to maximize returns and minimize risks, what about the average investor? Fortunately it does not take billions of dollars to create a portfolio of alternative investments that can provide similar double-digit returns as seen with the Harvard and Yale endowment funds. Let's look at an example of an investor who has found significant success.

Harriett, a theater producer and Equity Trust client, is an award-winning producer of Broadway shows, including *Stomp*, *The Crucible*, and *The Diary of Anne Frank*. Since theater production is what she knows best, she jumped at the chance to invest in Broadway productions in a self-directed IRA. This enabled her to tap into her tax-advantaged IRA funds, instead of using her taxable personal funds.

Recently Harriet was able to invest in a show that was produced in Las Vegas. This was a passive investment for her, which has enabled her to gain high returns in a market she understands intimately. Her first investment will provide a return between 50 and 100 percent, by the time the production stops running. These high rates of return have her looking for other investment opportunities within the theater industry. This is an industry she understands and therefore can make wise investment decisions about productions that will be the most successful, thus providing her with the highest rate of return possible.

Looking for the Upside in a Down Market

Alternative investments can become even more profitable when funded with a self-directed IRA. Self-directed IRAs provide all of the tax benefits that are seen in a 401(k), 403(b) or other tax-advantaged accounts, as long as the IRS rules are strictly followed. Don't worry, we'll explain these rules and will guide you the self-directed IRA investment process in a later chapter.

IRAs can be funded each year by individuals or can be funded through a 401(k) rollover. While job changes can be a stressful time, this is also an opportunity to convert the 401(k) into a self-directed IRA.

Another Equity Trust client, Stan, was suddenly laid off from his job in the aerospace industry when he discovered self-directed IRAs and rolled over his existing retirement accounts to self-directed accounts. What seemed to be a tumultuous life change turned out to be an opportunity of a lifetime for Stan. He took the time to study various investment opportunities and has found success with real estate, private lending, and equipment leasing. Stan has run a successful entrepreneurial business as well as being a full time investor. Stan remarks, "There are investment opportunities around if you are willing to take advantage of them." Stan is living proof that opportunity is what you make of it, especially when it comes to alternative investing, as he now has over a million dollars saved for retirement and routinely invests with a combination of 15 accounts to grow wealth for himself and each member of his family.

Chapter 4: Understanding IRAs – Types of Accounts

All of the alternative investment opportunities we discuss can be utilized without an IRA; however, removing taxation from your investment returns can significantly improve your ROI. If you invest in alternatives such as real estate, and you do not utilize self-directed retirement accounts to do so, you are flat-out leaving tax-free dollars on the table.

What is an IRA?

The acronym IRA stands for Individual Retirement Account. When an employee puts money away for retirement it is usually set aside in a 401(k), 403(b), or other similar program that provides a way to save money for retirement through an employer plan. When an employee changes jobs, they can no longer contribute to the company account and one option may be to "roll over" the funds into another qualified retirement plan, such as an IRA. Individuals can also open an IRA to set money aside for their retirement needs without an employer plan.

According to the Investment Company Institute's research[21], there is a total of $24.9 trillion in total U.S. retirement assets as of March 31, 2015. Over the last 15 years IRAs have increased in popularity and now hold the largest percentage of retirement assets in the country – accounting for 30 percent of U.S. retirement wealth. Defined contribution plans, such as 401(k)s, 403(b)s, 457 plans, and Thrift Savings Plans are the second largest category and accounted for 27 percent of the market share.[21] In what some have called "The Great Retirement Migration," investors continue to turn to IRAs to help support their retirement needs.

The IRA itself is not an investment. Think of it like a house. The IRA is the general account type, or the structure of the home, and you will choose where to invest your funds within the IRA. Similar to the different rooms in your home such as the kitchen, living room, bedroom, and bathroom, each room serves a purpose for you to live comfortably. Retirement investments work the same way – each investment avenue provides a different benefit. Having several different types of investments provides a more diverse portfolio and can potentially provide a more comfortable retirement.

As long as the investments are in the "house" they will receive all the favorable tax treatments that IRAs provide. The funds can be withdrawn from an investment without withdrawing it from the IRA. You can change the rooms in your home without changing the structure of your house. If each room represents a type of investment, you can have many different rooms (investments) within your house. You can change investments (rooms) whenever you'd like, without tax consequences. There may be one room with cash in it, a room with stocks, a room with mutual funds, a room with tax liens, and a room with rental property. You can move the money from room to room (or different investment types) as you see fit, and still gain all the tax benefits, as long as they do not leave the house. When you take the investment out of the house (out of your IRA) it is considered a withdrawal and will receive the tax treatment based on

---

[21] Investment Company Institute. (2015, March 31). The U.S. Retirement Market, First Quarter 2015. Retrieved from
https://www.ici.org/research/stats/retirement/ret_15_q1

the type of IRA and according to the tax laws of that particular account.

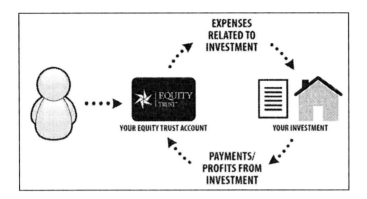

History of the IRA[22]

The Employee Retirement Income Security Act (ERISA) was passed in 1974. Prior to the establishment of this Act, most Americans relied solely on Social Security or pension plans to fund their retirements. Unfortunately, during the 1960s and 70s there were a number of corporations that had not contributed enough to their pension funds in order to make the promised payouts. This resulted in insolvent plans, and workers lost a significant amount of retirement income they had relied on. To address this concern, Congress enacted and President Gerald R. Ford signed into law the Employee Retirement Income Security Act (ERISA). The purpose of the Act was to protect and enhance Americans' retirement security by establishing comprehensive standards for employee benefit plans. The Act also created the Individual Retirement Account, or IRA.

To give the new account flexibility in accumulating assets for retirement, Congress designed a dual role for the IRA. One was to give individuals not covered by retirement plans at work an opportunity to save for retirement on their own in tax-deferred accounts made available through private financial institutions. The other was to give retiring workers or individuals changing jobs a

---

[22] Holden, S., Ireland, K., Leonard-Chambers, V., & Bogdan, M. (2005, February). The Individual Retirement Account at Age 30: A Retrospective. Investment Company Institute Perspective, 11. Retrieved from https://www.ici.org/pdf/per11-01.pdf

means to preserve employer-sponsored retirement plan assets by allowing them to transfer, or roll over, plan balances into IRAs.

Financial advisors were the first to tap into the market by providing the IRA through services they already offered. This enabled customers, who were already clients of the broker, to set aside additional money in an IRA with the stock and bond options the financial advisor offered. Banks came on board by offering IRAs that could be used to purchase CDs and other money market securities, as well as bank investment products. Over the last few decades banking has changed significantly and the product offerings have expanded to brokerage products, including stocks, bonds, and mutual funds.

Important Updates to the Law[22]

The industry has evolved over the last four decades since Congress created the original, or Traditional, IRA. New types of IRAs were added and eligibility and contribution rules have been updated several times. In 1978, Congress established the Simplified Employee Pension (SEP) IRA — an employer-based IRA. Between 1982 and 1986, Congress made the Traditional IRA available to all workers under age 70½, expanding the eligibility beyond those who were not covered by an employer plan and allowing anyone with earned income to make tax-deductible IRA contributions. Beginning in 1987, Congress eliminated the universality of tax-deductible IRA contributions, but permitted workers meeting certain income limits to make such contributions even if they were covered by employer-sponsored retirement plans. In addition, after-tax, or nondeductible, contributions were permitted. In 1996, Congress added the Savings Incentive Match Plan for Employees, or SIMPLE IRA, an account targeted to small businesses.

Throughout the 1990s, additional changes were made to the IRA, including adjustments to spousal IRAs and income limitations. The biggest change was the introduction of the Roth IRA in 1997. The Roth IRA has revolutionized the IRA market and provides additional tax benefits in regard to growth, allowing individuals to keep their earnings tax-free. Contribution limits have periodically increased since the inception of the IRA, allowing for more meaningful annual contributions.

With each adjustment to the IRA, new opportunities for investors have emerged. The IRA is still in its infancy as far as policy is concerned. As more individuals realize they must take retirement into their own hands rather than rely on employers or the government, these changes are increasingly important.

Discovering the Tax-Advantaged Account Types

To decide which type of IRA is right for you, you must first determine how the invested funds will be taxed. Reviewing these accounts and their differences will enable you to select the account that will meet your needs in the most tax efficient way. When you hear the term "self-directed" as it refers to IRAs, 401(k)s, and other retirement accounts, don't be thrown off. The term self-directed refers to the freedom you have with your account. The large majority of banks and custodians limit (whether intentionally or unintentionally) your IRA investments to traditional investments. Custodians, such as Equity Trust Company, that specialize in "self-directed" IRAs, put the freedom and control in the hands of the investor, and allow you to "self-direct" your investment in whatever avenues you see fit, granted that they are within the confines of the rules provided by the Internal Revenue Service.

We will first review the individual account types before moving into qualified plans available to small business owners, and then will conclude with special accounts that help to reduce healthcare and education costs. You will notice many accounts have both a Traditional and a Roth account type, which is an important distinction to understand.

Individual Account Types

Traditional IRA

The Traditional IRA is an account with three key features:

1) Contributions are tax deductible as long as requirements are met, meaning you could potentially reduce your current tax liability with annual contributions.

2) The funds in the account will grow tax-deferred, meaning they grow within the account without tax until they are withdrawn or taken as distributions.

3) When the money is withdrawn it will be taxed as ordinary income. In other words, it will be taxed at the rate your income is taxed. Although the money is taxed on the way out of the account, often owners are in a lower tax bracket at that point in their life and still benefit from the tax-advantaged compounded growth they had received investing their IRA dollars.

This retirement account dictates that the funds must remain in the account until the account owner is 59½. If they are withdrawn before that time they will be taxed and may be charged an additional 10 percent penalty for premature withdrawal, unless it is on the IRS list of exceptions. Contributions cannot be made beyond the age of 70½, at which time mandatory withdrawals are required each year. These withdrawals are commonly referred to as Required Minimum Distributions (RMDs).

You can fund an IRA through three different methods: rollovers, transfers, and annual contributions.

A rollover transfers funds from an employer-sponsored retirement account such as a 401(k), 403(b), 457, TSP, etc. into an IRA. Many workers do this when they change jobs. Rolling over a 401(k) to a self-directed IRA benefits the individual by increasing the available investment options from a dozen mutual funds and company stocks, to an array of both traditional and alternative investments. It also reduces the expenses, as 401(k) fees are generally higher than IRA fees and their accompanying investments.

IRAs and cash within the accounts can also be transferred from one custodian to another. These transfers are generally sent directly from an existing custodian to the new custodian, without the account owner handling the funds. Assuming a direct trustee-to-trustee transfer or rollover occurs from one like account to another, there is no tax liability for either a transfer or a rollover and they do not impact the individual annual "out-of-pocket" contribution limits in the year the transfer is made.

The last method is through yearly "out-of-pocket" contributions. These contributions can only be made by cash, so you cannot move a $5,000 non-cash asset into your IRA, for example. Each year, cash deposits can be made into an account until April 15 of the following year. For example, when you file taxes for 2015, you can make an IRA contribution until April 15 of 2016, for the tax year ending December 31, 2015. As of 2015, the maximum contribution that can be made is 100 percent of earned income or $5,500, whichever is less. Non-working spouses can make contributions under a special provision in the IRS rules. If the account owner is over age 50 an additional $1,000 can be added to the contribution each year. The household income will determine if the contribution amount is tax deductible or not. Contribution limits may change from year to year and are tied to the rate of inflation.

You can set up and make contributions to a Traditional IRA if you meet BOTH of these requirements:

- You (or, if you file a joint return, your spouse) received taxable compensation* during the year

- You were not yet age 70½ by the end of the year

If both you and your spouse have compensation and are under age 70½, each of you can set up an IRA. You cannot both participate in the same IRA.

*Compensation is defined as the wages, salaries, commissions, bonus, alimony and any other amount that you receive for providing personal services. For individuals who are self-employed, sole proprietors and partners in a partnership, "earned income" is another term for compensation. Passive income such as interest, dividends and most rental income are not considered compensation for the purpose of funding an IRA.

Roth IRA

Senator William V. Roth introduced the Roth IRA to U.S. retirement savers in 1997. The Roth is similar to the Traditional IRA, but with one powerful difference – the investment profits in a Roth IRA are tax-free. The difference between Traditional and Roth accounts is important to understand because most investors must choose between the two when electing to make their individual contributions.

The Roth IRA contributions do not offer a tax deduction in the year the funds are deposited. In exchange, the after-tax dollars grow tax-free and all money taken out of the account is tax-free, assuming account requirements are met. Because contributions are made with money that has already been taxed, the amount you have contributed (excluding earnings) can be withdrawn at any time without early withdrawal penalties after the account has been established for five years. All profits and growth are required to be left in the account until the account owner is 59½ and the account has been established for five years or longer. These requirements help to protect their tax-free growth and encourage retirement saving.

You can contribute to your Roth IRA regardless of your age and can also contribute to a Roth IRA for your spouse. Contributions can be made through a 401(k) rollover, a custodian transfer, or annual contributions, much like the Traditional IRA. The annual contribution limits are the same as the Traditional IRA and an account owner can make combined contributions between both a Traditional and a Roth IRA, if desired. The total contributions to both accounts cannot exceed the annual contribution limits provided by the IRS.

You must meet the Modified Adjusted Gross Income (MAGI) limits (found in the link at the end of the chapter) to be eligible to invest and/or contribute to a Roth IRA. This may disqualify high income earners from directly contributing to the Roth IRA. Fortunately rollover contributions do not have the income restrictions that apply to direct (out-of-pocket) contributions, so you may still be able to transfer an existing plan into a Roth IRA. Additionally, if you do not qualify to directly contribute to a Roth IRA, you may still be able to fund a Traditional IRA and execute a Roth conversion so the funds can still be available for tax-free growth by way of your investments. It is important to consult with a tax professional, CPA, or financial advisor when considering these options.

One of the main benefits of a self-directed Roth IRA is that there is no mandatory distribution (RMD) at age 70½ and you can continue to contribute as long as you have earned income, while still maintaining tax-free withdrawals. Additionally, you may be able to pass along your Roth IRA earnings to beneficiaries tax-free so they can also benefit from the tax-free savings you've accumulated.

When you roll over a 401(k) or IRA it will be transferred under the same structure of the existing account. This means if you roll over a Traditional 401(k), it will become a Traditional IRA and the tax treatment will remain the same (tax-deferred). In the same manner, a Roth 401(k) will roll over into a Roth IRA with the same tax-free treatment. As of 2010, you are able to roll over accounts from 401(k)s directly into their Roth counterparts as well as Traditional IRAs to Roth IRAs via a Roth conversion. It is important to seek tax advice for either of these transactions as the amount of the rollover may be taxed in the year of the conversion. Many investors still find this as an attractive option because of the tax-free growth capability.

When deciding between the Traditional or Roth account options you should ask yourself, "Would I rather pay taxes on the seed or would I rather pay taxes down the road when I harvest the crop?" A Traditional IRA allows you to deduct your contribution amounts from your taxable income, thus reducing your tax liability for that year. Since it is a tax-deferred account you are able to reinvest your money and grow it faster than if the investment gains were taxed, but with the understanding that when you remove the money from your account you will have to pay taxes. You are deciding to defer your taxes until the harvest. On the other hand, Roth accounts are taxed on the seed, or when you put money into your account. While you might not see the benefit instantaneously, when you turn that $5,000 into $20,000 the additional $15,000 you just earned will never be taxed. When the harvest comes, what you've cultivated is yours and not Uncle Sam's. It is important to consider your unique situation and retirement goals and to consult with a trusted tax accountant or tax advisor when making these decisions.

Traditional 401(k) and Roth 401(k)

The Traditional 401(k) is a savings plan offered to employees that allows them to set aside tax-deferred income for retirement. The 401(k) is attractive to employers and employees because of the high contribution amounts and large tax deductions available. Plus, at a custodian like Equity Trust, investors still have the ability to self-direct 401(k) investments in both traditional and non-traditional assets.

The Roth 401(k) possesses the same benefits of the 401(k) but with the ability to designate a portion of funds as Roth contributions. Roth contributions may be withdrawn tax- and penalty-free as long as the participant is at least 59½ years of age and has held the account for at least five years. Investors don't have to worry about income limits and they still receive tax treatment similar to a Roth IRA. This plan is available to anyone with a 401(k) and is a benefit to higher-paid employees and self-employed individuals who may have been excluded from having a Roth IRA because of income limitations. Contributions to a Roth 401(k) are irrevocable, meaning once the money goes into the account participants may not later decide to move the funds into a regular tax-deferred account.

The Roth 401(k) has the same distribution requirements as the Traditional 401(k) and participants must begin taking minimum distributions by age 70½, which contrasts with requirements for the Roth IRA. Account holders can often avoid this distribution requirement by rolling over their account into a Roth IRA.

Small Business Account Types (and Why You May Qualify as a Small Business)

Whether you know it or not, you may be eligible for government-sponsored small business retirement plans such as the SIMPLE IRA, SEP IRA, Solo 401(k) and Roth Solo 401(k). Being an investor often qualifies you as self-employed, a sole proprietor or even as your own small business. The advantages of a self-directed SIMPLE, SEP, Solo

401(k) and Roth Solo 401(k) plan over a Traditional or Roth IRA are clear: higher contribution limits and larger tax-deductions. In addition, you are able to contribute to both an individual account such as a Traditional or Roth IRA *and* a small business plan—truly maximizing the investing power of your self-directed retirement accounts.

It's important to know the basic facts about each plan before making an investment decision that will impact your future. The following is a brief overview of the SIMPLE, SEP, Solo 401(k) and Roth Solo 401(k):

Simplified Employee Pension (SEP) IRA

This is a retirement account that is available to small business owners who typically employ fewer than 25 employees and allows individuals to make contributions toward their own retirement without getting involved in a more complex qualified plan such as a 401(k). Any employer (whether a corporation, partnership or self-employed individual) may establish the plan, even if there's only one employee. The SEP IRA operates much like a Traditional IRA in that the contributions are tax deductible to the business, the earnings grow tax-deferred, money cannot be withdrawn without penalty until the account owner is 59½, and withdrawals are taxed as ordinary income. SEP IRA owners are also required to make RMDs when they turn 70½. Small business owners like these plans because they are simple to set up and are a cost effective way to plan for retirement.

The advantage of a SEP IRA over a Traditional IRA is that the contributions limits are much higher. An account owner can contribute up to 25 percent of the earned income of each employee, up to $53,000 per year, compared to the $5,500 limit for the IRA (for 2015). This plan is an employer contribution plan and employees cannot contribute directly. The plan must cover all employees who earn at least $550, are at least 21 years of age, and have worked for the employer in three of the last five years. For a full list of exemptions consult with your tax advisor or visit the IRS website.

Savings Incentive Match Plan for Employees (SIMPLE) IRA

A SIMPLE IRA is another plan option for small business owners and is popular with investors who pay themselves $45,000 or less. It's an incentive-match plan designed for small businesses with 100 or fewer employees that have no other qualified plan. With a SIMPLE IRA, an employer contributes a percent-based salary match to its employees' SIMPLE IRAs, while the employees make elective salary deferrals. The basic framework of this account is similar to a Traditional 401(k) or IRA with the same tax deduction, tax deferment and withdrawal rules.

The SIMPLE IRA was designed specifically to help small business owners (you, if you're self-employed or a sole proprietor) offer a retirement plan to their employees. The main advantage of this plan is that the account balances compound tax-deferred until funds are withdrawn. Plus, an employee can contribute 100 percent of his or her annual compensation, up to a maximum of $12,500 for those under the age of 50 and $15,500 for those employees over the age of 50 (for 2015). Employers are generally required to provide a company match, rather than a set contribution amount to all employees. If the employee does not make a contribution with his or her own funds, the employer is not required to contribute to that employee's account.

You can set up a SIMPLE IRA plan if you meet BOTH of the following requirements:

- You meet the employee limit.

- You do not maintain another qualified plan, unless the other plan is for collective bargaining employees.

Solo 401(k) and Roth Solo 401(k)

The Solo 401(k) is often the most attractive plan to investors, if they qualify, because it combines elements of both the SEP and SIMPLE. This plan is designed for owner-only businesses and spouses. It can be established by both incorporated and unincorporated businesses, sole proprietorships, partnerships and corporations. You can contribute annually through salary deferral, plus a profit-sharing portion of 0 to 25 percent of your salary.

The Solo 401(k) is derived from the 401(k) plan. The only difference is that the Solo 401(k) was designed for owner-only businesses and spouses, while the 401(k) plan is sponsored by companies with multiple employees. The Solo 401(k) plan must be the only plan maintained by the business and the business can't be considered part of a controlled group under tax law.

Two components comprise the maximum Solo 401(k) plan contribution:

- An employee salary-deferral contribution – The employee can contribute up to $18,000 annually ($24,000 if age 50 or older) through salary deferral in 2015, although this may not exceed 100% of the employee's pay.

- An employer profit-sharing contribution – The annual limit for this is $35,000 or 25% of the employee's pay (20% for a self-employed person) for 2015.

The total annual contribution limit from both sources for those under age 50 in the year 2015 is $53,000.

As you can see, for those who meet the eligibility requirements, there is the potential to contribute as both the employer and the employee to maximize your tax-advantaged retirement savings.

Would you like the same benefits of the Solo 401(k) but with the tax benefits of Roth-type contributions? Consider the Roth Solo 401(k). In 2006, Congress merged two of the most popular types of retirement savings plans, the Roth IRA and the Solo 401(k) into a Roth Solo 401(k). The Roth Solo 401(k) possesses the same benefits of the Solo 401(k), but with the tax benefits of Roth-type contributions. If you want Roth tax advantages (tax-free distributions) with a substantial contribution limit, then the Roth Solo 401(k) is for you. Also, if you are interested in a Roth IRA, but you don't qualify because of income limits, then the Roth Solo 401(k) is an option to consider. The same contribution limits apply as the Traditional Solo 401(k) but you can designate the salary deferral contributions you make as Roth contributions. The portion you contribute as Roth does not qualify for a tax deduction but the profits from these contributions grow tax-free, plus all qualified distributions are tax-free. The profit-sharing portion (0-25 percent of your salary) of the Roth Solo 401(k) is just like the Traditional Solo 401(k) and is tax-deferred.

The advantages of a Traditional or Roth Solo 401(k) plan over a Traditional or Roth IRA are clear: much higher contribution limits and larger tax-deductions. It truly is the most powerful retirement plan you have at your disposal!

Specialized Account Types

Finally, as discussed in the Introduction, the cost of healthcare and education continues to rise. Fortunately, there are tax-advantaged self-directed accounts available to help save for both healthcare- and education-related expenses.

Coverdell Education Savings Account (CESA)

The importance of education is clear, but figuring out how to pay for it has become a serious dilemma for students and their parents. An account is available at Equity Trust to help you pay for education costs and ease the burden of debt after college. The Coverdell Education Savings Account (named after creator, Senator Paul Coverdell of Georgia) is a trust or custodial account created for the purpose of paying the qualified education expenses of the designated beneficiary of the account.

When you're ready to establish a CESA, you must have a child under age 18 or with special needs. Unlike other savings plans that require earned income, you don't need income to open a CESA. However, if you do have earned income, you must fall within certain modified adjusted gross income (MAGI) limits. You are not the only one who can open a CESA for your child, however. If a relative or friend wants to help save for your child's education, it's possible for more than one individual to open a CESA for the same beneficiary.

You can contribute $2,000 annually to a CESA until the beneficiary turns 18. For example, if you contribute $1,400 to your child's account, then a relative can contribute the other $600 (you're not permitted to exceed $2,000 for the same beneficiary's CESA in a year). In addition, there's no rule requiring earned income to contribute, allowing your child to use birthday money, holiday money, or even money you give them to contribute to their own CESA.

CESAs have similar tax treatment to the Roth IRA. This includes tax-free growth along with the lack of a tax deduction for contributions. The money can be withdrawn tax-free without penalty when used for qualifying primary or secondary educational expenses. The CESA covers more than just tuition to an accredited college, university, vocational or private grad school however. Funds can also be used to pay for fees, books, supplies and certain expenses related to room and board.

When the beneficiary reaches age 30 the account must be distributed or the remaining funds moved to an account for another qualifying family member (this rule does not apply to special-needs beneficiaries).

Health Savings Account (HSA)

Affordable health care has become a priority for many Americans because the cost of medical care and insurance continues to skyrocket each year.

Fortunately, an option exists that gives you control over your medical expenses and how to save for those expenses – the self-directed Health Savings Account (HSA). Taking advantage of an HSA requires two parts: a high-deductible health insurance policy to cover large hospital bills and an investment account from which you can withdraw money tax-free for medical care. Contributed funds accumulate with tax-free interest allowing you to use those funds to pay for any qualified medical expense you choose.

Imagine lowering your health-care costs today (up to 70 percent less in premiums), while saving for future medical costs by investing in what you know. It's possible with a self-directed HSA. Plus, you take control of what medical expenses to pay. It's not decided for you by a complicated health plan. The items below are just some of the benefits a self-directed HSA provides:

- Contributions are tax-deductible (subject to limitations)

- Contributions can be invested in the same way as a self-directed IRA, accumulating profits without tax

- Distributions are never taxed if used for qualifying medical expenses

- Account balances are carried over one tax year to the next; forget about "use-it-or-lose-it" medical savings accounts

First, you must be enrolled in a High Deductible Health Plan (HDHP). HDHPs are typically defined as a health insurance plan with a minimum deductible of $1,300 for self-only coverage or $2,600 for family coverage. Annual out-of-pocket expenses, including deductibles, can't exceed $6,450 for self-only coverage or $12,900 for family coverage (for 2015).

Next, you contribute pre-tax dollars to an HSA. For 2015, individuals under the age of 55 can contribute $3,350 and families can contribute up to $6,650. You can invest into almost anything you want with your HSA – from stocks, bonds and mutual funds to real estate and other alternative assets – which makes a self-directed HSA unique compared to other medical savings plans. Invested funds grow tax-free. When it's time to pay for routine medical expenses such as prescriptions or routine doctor visits, you decide whether to pay for them out of your HSA or pay out-of-pocket and save your HSA for future medical costs. Your HDHP can cover the larger medical expenses.

By joining an HDHP, you can immediately cut your health costs by as much as 70 percent. How? Premiums for HDHPs are generally much lower than low-deductible health plans. Unlike certain IRAs, there are no income requirements or restrictions for HSAs. However, to be eligible for an HSA, you must be covered by an HDHP, must not be covered by other health insurance (this does not apply to specific injury and accident insurance, disability, dental care, vision care, or long-term care), must not be enrolled in Medicare, and can't be claimed as a dependent on someone else's tax return.

HSAs are tax-advantaged as long as they remain Health Savings Accounts. Funds contributed or earned within the account are never taxed if used to pay qualified medical expenses. However, funds not used for qualified medical expenses are subject to a 10-percent penalty and are taxed as ordinary income for individuals under age 65. Individuals over 65 aren't subject to the 10-percent penalty, but the funds are taxed as ordinary income.

Your HSA is entirely portable and follows you if you change jobs. Plus, you determine how much is contributed to it each year and whether to pay current medical expenses from the account or save the money for future expenses. If you're unemployed or laid off and are collecting unemployment insurance, you may use funds from your HSA to pay for your health insurance premium and routine health expenses – all tax-free. You may also spend tax-free money out of your HSA for long-term care insurance. However, if your new job has a low-deductible health plan, you will no longer be able to contribute but still can invest your current funds.

> For the updated contribution limits and details for each account, please visit:
>
> https://www.trustetc.com/contributions
>
> If you are interested in learning more about the various account options, or have questions regarding your eligibility, **please contact a Senior Account Executive at 855-673-4721 for a free consultation.**

Summary

This chapter does not review the intricacies of each account, but rather provides an overview of the account requirements and available tax benefits.

A self-directed account can provide the flexibility for whatever your retirement goals may be. You can plan to offset healthcare expenses by growing your HSA through successful real estate deals, rather than a small contribution to your other plan each year or you can set your children and grandchildren up for future success by establishing CESAs. As you grow more comfortable and dive into the resources Equity University has available, you can learn creative strategies other clients have implemented to leverage multiple accounts at one time, thus spreading your tax-free or tax-deferred earnings across the various rooms of your investment "house."

Chapter 5: How Self-Directed Accounts Can Offer Diversity with the Most Power

At this point we've reviewed the history of the IRA and showcased the various account types available to investors today. We've touched on the benefit of diversification and how alternative investments have helped strengthen the portfolio of investors both large and small and we've discussed some of the social and economic factors and challenges facing retirees today. Now, it's time to explain how self-directed IRAs can help.

The Do-It-Yourself (DIY) movement has become increasingly popular in recent years. This is now part of nearly every industry and more than a dozen hit TV shows showcase the efforts of DIY. Technological advancements, an increase in free and user-created content, and the use of the Internet can provide more than enough resources to get started and find success on your own.

Two of the biggest problems with the DIY movement are first: knowing what resources and information is reliable, and second: actually being able to implement what you've learned or follow the instructions. For every successful DIY home improvement project there is an equally engaging story of failure. This very hurdle keeps many investors from branching out on their own into the world of self-directed IRAs.

Today there are a variety of "crasher" shows. You may be familiar with shows such as *Kitchen Crashers, Bathroom Crashers, House Crashers* or *Yard Crashers*. These shows select ordinary people with home improvement skills of varying degrees. A general contractor organizes the project and works with the contestant to create a plan and a strategy to implement the plan. While the homeowners receive help from the show's general contractors, they are required to do much of the work themselves.

Self-directed IRAs operate much the same way. Though all decisions are ultimately the investor's, he or she is not left out in the cold. Equity University offers a library of resources that enable you to learn more about various investment options and learn from client investors and industry experts who have found success doing it themselves. Equity Trust's experienced staff and Senior Account Executives are available to answer questions during the execution of your selected investment and can speak to the self-directed IRA rules and investment process. For the investor, this is like completing a renovation with a general contractor present. This additional level of assistance can reduce the learning curve. Then, as you gain more confidence, you can self-direct your retirement investing however you see fit.

Richard, a client from Kansas, recently shared:

> "My experience with Equity Trust is somewhat limited. I have an IRA and a Roth with them and my first investing experience has been in buying tax liens. Not having done anything like this before, the hands-off approach and additional steps required to keep everything legal was uncomfortable initially, but that is where Equity Trust really shines. They were always available to answer my questions and did so in such a way that it was obvious they were knowledgeable and seasoned with these types of investments. The one thing I really appreciate is their willingness to spend as much time on the phone with me as I needed to insure that I understand. As a real estate agent, I have recommended

Equity Trust to all the agents in our office as a resource for their investor clients. I wish I knew about Equity Trust earlier. I would have viewed my IRAs much differently."

Benefits of Self-Directed IRAs

Investor control is one of the most attractive features of self-directed IRAs. Investors are able to move in and out of investments as they see fit. With the proper tools, they can evaluate each investment, its risks, potential return, and the time horizon that the money will be invested. Self-directed IRAs provide tremendous flexibility and allow investors to hand-select investments that not only meet their portfolio needs but are also within their comfort level.

No longer must investors be subject to the whims of an unstable market, not knowing if and how much of a return they might receive. Investing money into an account and hoping that the markets do not decline around the time the funds are needed can be very stressful. The ability to evaluate and make decisions with an understanding of the investment from the outset can bring peace of mind and a greater sense of control.

Why rely solely on the stock market, especially if you don't have expertise in that area, when it's possible to invest in assets you know and understand? Combining your personal expertise and the advantages of an IRA's tax-deferred or tax-free growth can be a powerful investment strategy that allows you to capitalize on the benefits discussed in the following sections.

Compound interest has been called the most powerful force on earth by Albert Einstein and has the ability to increase investment returns exponentially. Einstein was famously quoted as saying, "Compound interest is the eighth wonder of the world. He who understands it, earns it. He who doesn't, pays it."

Compound interest is the interest you earn on both the principal amount and the interest earned on the principal. So, for example, let's say you have $1,000 and you earn 10 percent for a $100 return. The power of compound interest is that you now earn 10 percent on

$1,100, for a $110 return, instead of the original thousand. And on and on it goes.

Time is the most important factor when it comes to compound interest and it's your most powerful ally. Because an IRA is established for long-term use and will not be used until retirement, your funds will compound with each succeeding investment.

For example, if your IRA invests $10,000 in a tax lien and at the end of the year sells the property for $25,000, your IRA has received a $15,000 profit. This provides a 150-percent return on the investment. Due to the tax treatment of an IRA, you are now able to use the original $10,000 plus the $15,000 in profit to invest in the next project without taxation. This compounds the amount of tax-advantaged money available to invest and can therefore increase retirement funds much faster than if you were only re-investing the original amount with each project. This is the benefit of tax-advantaged compound interest.

For a simple example, let's say you begin to take the $4 you spend on coffee each day and start putting it toward retirement when you are 25. At this rate you'll save $121 a month, or $1,460 each year. If you received 9 percent in compounding interest each year, you would have $23,415 after 10 years. After 20 years, you'd have $221,520 and after 30 years, when you are 55, you'd have an amazing $566,440 as indicated in the chart below.

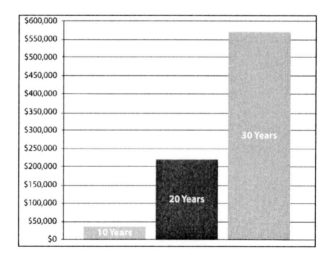

The power of compound interest is that you are earning the 9-percent return on the lump sum of the account and not just on the amount you contribute each year. For example, after investing for ten years you would earn the 9-percent return on a balance of $23,415 instead of simply the $1,460 you put into your account that year.

Compounding interest is an extremely powerful concept, but investors often fail to account for taxation when performing these compounding calculations. If we remove the variable of taxation from your compounding calculation you will see that you can accelerate the accumulation of wealth. And how can you eliminate this variable of taxation, you ask? – Simply by using a self-directed IRA or other tax-advantaged investment account. Let's illustrate this for you and demonstrate the tax related efficiencies of a self-directed IRA.

Tax savings are one of the key reasons investors use self-directed IRAs rather than investing in the same instruments outside of an IRA. Tax savings will either be tax-deferred or tax-free, depending on the type of account that has been established. Either option will provide compounded growth faster than in accounts that are taxed each year. Plus, in tax-deferred accounts you may be eligible for a tax deduction on annual contributions, thus reducing the amount you pay in taxes that year.

For example, if a home was purchased, renovated and resold in less than a year outside of an IRA, all gains would be taxed at the ordinary income tax rate. Let's say the home was purchased for $50,000 with an additional $20,000 in renovations and the home was sold for $100,000. Your $30,000 profit would be taxed as ordinary income in addition to any other applicable taxes. In a non-tax-advantaged account your taxable income would be increased by the profit from the sale and may even move you to a higher tax bracket, adversely affecting *all* of your income's tax liability. If, for example, you were in the 25 percent income tax bracket it could result in paying $7,500 in taxes on that investment, reducing your profit to $22,500. In a self-directed IRA however, that $7,500 does not leave the account and can be re-invested for even more growth. Let's make this even clearer and remove the real estate investment from the equation.

If you were to contribute $4,000 a year to a tax-advantaged account (like an IRA) and assume an 8-percent compounded interest rate of return for 30 years, your self-directed IRA would be worth $449,133 at the end of year 30. If you made the same investment in a non tax-advantaged environment (a brokerage account), assuming a 31-percent tax rate, it would be worth $286,752 instead of $449,133. That is 43 percent less, a difference of $162,381!

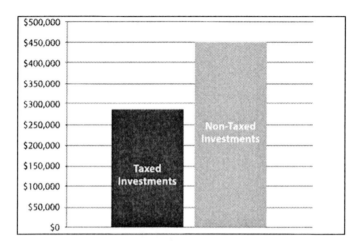

The tax savings available with IRAs is clear, but when you combine the added power self-directed IRAs give you by investing in alternative assets like real estate, the difference grows even more. Savvy investors have been using this strategy for decades, and now it's time you join them.

Calculators: Compound Interest and Investment Returns

Compound Interest – How interest is calculated can greatly affect your savings. The more often interest is compounded, or added to your account, the more you earn. This calculator demonstrates how compounding can affect your savings, and how interest on your interest really adds up:

https://www.trustetc.com/resources/tools/calculators/compound-interest

Investment Returns – Meeting your long-term investment goal is dependent on a number of factors. This not only includes your investment capital and rate of return, but inflation, taxes and your time horizon. This calculator helps you sort through these factors and determine your bottom line. Click the 'View Report' button for a detailed look at the results: https://www.trustetc.com/resources/tools/calculators/investment-return

Asset protection and generational wealth building are two additional benefits self-directed IRAs provide. IRAs are afforded protection under federal bankruptcy law and thus generally are shielded from creditors in bankruptcy proceedings. Consult a tax attorney for further guidance on this topic. Additionally, certain IRAs allow assets to be passed to beneficiaries while generally avoiding probate and taxes. Self-directed IRAs can benefit your family's financial future with estate planning that leaves valuable IRA assets to loved ones without the burden of taxes.

Raising capital with self-directed IRAs is one of the lesser known, but powerful aspects of these accounts. It's conceivable to use your self-directed IRA or other people's retirement plans to fund your deals, as we demonstrated in Chapter 2 when discussing the "democratization of capital." Recent estimates place over $24.9 trillion within IRAs, 401(k)s and other qualified programs across the country, with $7.6 trillion of assets held in IRAs.[21] These funds could potentially be used to invest in a variety of alternative investments, such as real estate, private entities, start-up businesses, notes and many more. Some investors may be willing to loan you the capital needed for your investment with terms secured by the investment for an agreed upon rate of return and others may be willing to partner on the deal as co-investors. Often times the first step is to make others aware of the possibilities of their own retirement plans – the ability for them to be in control and to invest in alternatives to the market.

Selecting the Right Custodian

Choosing which company will custody your IRA often determines which investment options are available. The company that holds your IRA is the account custodian; as such, there may be specific investments that an IRA custodian offers or specializes in facilitating, and by selecting a custodian you may be selecting your investment options as well. It is important to understand the IRS requirements and characteristics of an IRA (pursuant to IRC §408) when selecting a custodian:

1) IRA investments must be held in the name of the IRA and not in the name of the account owner or beneficiary.

2) The Trustee of the IRA has the authority to act for the IRA; the IRA account owner gives instructions to the IRA custodian.

3) The Trustee of the IRA must be a federally chartered bank, federally chartered credit union, or state-chartered financial institution.

4) You cannot serve as your own Trustee or custodian of the IRA since the law requires the Trustee of the IRA to be a financial institution or state-chartered trust company.

Custodians are not required to offer an entire range of investment options, even if the investment is acceptable under the IRS guidelines (IRC §4975). As a result, finding a custodian that will allow the investment types you are interested in (or may be interested in down the road) is the most important consideration. From there, fees, customer service, security, and other account details should be evaluated. Even among companies who offer self-directed IRAs the product availability will vary widely.

Equity Trust Company is one of the longest standing companies offering self-directed IRAs and is an industry leader in experience and expertise. The Company offers a full range of options that are not limited to one sector or one type of account. Equity Trust is proud to offer truly self-directed IRAs, thus allowing investors like you the most control and opportunity.

Taking the Important First Step

If you are looking to take advantage of the self-directed IRA benefits we just went over, the most important thing you can do is get started. There is no substitute for starting early, primarily due to the benefits of compounding interest. The longer you allow your account to grow, the greater the chance of success.

The challenge to getting started is there are a lot of distractions and demands on your time and money. Plus, retirement may seem too far away or too overwhelming to worry about now. Yet if you start saving and investing as soon as you are hired for your first "real" job, you will get in the habit of setting aside money for yourself. This habit will help develop better money management skills and will help you build wealth for retirement.

I've seen it time and time again with our own clients. After discovering the power of self-directed IRAs and benefitting their own retirement, many clients open accounts for their children as soon as possible. They've seen the power of compounded tax-free growth first-hand and want their children to benefit for as long as possible.

If you are well into your career, however, there is no time like the present. By starting a self-directed IRA now, you can take advantage of compound interest for your remaining working years. While the final amount you have at retirement may not have compounded for as long it could have if a savings plan were implemented at an earlier age, it will put you ahead of where you will be if you continue to wait. With every second you decide to wait, that's another second your money isn't working for you, and another second you decide to accept the crushing blow of taxes.

Take a look at this chart for a second because I want to show you the importance of starting now.

Age	Scott Invests	Scott's Return	Michael Invests	Michael's Return
19	$2,000	$2,240	$0	$0
20	$2,000	$4,749	$0	$0
21	$2,000	$7,558	$0	$0
22	$2,000	$10,706	$0	$0
23	$2,000	$14,230	$0	$0
24	$2,000	$18,178	$0	$0
25	$2,000	$22,599	$0	$0
26	$2,000	$27,551	$0	$0
27	$0	$30,857	$2,000	$2,240
28-65	$0		$76,000	
Retirement Totals	$16,000	$2,288,966	$78,000	$1,532,166

Scott began investing $2,000 per year eight years sooner than his friend Michael. Scott only contributed annually for the first eight years while Michael tried to play catch-up by contributing $2,000 for the next 39 years. They both earned 12-percent interest on their money until they were 65. So who do you think benefited most from the compound interest? This is why Einstein described compound interest the way he did. Scott was able to invest $62,000 less (and in less time) than his friend Michael but earned over $700,000 more because he leveraged the power of compound interest. Not only that, but compound interest and an attractive 12-percent return turned Ben's $16,000 into almost $2.3 million that he can use for retirement.

Saving early gives you the advantage of being able to start with a small amount and build wealth steadily over many years. The longer you wait, the less time there is to build for retirement and reach your goals. The result is one of three things: more money must be invested, more risk must be taken in an attempt to obtain a higher rate of return and catch up for lost time, or you must work longer and delay your retirement. Either that or you may have to modify the plans and goals you are looking forward to in retirement, which no one deserves.

These are the steep consequences that millions of Americans face today because they have delayed adequately funding a retirement account. While it is not possible to turn back the clock, it *is* possible to start today, set a strict budget, establish a retirement account, and begin taking advantage of the powerful benefits we've reviewed.

With the cost of living rising rapidly and improvements in healthcare and technology extending life expectancy, it is more important than ever to have a well-thought-out retirement plan.

Where to Invest? – Understanding the "Why" and "How" First

Where or what you will invest in is not nearly as important as understanding how and why. It is not necessary to have an alternative investment in mind before establishing a self-directed IRA, because when you open an account you are opening the door to take advantage of opportunities as they occur. Many alternative investment opportunities come and go quickly. If you are not prepared to act on the opportunity there will be others who will recognize its value and they will be the ones to invest. It is always better to have an open door than a closed one.

For this reason it is best to set up and fund an account before determining which specific opportunity to select. This will give you time to research areas of interest, identify opportunities, and perform your due diligence knowing when the time is right you can act.

If you know how you would like to invest (in a tax-advantaged retirement account) and why (to take advantage of compound interest, tax savings, asset protection, and the ability to raise tax-advantaged money for investments you know and understand) then you are already in position to take advantage whenever the "where" comes about. Allowing time to research opportunities and understand the investment thoroughly will always provide the best scenario for success.

Fortunately self-directed IRAs do not require an all or nothing approach. It is possible to invest a portion of your retirement funds in a self-directed account while leaving other funds in traditional investments. This will allow you to gain knowledge and become comfortable with the various alternative investment opportunities and the self-directed IRA investment process. Many investors start out self-directing a small percentage of their portfolios into alternatives and gradually allocate a greater percentage of their overall portfolios into their self-directed account as they find success and gain more confidence.

Often investors are told that it is not possible to invest their IRA in real estate or other alternative assets. You may still encounter CPAs, banks, and other financial professionals who are not aware of the opportunities available with self-directed IRAs. This is merely due to an education gap. For this reason it is important to perform your own due diligence before making any investment decisions. Equity University provides a vast array of resources to educate both you and your support team regarding the legality of self-directed retirement account investing.

Chapter 6: Toolbox of Options – What Makes Sense for You?

When it comes to investing, everyone has a different comfort level. Fortunately there is a vast array of investment options that may meet the needs of different investors. The options you pursue will greatly depend on your preferred investment style, tolerance for risk, and overall investment goals. We recommend that you meet with a financial advisor to identify your goals and the investment style right for you.

Types of Investors

Conservative investors. These investors are often referred to as savers and are looking for safe instruments they understand. They seek returns that are known upfront with very little left to chance. As a result, conservative investors are willing to sacrifice higher rates of return for the comfort and stability of knowing exactly how much money will be coming in.

Speculative investors are willing to take a greater level of risk in exchange for higher potential returns. Speculative investors generally are not as sensitive to losses as conservative investors and feel they will recover with the next great investment. They understand that not every opportunity will be a winner but, when it works, it is well worth the risk. They are willing to speculate and take the risk.

Moderate investors understand logically that they need to take risks to make money, but are still sensitive to aggressive risks. They like a middle-of-the-road approach – not too conservative, but not too risky either. This is perhaps the most common investor type. Many moderate investors have saved conservatively over the years but, as they approach retirement, worry if the lower returns of their conservative investing will be enough to accomplish their financial goals.

Specialists are investors who understand a few industries extremely well and choose to invest heavily in those industries. Specialist investors believe that understanding the industry is the number one factor in finding a good investment and trust their specialized knowledge to lead them in the right direction. For example, specialists may be small-business owners who have mastered the intricacies of their market or someone with a particular skill or experience in a certain industry.

Passive versus Active Investing

As you and your advisor consider your investment style and risk tolerance, also consider the level of involvement you'd like to have in the process. Active investors seek out new opportunities and prefer to be directly involved in their investing. They get excited about finding real estate deals and overseeing the project. They are willing and able to attend tax lien auctions, actively scour MLS listings, or actively network to source more deals. These investors are energized by the projects they find and are motivated to learn, study potential opportunities, and find more deals.

Passive investors are typically less interested in being involved with the investment process and would prefer to stay hands-off and allow the returns to trickle in. These investors may be more apt to invest in lending opportunities where they might finance the project of an active investor. A good comparison between active and passive investors can be found in real estate. An active investor may be more interested in a rehab project where he or she can directly oversee a subcontractor's renovation of the home and have a hand in selecting the appliances, layout, and décor of the home. Meanwhile, a passive investor might be drawn to turn-key real estate or rental properties that are managed by a property management company. If a passive investor wants to invest in tax liens, he or she is more likely to hire a tax-lien service agency to identify properties for his or her portfolio rather than attending the auctions personally. The passive investor might also gravitate toward a Real Estate Investment Trust (REIT), as opposed to a physical piece of real estate.

The important point is that whether you are an active or passive investor, whether you are more conservative or willing to accept risk, there are opportunities in the alternative investment space. The key is to understand what makes you tick and what makes you successful, and then leverage that knowledge with a self-directed IRA.

Areas of Expertise

Self-directed IRAs make it easy to take advantage of your areas of expertise. Starting in markets or industries you understand or are passionate about can shorten the time it takes to learn the investing side. Every industry offers investment opportunities, and to find those opportunities you must look at the industry through a different lens. Not as a consumer, employee, or industry specialist, but as an investor. People often can't get over the anxiety of making an "investment." But if you reframe your mindset and begin to look for needs in the market instead of "investment opportunities," you may find opportunities available that you never previously considered.

Take Patrick from Maryland for example. He used his experience in the medical technology industry to build for his retirement. Patrick had an interest in technology from a young age and even ran a part-time television repair business for some extra cash at the age of 15. As he grew older and more experienced Patrick eventually became a medical electronics technician and then worked as a field technician for various X-ray and medical imaging technologies. A few years ago Patrick found an interest in real estate and discovered the concept of self-directed IRAs. As he explained, "I decided that this was something I wanted to do but wasn't comfortable investing in real estate yet, but I wanted to at least get a Roth IRA started. I really believe you need to start by building your Roth with what you know best and leverage your mind for your retirement."

Patrick decided to leverage his knowledge of the medical imaging industry to grow his Roth IRA. He began purchasing older models with his Roth IRA and reselling them to small doctor's offices and medical practices. Patrick discovered that hospitals (with larger budgets) were willing to sell their outdated equipment at a discount when they decided to upgrade their technology. Patrick's Roth IRA purchases the equipment and then identifies a smaller office that is looking for a piece of equipment on a budget. These smaller offices are willing to accept a perfectly functioning, though slightly outdated, model for the right price. On one of his recent deals, Patrick's Roth IRA purchased the OEC 9600 C-Arm 1994 Model for $8,000 and resold it to a doctor's office at the market value of $16,000.

This strategy has enabled Patrick to invest where he feels comfortable and in what he understands. He's been able to grow his Roth IRA tax-free as he continues to learn more about real estate.

When deciding where to begin, start with what you know. Is there an industry you know extremely well? Is there a hobby where you have developed a skill you can turn into an investment opportunity? Consider your own skill set, and the knowledge of your peer group, and opportunities are sure to emerge if you begin to take control and think creatively.

Other Factors to Consider

What kind of investor are you? When establishing an investment strategy, begin in your comfort zone and you can always branch out from there. If you start as a conservative investor you may not remain there. As you gain more knowledge and experience you may find you are willing to take on more risk with investments you have researched and now understand.

On the other hand, if you are currently an aggressive and speculative investor, you may adjust your investment strategies to a more conservative approach as time passes and you near retirement. The key is that there is no right kind of investor. There is no one style that works for everyone. It is a matter of assessing where you are in life, what your goals are, and what investment style best meets those needs.

Identify specific goals. After gaining an understanding of your investment style (or during the process), write out your financial goals. The more specific, the better. Look at all your financial goals, long- and short-term. How many years are there until retirement? Are you in a place where you need growth or steady income? Look at your overall job and family situation. Are you and your spouse close in age and on track to retire at the same time? Do you own a home that is building equity or is a home purchase still on the horizon? Do you have children and anticipate upcoming college expenses?

These questions can help to establish both short- and long-term goals. While retirement is a long-term goal, there are many other family goals that also require financial planning and there are accounts that specialize in tax-savings for many of these goals and needs.

It is always best to consult with your financial advisor or other trusted financial professional to help with this exercise. You can use what is presented in this material as a starting point for deeper and more specific conversations with your support team.

There are a variety of calculators that can help when considering your retirement plan. Feel free to browse our website's resource calculators at: https://www.trustetc.com/resources/tools/calculators

Understand tax implications. When evaluating which funds to invest within an IRA, CESA or other tax-advantaged account, consider your tax situation. Most people feel they pay too much in taxes and want to make financial decisions that will minimize the amount of money they owe the government each year. Planning is the best way to mitigate taxes. Meet with a financial professional or tax advisor to discuss ways to reduce taxes. Consider the immediate deduction offered from Traditional IRAs and 401(k)s and the tax-free growth offered in Roth accounts. If you have a low income year it might be a good time to consider rolling over a Traditional IRA to a Roth IRA while your income tax rate is reduced.

Just like you get an annual checkup to safeguard against health issues, meeting with a tax advisor or financial professional will help to ensure the financial decisions you are making each year will provide tax benefits that are consistent with your overall investment strategy.

Retirement and estate planning. Retirement planning should consist of more than just accumulating cash for retirement. Combining financial planning and estate planning will help to account for the bigger picture. Too often we think that estate planning is for the "other guy," the guy with more wealth or more property. The reality is that if you have children, if you own anything, if you have loved ones – you are in need of estate planning.

Estate planning not only considers the cash needed for retirement, but also additional costs and expenses such as education, healthcare, and the cost of raising children. It considers insurance such as life, disability and health insurance. It creates a tax-efficient strategy that will impact all of your financial decisions and allows you to be better prepared, regardless of what events transpire during your working and retirement years.

The reality is that we never know what our life is going to look like. Primary income earners become disabled, children lose parents to accidents, and family members get sick with illnesses. While we all hope that these events never come our way, no one can predict the future. Lack of planning can lead to financial disaster. The better prepared you are, the better you can handle unexpected events as they occur. This requires estate planning in addition to retirement planning. IRAs have the added benefit of designating beneficiaries. You have the opportunity to pass your wealth to future generations while maintaining the tax advantages and can set your children up for financial success. In addition, IRAs are afforded protection under federal bankruptcy law and thus generally are shielded from creditors in bankruptcy proceedings.

Setting up an Account

Once you have a basic understanding of your investment style, how you want to invest, what risks you are willing to accept, and the best way to create tax-advantaged growth, you are ready to open an account.

As we discussed earlier, there are three ways to fund a self-directed IRA. You can make annual contributions to the Traditional or Roth IRA. This contribution can be made every year going forward. CESAs, small-business retirement accounts, and HSAs all have different contribution limits previously discussed.

If you have IRA funds with another institution you can transfer some or all of those funds into a self-directed IRA. This will be a custodian-to-custodian transfer. If you are not sent a check, there is no IRS reporting necessary and no tax consequences to the transaction. If you choose to have the check mailed to you and take active receipt of the funds, you have a 60-day window to return the funds to a qualified plan. If you miss the window there may be taxes and penalties owed and it will be considered a withdrawal. This is referred to as a 60-day rollover and you are only permitted to perform this once in a 12-month running period across all plans in your name.

Rollovers can be completed from 401(k) plans with former employers. This process will be dictated by the former employer and if you elect this method, we can walk you through the process. In this case, often the previous custodian of the 401(k) will issue the individual a check and it is important to deposit it immediately as the same 60-day rules apply.

The last of the account open options is a conversion. This includes taking a Traditional IRA (or other tax-deferred account) and converting it to a Roth IRA. As the rules have recently changed, this has become a transaction that is in high demand. This transaction triggers initial tax consequences and may not be available to everyone due to income limitations. Meeting with a tax advisor or financial planner prior to a planned conversion is recommended to help minimize taxes and understand the financial consequences of the transfer. For many, taking a tax hit one year, in exchange for tax-free growth over the next several decades makes sense, although you want to understand all your options before completing a conversion.

It's possible to combine several account funding methods for your self-directed IRA. It is also important to remember that conversions and transfers do not count against your accounts' contribution limits each year.

Chapter 7: It's Time to Start Self-Directed Investing! Understanding the Process

Once your account has been established and funded, identifying an investment that will meet your established strategic goals is the next step. The process of investing is simple, but there are a number of rules and regulations set in place by the IRS that must be followed to ensure the tax advantages for the account remain in effect.

Equity Trust supports a wide range of investment options to choose from, some of which will be detailed in the following chapters. Before we discuss the investment options, it's important to understand the investment process, rules and regulations. It will help set the framework for any of the self-directed IRA investment options you consider.

Follow this six-step process and you could be on your way.

Step 1 – Identify Your Investment

Review the investment chapters to determine which avenues most interest you and can help meet the goals for your portfolio and your retirement. Our goal is to help get the wheels turning and help you think creatively now that you know your investment options are not limited to traditional investments. Study the investment opportunities and decide which resources are needed. Seek to find opportunities within the investment field you have identified will meet your goals. Always consult with your tax, legal, or financial advisor to determine if an investment is right for you.

Once you've identified a qualifying investment opportunity for your self-directed IRA, you are ready to move on to the next step.

Step 2 – Perform Your Due Diligence

Carefully examine the investment for risk and return potential. Research every aspect of the investment and make sure you feel comfortable with all parties involved and the terms and conditions of the deal. Consider possible worst-case scenarios and make sure you have a contingency plan in case things don't go as planned. Verify that all IRS rules will be followed and the investment is not listed among the prohibited investment options. Then, verify that the transaction will avoid all prohibited transactions and will not involve a disqualified individual. Seek counsel from a tax, legal, or financial advisor who can help you understand how to follow the rules in your particular case.

Step 3 – Request Funds for Investment

When you are ready to make your investment, you must complete a Direction of Investment form that details information about the investment, how much it costs, and where to send the funds. There are various forms that need to be completed depending on the type of investment you have chosen. These forms will describe the terms of the transaction, will include any supporting documentation related to the investment, and provide Equity Trust with the direction of the amount of funds needed, including where the funds should be forwarded. Part of self-directed IRA investing is that the IRA is for your benefit, but you cannot touch the funds directly.

It is important to remember that all documents related to the investment must be titled in the name of your IRA; not you personally:

Equity Trust Company Custodian FBO (your name or account number) IRA

All funds, expenses and profits must flow to and from the IRA without passing directly to the account owner or the individual. It is important to follow these steps to qualify for the tax benefits the account provides.

Equity Trust has years of experience and can answer any questions you have regarding how to fund an investment or how to arrange for proceeds to be properly deposited into the account.

Step 4 – Process the Investment

Once all appropriate documentation is received, Equity Trust processes your Direction of Investment form and will send funds for the investment based on your directions. Equity Trust will retain all documents you provide pertaining to the investment (such as real estate deeds, original notes, operating agreements for LLCs, etc.). It is your responsibility to locate and provide these documents.

Equity Trust will process the request and send funds to the appropriate party as instructed by you on the completed forms.

Step 5 – Manage the Investment

Once your IRA owns the investment, all expenses and profits related to the investment must come from and return to the IRA.

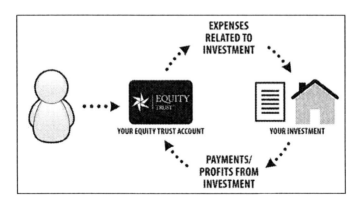

You will make all account decisions regarding when to collect payments, sell, upgrade, or repair an investment, or request additional funds that are needed to manage the investment. As a passive custodian, Equity Trust will complete the instructions based on your discretion, but will not offer advice on how to manage the specific investment.

As the investor/owner of the IRA, investment choices will fall on your shoulders. Equity Trust will assist with procedural issues that keep the account in compliance with the IRS rules but will not offer advice on which investments the investor should choose.

Think of self-directed IRA investing as a three-way partnership that forms a three-legged stool. The first leg is you, the investor, who works with your support team to select the goals for the account and the investments that will be pursued. The second leg is your tax, legal, or financial advisor. They offer valuable advice on how your investments factor into your overall portfolio and how to manage the account in a way that follows all of the IRS rules. The third leg is the custodian of the account. They provide the administrative support needed for the account. This includes storing documents provided by the investor, processing investment funds according to the investor's instructions, accepting deposits, etc. Each leg is essential in order for the stool to stand.

Step 6 – Sell the Investment

Once you've negotiated the sale of an investment with a buyer, you must complete a Direction of Investment form which instructs Equity Trust to remove the asset from your IRA.

When the time comes to sell the investment, all profits will be returned to the investment account without being taxed, freeing up funds for the next opportunity.

> **Infographic: How Does a Self-Directed IRA Investment Really Work?**
>
> For an infographic depiction of the self-directed IRA investment process portrayed as a road map, set up or log in to your user account to view it here:
>
> https://equityuniversity.customerhub.net/process

As you can see in the 6-step investment process, you must provide direction to the custodian regarding all investment decisions. This adds an extra step to the investment process, however the tax-advantaged growth makes it well worth the extra step.

Equity Trust is available at any time to answer questions about a particular transaction and can add clarity for the investment rules that must be followed. Feel free to give us a call at 855-673-4721 and a Senior Account Executive will be happy to assist.

Prohibited Transactions and Disqualified Individuals

This topic will be covered more extensively in a later chapter. The basic concepts are outlined below.

Prohibited transactions include:

- Certain collectibles, such as:
    - Artwork
    - Metal (with some exceptions)
    - Rugs
    - Antiques
    - Gems
    - Stamps
    - Coins (with some exceptions)
- Life Insurance
- S-Corporations

Disqualified individuals include:

- Yourself
- Your spouse
- Parents and step-parents
- Grandparents and step-grandparents

- Children, step-children and their spouses

- Grandchildren, step-grandchildren and their spouses

- Any fiduciary (examples may include a stock broker, tax attorney, accountant, or financial planner)

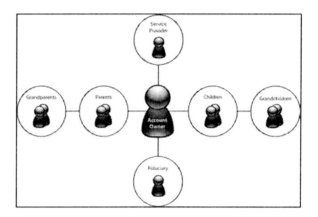

For more information, consult a tax, legal, or financial advisor or visit the IRS website and see Publication 590, which covers specific requirements for IRAs. There are many transactions that require additional attention and it is important to be aware of the rules and seek professional advice before acting.

> ## YouTube Video: Self-Directed IRA Rules and Regulations
>
> You can also watch a 3-minute video from Equity University's National Education Specialist regarding the self-directed IRA rules and regulations. Visit out YouTube channel to watch it today:
>
> https://youtu.be/_bj_gzjuNjY

The consequences for not following IRS rules are that the account may no longer receive preferential tax treatment, and the entire account may be considered a distribution and taxed as ordinary income. This may result in a loss of up to 50 percent of the funds to taxes when considering both the high tax rate and penalties involved.

Investment Options

The next set of chapters will take an in-depth look at possible investment opportunities. While it is in no way an all-inclusive list, it will cover popular alternative investments as held in other customers' accounts at Equity Trust.

These will include real estate investments such as rehabbing homes, rental income properties, raw land, commercial property, foreclosures, and tax liens.

Notes and mortgages can include both buying and lending opportunities. Real estate options, probate, precious metals, private equity and business opportunities are all available within an IRA, where all gains and profits are either tax-free or tax-deferred depending on the account type.

Richard Desich, Sr.

Chapter 8: Investing in Rehab Properties

Rehabbing real estate is an investment option which can be very profitable for investors and is probably the example you see most often in your self-directed IRA research. The idea behind this type of investing is that the appreciation and value of the home can be accelerated through improvements to the property rather than relying solely on the markets and the passage of time to increase the property value.

If you understand how to inspect a home to gain an understanding of upgrades and repairs that can improve the property value and can work closely with contractors to accomplish the project, rehab investing has the potential to provide profitable returns in a relatively short time period. Rehab projects generally have a shorter time horizon and can even close within 90 days or fewer, depending on the necessary upgrades or repairs. When a rehab investment is successful, it can provide a significant boost to a retirement account, often in less time than could have been accomplished through traditional practices. In the example we shared of Wayne and Alicia's rehab in New Orleans, they returned more than $37,000 tax-free into their Roth IRAs in just 102 days, a 35-percent ROI.

How Does Rehab Investing Work?

Sometimes a rehab is a home that has gone into foreclosure. A foreclosure is created when a homeowner has failed to pay the mortgage for an extended period of time, sometimes a year or more. The result can be a home damaged from abuse, neglect or lack of maintenance. These homes often will require upgraded or replaced appliances and need a fair share of cosmetic work. Depending how long the home was vacant, other issues may arise such as broken pipes, vandalism or structural damage.

Homes suitable for rehab may also come from homeowners who are relocating to a new job, elderly individuals who are moving into a retirement living situation, or from those who have recently passed away and the family wants or needs to dispose of the home quickly. When an owner has a change in life circumstances, change of health or suffers the death of a spouse, they become motivated sellers. Often they have a lot of equity in their home and, due to the circumstances, are willing and able to sell the home below market value in exchange for more liquidity. These opportunities can result in low-priced purchases that can occur quickly. The homes have generally not been updated over the last several years, but do not suffer from the abuse commonly found in foreclosures. Homes can be more difficult to locate before they are listed with a real estate agent, which can slow the process. Looking for auctions and estate sales is one way to locate properties that are sold below market value and can make excellent rehab investments.

Not all rehab investments involve a distressed property or distressed seller. Many investors use their knowledge of the real estate market and seek to find properties that can be made more desirable for a particular market, even if the home's original condition was in pretty good shape. They may find opportunities in growing housing markets or feel confident in their ability to improve the property enough to make a profit on their upgrades.

Key Things to Consider

Profitability. It can be easy to make a costly mistake when rehabbing a piece of real estate. Sometimes it's buying a home that needs more repairs than anticipated or a home that takes longer than anticipated to sell. In the rehab market, these factors can be the difference between being profitable or not.

To determine profitability, calculate the cost of the home, the cost of needed upgrades or repairs, the carrying costs or cost of holding the property, and the cost to sell the home. These must be weighed against the amount you think you can make on the sale. The best way to determine the profitability is to inspect the home carefully with a certified inspector before the home is purchased. Discuss a timeframe for upgrades and repairs with a contractor. This will help to establish realistic time frames and the costs associated with the investment property. The more you understand the rehab and home improvement markets, the better.

Cost. The cost of the home includes the purchase price and any additional costs such as inspection fees, appraisals, attorney fees, filing fees, etc. The repair costs must then be added to the price of the initial investment. You will typically want to sell the rehabbed home quickly to reduce the cost of holding the asset. This may mean not seeking the highest dollar for the home, but rather a price that will move the home quickly while still producing a desired return. Once these costs have been considered and the estimated sales price established, you can determine how much profit can be made over the months it will take to rehab and sell the property and can plan accordingly.

Market conditions. One key to successful rehabbing is finding homes that are located in hot real estate markets. Finding a location and neighborhood in high demand is a key to success. If the current owner is having a hard time selling, it may be a red flag for a buy-and-rehab approach and may better serve as a rental investment instead.

Hot markets are also where others are looking to buy so there will likely be more competition as market conditions improve. You may not be able to find homes at extremely discounted prices since other investors may have identified the same potential in the area and compete to drive up the prices.

It is important to understand exactly what you will need to put into your investment so you can forecast your profit potential. Diligent home inspections and selecting cost-effective improvements are a close second to location when you are setting your priorities. Understanding market conditions, inspections and repairs, or partnering with someone who does, can help prevent buying mistakes that can reduce or eliminate profits.

Cost-Control Case Study

Scott is an Equity Trust client from Ohio who utilized a creative deal structure to ensure the expenses of his rehab project did not cripple his profit potential. Scott found a home in a sought-after part of town that had a reputation as a public nuisance.

He bid on the property and his self-directed IRA purchased the home for $68,404. Scott worked with a local contractor who hired employees recently released from prison and trying to make a living and get their lives back on track. (This again speaks to the larger benefit self-directed IRA investments create. Scott's investment created local jobs and provided gainful employment to Americans needing a second chance while also renovating a public nuisance property.)

The strategy Scott used on this deal included an agreement with his subcontractor that specified a fixed amount for the rehab and renovation of the home. His subcontractor agreed to complete the entire rehab process for $24,000 – allowing Scott to more easily factor his expected return on his investment. It also reduced the risk that he got caught up in the project and overextended his funds on extra improvements that were not necessary to make a profit. The fixed expense allowed his subcontractor to budget exactly what needed to be done to improve the property. The subcontractor agreement was actually finalized before Scott's IRA closed on the property. He was able to start the project with a clear and concise financial projection.

Scott's subcontractor ended up going over budget by an additional $1,000 but did not miss the expense goal of $24,000 by much. In just four and a half months Scott was able to sell his rehabbed property for a 45-percent ROI. That's an annual yield of more than 100 percent on his investment – something rarely found outside of self-directed IRA investing. All told, Scott's investment breaks down like this:

- Initial Purchase: $68,404.55

- Subcontractor Expense Budget: $24,000

- Subcontractor Additional Expense: $1,000

- 4½ Months of Utilities: $947.63

- Total Expenses: $25,947.63

- Total Costs (expenses + purchase price): $94,352.18

- Sale Price: $125,265.39

- Total Profit: $30,913.21

- Return on Investment: 45.19% in 4 ½ months

- Annualized Return on Investment: approximately 135%

By capping his expenditures, Scott was able to more accurately predict and anticipate his investment return. Since real estate is a tangible asset, something you can walk through and inspect, it is much easier to predict and plan for the investment, especially when compared to the rise and fall of the stock market. While the value of real estate is affected by market conditions and a host of other factors, you have much more control over the value of your investment property. When you upgrade a dilapidated kitchen with new kitchen cabinets, appliances and floors, you can see the increase in value with your own eyes. You have control over how the investment performs by controlling the management, improvement, and sale of the asset.

What are the Benefits of Rehabbing Homes?

Fast profits. One of the biggest advantages of rehabbing real estate is the relatively quick returns. Real estate is generally a market that is characterized by slow and steady appreciation, which over time converts into a nice nest egg of equity for owners to enjoy. The rehab market is the stock car race of the real estate world. It provides the ability to purchase neglected homes whose current owners were unwilling or unable to improve, and reap a higher return through sweat equity. (Please note: Rehabs in a self-directed IRA require the sweat equity to be completed by a non-disqualified third-party, not the IRA owner. We'll discuss the rules in further detail in a later chapter.)

I want to share the story of Michael and Janet, and the successful rehab they completed in Concord Township, Ohio (pictured below). They said they look for homes in good areas and that have "curb appeal." The home in this scenario was located in an excellent school district with proximity to a beach, community pool, and a playground. They purchased the home for $41,000 and then scoured *The Home Depot* and *Lowe's* for the best deals on rehab supplies. They instructed their contractors to update the interior of the home with a new furnace, lighting, flooring, and kitchen. They also improved the curb appeal with a new front door and paint job. In just 131 days they were able to sell the home for a profit of $18,313 tax-free into their Roth IRA. There are few investment vehicles available that allow you to make such a substantial profit (44.6-percent ROI) in a mere four and a half months.

Secured collateral. Real estate can be considered a safe investment in terms of its role as collateral. Regardless of what happens, the property will have some type of intrinsic value. Many investments outside of real estate can put the entire investment at risk. If you put $100,000 in the stock market, it is possible to lose the entire investment amount. Real estate, on the other hand, typically holds some intrinsic value and is more a matter of finding someone to purchase or fill the property you are holding, rather than taking a total loss.

Slower market transitions. The rehab process could take a matter of months instead of years. This reduces the risk of market fluctuations impacting the value of the investment. While it is possible for the market to suddenly turn, real estate market fluctuations are generally slower.

Backup plan. If for some reason the costs are higher or the market changes, causing home sales to lag, it is possible to convert a rehab into a rental, thus reducing or eliminating the possibility of losing money on the property. This may create a challenge to convert short-term financing to a long-term solution, but if things do not turn out as anticipated, there is a built-in backup plan that can also result in a profitable investment with cash flow.

Robert from Kennesaw, Georgia found success in his very first rehab (pictured above). He identified a 60-year-old ranch house that was "a neglected mess," as he put it. Robert purchased the home for $56,000 with his IRA and had to sink about $45,000 of renovations (paid from his IRA) into the home. After updating the wiring, plumbing, paint job, and roof he decided to gut the inside to create a better flow by knocking down walls and moving doorways. He says the home is probably worth $120,000 now and decided to generate a steady cash flow by renting the home for $1,000 per month. He did such a wonderful job on the rehab, his first tenant agreed to pay the entire first year in advance! The monthly rental checks are returned into Robert's IRA tax-deferred. The best part is summed up in Robert's own words: "Equity Trust made it all pretty easy for our first rehab, from buying the house through the rehabbing project. We had a ball fixing it up and the neighbors love us for upgrading the neighborhood." Not only do self-directed investors generate exciting profits for their own retirement, but they are improving neighborhoods around the country one rehab at a time.

What are some Risks of Rehabbing Investments?

Higher than expected costs. The biggest risk is when the cost of repairs is higher than expected. This could include finding mold, needing to upgrade the electrical system, or needing a new HVAC system. High-dollar repairs can impact profits significantly. They can also result in delays that extend the time the property is held. If you secured short-term financing, this can impact the carrying costs and thus reduce profitability.

The best way to mitigate this risk is by working with an inspector who will provide a thorough evaluation of the property before the purchase price is secured. The other is to work with a contractor who can complete the repairs at an affordable price and in a timely manner. This is especially important when you are just starting out. Having a trustworthy team in place that provides reliable information will help you steer away from money-pit properties and invest in those that will be the most profitable.

Another risk is if the property does not sell as quickly as expected. When you are paying interest by the day, week, or month, every delay means the cost of the money borrowed goes up. If the property was paid for with cash, this is less of an issue; however the profits will be delayed by the longer sales cycle. Carrying costs can also become an issue if the home cannot be sold in the amount of time expected.

Higher-than-expected cost is a risk factor that becomes especially important for self-directed IRA investments. Since all expenses and profits must flow directly from the retirement account, it is imperative that you factor some cushion into your investment plan in the event your IRA must pay more than expected. Running out of available IRA funds can put your entire investment at risk.

Over- or under-renovating. Understanding the market and the expectations of buyers at a particular price point is very important in rehab work. In the wrong market, selecting expensive upgrades at a higher price point may make the home more difficult to sell. While selecting lower-grade improvements may result in the inability to ask for a higher price that would maximize profits. Understanding the current market and visiting homes currently for sale at the price point of the investment you are considering will help to establish what upgrades are most appropriate for the investment. Adding luxury appliances and amenities in a middle-class neighborhood may out-price your market and make it more difficult to find a buyer. Another danger investors run into is when they begin to see themselves as the interior decorators they see on television rather than investors. Does the rehab property really need a granite counter top or can you replace it with a less costly, but comparable, surface? Remember, this is your investment, not a fun renovation project (though it can often be both).

Profits, Taxes and IRS Rules

Tax implications are important to understand in real estate investments. If a property is purchased outside of a tax-advantaged account and sold within a year, profits are considered ordinary income. When there are significant profits, this can result in substantial taxes up to 39.6 percent of what was earned. Often investors think real estate is taxed at a low rate (capital gains) even when it is purchased through a taxable vehicle. While this is true for properties held for more than 12 months from the purchase date, it will not generally be applicable for rehabs because of the quick turnaround.

If a property is purchased in a Roth IRA the profits will be tax-free and you will have access to the initial investment and all profits for the next purchase. This enables you to start with smaller homes at a lower price point and work your way up to more expensive homes, which can result in even larger profits over the same time period.

Properties purchased within a Traditional IRA or other tax-deferred vehicle will allow all profits to return to the account without tax, making them available for future investments, and compounded growth, and taxes will be paid when distributed in retirement.

It is important to review prohibited transactions when completing real estate rehabs in an IRA. For example, you cannot complete any of the work on your own. Work must be contracted to a non-disqualified third party.

There are also specific rules regarding lending practices and what options are available for financing a property within an IRA. These will be discussed in a later chapter. Many banks are hesitant to finance property held within an IRA because the loans must be non-recourse, but there are those that specialize in self-directed IRA financing. Many investors also utilize private lenders to help finance the purchase of rehab homes. It is best to check with a tax, legal or financial professional to ensure no mistakes are made in regard to the IRS rules for self-directed IRA real estate investments.

Rehabbing Overview

Real estate rehabbing can be a great way to convert retirement funds into significant profits. It's an investment option that is best for active investors who have the time to oversee the purchase, renovation, and sale of the home, or have someone they trust who can oversee the work.

The ability to finance the investment with non-recourse loans, private money lenders, or a combination of multiple retirement accounts makes it possible to invest in rehab homes without needing a large amount of money in your individual account.

As an active investment the rewards can be high, as long as you purchase a home at the right price and are able to repair and sell the home for a profit. Rehabbing is an opportunity many do not realize can be used to build for retirement, but it has helped thousands of investors take control of their financial futures.

Webinar: Maximizing Your IRA with Rehab Investing

Andrew Holmes, an experienced real estate investor, reveals how it's possible to turn real estate rehabs into cash flow for your IRA. Set up or log in to your user account to watch it now:

https://equityuniversity.customerhub.net/rehab1

Webinar: "How I've Turned Real Estate into Pots of Gold in my IRA"

Equity Trust client and experienced real estate investor/educator, Robyn Thompson, and Equity University National Education Specialist, John Bowens, host a free webinar to share the profit-making, tax-saving real estate investments she's used to grow her IRA. Set up or log in to your user account to watch it now:

https://equityuniversity.customerhub.net/rehab2

Richard Desich, Sr.

Chapter 9: Investing in Rental Properties

Rental property investing is all about cash flow. It is important to find homes with low debt payments and high rent values to cover your expenses. This is especially true when investing in an IRA. You must be able to pay all expenses from the IRA, ideally through the income (rent) received from the property.

Rental investments can provide steady income and can be a fantastic investment for those reaching retirement age or looking for additional streams of income. Creating residual income has become a popular topic among investment circles. Residual income is income that comes in regularly without requiring a lot of additional work to generate the income.

Previous generations have looked to Social Security and pensions to provide residual income during retirement years. With pensions drying up and becoming a rarity and with the threat of Social Security being underfunded, investors are seeking vehicles that will provide steady, consistent income to provide for retirement needs. Rental properties can be a great source of residual income, while not significantly impacting the value of the asset.

For the past 10 years, Neil, a retired attorney and Florida resident has experienced the value of buying real estate in his Roth IRA first-hand by acquiring rental properties. A few years ago when the real estate bubble burst, Neil leveraged the market conditions to bolster his portfolio while also helping less fortunate residents weather the same market.

He recently had a tenant in one of his rental properties tell him that her mother and her mother's husband were being forced out of their rental unit. The owner wanted to sell it and they were wondering if he had any houses for rent.

Neil didn't have anything available at the time, but that didn't hinder him.

"These renters were good people, so I thought, well, why don't I just go ahead and let them look at some houses," he recalls. "And if it's one they want, let me go ahead and buy it for them if they sign a long-term lease."

He contacted a real estate agent he knew from the Central Florida Realty Investors Association, who rounded up three different properties that were close to his current tenant. He let the family pick one out.

They chose a house with a two-car garage and a swimming pool listed at $49,900. After learning the real estate agent paid less for the property than the listing price, Neil bargained the price down to $45,500 with no closing costs.

The tenants signed a five-year lease. The terms state the lease only changes if the Consumer Price Index increases. Neil also bypasses some of the expenses of updating the property because the tenants have agreed to paint and take care of other maintenance in exchange for discounted rent.

Neil collects $10,200 in rent each year, which means the house will pay for itself after four years, the rest will be tax-free income for his retirement. He has managed to receive a 25-percent annual return on his investment.

This is just one of several houses he has bought using his self-directed Roth IRA, a retirement account that he says "is the best thing for me since sliced bread."

What is Rental Property Investing?

Rental investments come in two primary forms. The first, as monthly rentals (typically with a one- or two-year lease) and the second, as weekly or vacation rentals. There are important distinctions, benefits, and risks to each type of rental investment.

Monthly rentals have a lower operating cost, as the tenant will generally pay additional home costs such as utilities. There is often less ongoing maintenance such as lawn care or basic upkeep of the home, which the renter generally provides depending on the lease agreement. Along with lower operating costs, income can be easier to predict which can help to manage costs more effectively. There are also lower management fees due to the single tenant feature as opposed to management of an apartment complex.

Weekly rentals can provide a higher weekly return (often close to what is collected for a monthly rental) but will also have a higher percentage of time the property is empty, depending on the location. These properties are typically located in a popular tourist or vacation destination and have the amenities that vacationers are looking for. This can include views, close proximity to activities, and features like hot tubs and pools.

Weekly rentals also have higher maintenance costs. Utilities must remain on, and the costs of homeowner's dues, pools or other amenities must be considered. It is necessary to have a maintenance person on call along with a reliable housekeeper that can clean the property between renters. As a result, management companies are often used to manage weekly rental properties. However, due to the higher operating costs, property management fees for weekly rentals can eat into the return from rental income.

Investor cash flow is critical to successful rentals and should be carefully considered. Higher management fees can impact the ability to create positive cash flow. This is especially true if financing is a part of the expense equation.

How Does Investing in Rental Property Work?

The goal of investing in rental properties is to create a positive cash flow each month. To accurately access annual costs, many factors must be considered. First is the cost of ownership. What is the monthly carrying cost of the property? Add taxes and insurance payments that must be paid each year and add the costs of upgrades or repairs. It is a good idea to set aside an additional budget for expected and unexpected repairs and maintenance. Another important consideration is deciding if you will manage the property or if you will hire a property management company. If you are planning on investing in rental property with your IRA it is important to ensure you are following the IRS rules and regulations, which will add an additional layer of decision-making when considering the factors that were just discussed.

What will those costs be? Research must be completed on the rental rates for the neighborhood as well as the occupancy rates. If there are a lot of empty rentals it may be more difficult to fill your property. Rates might have to be lowered, and you may find you must pay all the costs for the property for several months at a time while waiting to find a new renter.

What are the Benefits of Rental Property?

Rental properties create ongoing cash flow that can last for years. They have the potential to provide a steady stream of residual income for your retirement years.

Another advantage is the rental income is received while the property hopefully appreciates in value. This means that down the road, you may be able to sell the home and receive an additional profit from the principal investment, in addition to the rent that was received over the years.

We'll use an example to demonstrate this concept further, but keep in mind this is simply to represent the benefit of the rental income plus the appreciation of the asset. It is a simplified representation rather than a financial projection. Let's say you purchased a home for $100,000 and rented it for $1,000 a month for 10 years. (For this example we will assume that rental increases only covered the increase in expenses, holding expenses and rental income steady.) Assume the value of the home increased at 5 percent a year and the total operating expenses were 30 percent of rent (this assumes no mortgage, average expenses and upgrades as needed in addition to taxes, insurance and property management fees). Generally speaking, the numbers would look something like this:

Accumulative	After Year 1	After Year 3	After Year 5	After Year 10
Income	$12,000	$36,000	$60,000	$120,000
Expenses	$3,600	$10,800	$18,000	$36,000
Value of Home	$100,000	$115,762	$127,628	$162,887
Total Profits	$108,400	$140,962	$169,628	$246,887

This long-term investment can be attractive for those seeking to gain steady residual income. It also can be an excellent investment for those wishing to leave a legacy to their families as the value of the investment may continue to appreciate, even when rents are being withdrawn for retirement needs.

Paul, an Equity Trust client from Michigan, is a former financial analyst for Ford Motor Co. who, after researching many potential investment types, decided real estate was a relatively stable place to put his retirement funds.

"It's a tangible property, it's always going to have some value, and you have control over the property to some extent," Paul remarks. "It makes you feel better about the actual collateral (rather than investing in the stock market)."

Paul converted his Traditional IRA into a self-directed Roth IRA to allow his savings to grow tax-free. He finally pulled the trigger in January of 2012 and his Roth IRA purchased a 20-year-old single-family-home in nearby Wayne, Michigan for $32,000.

He currently leases the property to a Section 8 tenant for $850 per month in rent, which is paid jointly by the government and the tenant. After paying the property taxes, his Roth IRA nets nearly 26 percent in profits annually, which grows tax-free. He received 31 percent of his investment back in just the first year.

For the most part, owning a property and being a landlord has been "smooth sailing" for Paul, though he acknowledges it takes some work on the front-end to size up potential properties and make sure it's a solid investment.

Now that he's dug into one self-directed investment and it's been cash-flowing for a year, he's anxious to explore more self-directed deals – not just real estate.

He also intends to continue spreading the word about this investment funding source, with which few of his real estate industry peers and financially savvy friends are familiar.

"I'm shocked how few people know about self-directed IRAs," he says. His own accountant was one of the ones in the dark about the strategy before Paul told him about it. "He described it as a secret of the industry," he says about his accountant. "I got to thinking...it is kind of like that. I don't know why, but it is."

What are the Risks of Rental Property?

There are several risks involved with rental property that need to be considered. The first is when a renter signs the lease but doesn't fulfill their agreement to pay each month. If you have selected to hire a management company, they will typically handle the eviction procedures, which vary by state. However, you may still find yourself out of several months' rent while evicting the tenant and may need to invest in repairs before the property can be rented again.

Selecting good tenants is the best way to mitigate this risk. Performing adequate due diligence is key. Running credit, verifying employment and speaking with former landlords are all common and best practices. Speaking to the previous landlord will often provide a more accurate assessment of the kind of renter they are, but keep in mind that the current landlord may give a positive review in order to get a bad tenant out of his or her hair. It is also good to understand the laws of the state where the property is located. Any non-compliance of the law will extend the time the renter can remain in the home, costing you more money.

Another risk is the home will sit empty. If it takes two or three months to get the home rented, you must cover all the costs of the home from your IRA while receiving no income in return. This will often include additional costs like a home security system, maintaining the property and lawn, or leaving utilities on, which would normally be paid by the renter.

The other risk to consider is that maintenance costs could be higher than anticipated. Some investors choose to purchase annual home warranties which can spread out the maintenance costs and provide a more predictable expense structure. If the roof or HVAC system needs to be replaced, these can be very costly expenses that will reduce profitability.

Profits, Taxes and IRS Rules

If the property is invested in a tax-advantaged account, all profits are either tax-free or tax-deferred each year. If you do not need the funds to live on and refrain from taking the rental income as distributions, the rental income and appreciation will accumulate within the account without being taxed. When the property is eventually sold, all proceeds from the sale return to the account either tax-free or tax-deferred, depending on the type of account.

If the rental property is in a Traditional IRA it is important to note that the profits will be taxed as ordinary income when withdrawn from the account, which can be higher than the long-term capital gains taxation real estate would ordinarily receive. For this reason many investors who are interested in self-directed IRA rental investments will convert a Traditional IRA (or other tax-deferred account) into a Roth before investing.

It is critical that all IRS rules be followed with regard to prohibited transactions and disqualified persons. This means that if you have purchased a rental home on the beach, you and everyone who is considered a disqualified person cannot use the property. You cannot hire a disqualified person to complete work on the home, even if you pay market rates. This is considered self-dealing and is disallowed by the IRS.

Rental Property Overview

Rental properties can be an excellent investment for long–term retirement needs. They can provide income along with appreciation, much like dividend-paying stocks, but often with less volatility in the market. You can receive monthly or weekly income in addition to the overall appreciation of the asset.

After ending her 26-year career on the police force, Roxie from Florida has found a way to reinvent the way she earns income for herself using a method that she only recently discovered: self-directed IRA real estate investing.

Roxie had her retirement savings in stocks and bonds, only because she thought it was the only option for building her retirement savings. "I didn't really like stock investing; I like self-directed investing better," she says. "With stocks, you have to know when to sell, when to buy, when to do all that stuff. I know when to buy, but not when to sell."

Real estate investing, coupled with the capabilities offered through the self-directed IRA, turned out to be the perfect combination for Roxie.

"The self-directed IRA gives you cash flow," she says. "If you put everything out into stocks, you have nothing coming in. That's what I like about investing in real estate with my IRA – you have cash flow."

Roxie closed on her first property in June 2014: a single-family house that she's leasing with an option for the renters to own it. Her investing activity has taken off in a few short months. As of October 2014, she had seven self-directed transactions under her belt, consisting of six lease-to-own properties and a note. These investments have already gained more than $15,000 in income back to the IRA, mainly from the monthly rental payments the properties generate.

She sees her investments as a win-win. In addition to supplementing her retirement income, she's helping members of the community.

"It's hard to get bank loans now," Roxie says, adding "I'm helping people who couldn't get a note so they can become a homeowner."

During your retirement years, cash flow needs to cover expenses. Once the financing has been paid off, rental income can provide consistent residual income. The home could be paid for several times over through the rental income, before cashing in by selling the home.

Due to the favorable tax treatment of long-term real estate, the biggest benefit can be found in a Roth IRA where the profits may be accumulated tax-free. Outside of an IRA, depreciation is added back when a property is sold, improvements must be tracked to add to the cost basis, and selling an investment can be a very complicated process. Without solid recordkeeping, you could end up paying a lot more in taxes.

A Roth IRA reduces much of the tax complexity surrounding the sale of real estate because all profits are tax-free. To benefit, the IRS rules must be followed exactly while the investment is held within the IRA. All activity must be at an arm's length and it is important that you, or any disqualified persons, never use the property for personal use or work directly on the property, as defined by the IRS.

As long as the rules are followed, rental investments have the potential to provide tax-free or tax-deferred residual income through your retirement years. This investment option helps to mitigate the concern of running out of money during your golden years.

Audio: Real Estate Client Panel

A panel of Equity Trust clients and real estate investors discuss their experiences. They share their thoughts on the decision between a buy-and-hold or buy-and-flip exit strategy and provide cost-saving rehab tips they've learned over the years. Set up or log in to your user account and listen here:

https://equityuniversity.customerhub.net/real-estate-panel

Chapter 10: Investing in Foreclosures

The unforeseen real estate market collapse of 2008 brought news of foreclosures to the headlines and many investors flocked to foreclosed properties, purchasing them at a premium. On the surface, this seemed like an easy way to make money in real estate and became popular among the "get-rich-quick" speaking circuits.

Like most investments, a "get-rich-quick" mentality is dangerous. Success in the real estate market involves education, time, wise investments and understanding the risks involved in making the transaction. Foreclosures, in some ways, are one of the more complicated real estate investment options. While it may appear on the surface that you cannot lose, buying property at a significant discount, like any investment there are no guarantees. Taking the time to learn and understand the intricacies of this market will provide the best opportunity for a profitable return.

What is Foreclosure Investing?

Foreclosure investing involves purchasing property where the current owner has been unable or unwilling to make the mortgage loan payments. This can happen for a variety of reasons. Sometimes failure to make loan payments comes from a job loss or if a family is overextended and stops making payments on a second home to focus on keeping their primary residence. Another reason may be a correction in the real estate market where the homeowner experiences a decline in home values and finds themselves upside down – owing more on the home than what it is worth – causing them to default on the loan. Whatever the reason, it creates an opportunity for investors to purchase homes at a discount, and then potentially profit from the lower price.

How Do Foreclosure Sales Work?

There are three stages to a foreclosure, each with different risks and opportunities for the investor. The stages are pre-foreclosure, foreclosure, and post-foreclosure.

Pre-foreclosure is when the homeowner has fallen behind on the payments, but the bank has not yet taken control of the property. Generally in pre-foreclosure the homeowner still occupies the home. At this stage it is possible to work with the homeowner so they can purchase their home back.

As an investor, finding pre-foreclosures generally comes from having contacts in the industry or the local market. Often it is a bank or a real estate agent who can direct the investor to owners who have fallen behind on mortgage payments.

Short sales are common in pre-foreclosures. In a short sale the bank agrees to accept a sale amount that is lower than the amount that is owed. This process allows the homeowner to get out of the loan without owing the bank the full amount and saves the bank the expense of foreclosing on the property. While the bank is accepting a loss, it is a favorable option that allows the bank to dispose of the property, recoup some of its investment, and remove it from its books. The downside of a short sale is that they can often take a very long time to process, sometimes as long as six months. For an investor who is trying to make a profit on the home, money is tied up waiting for the sale to go through.

There are many risks with a pre-foreclosure. Each state has specific procedures that must be followed when the homeowner defaults on a loan and, if those procedures are not followed exactly, the homeowner may have legal recourse against the investor. There is also the risk of additional liens on the property that the owner fails to disclose. Doing your homework and performing your own due diligence on the property is critical. Another risk is if the homeowner files bankruptcy during the period of negotiation. If bankruptcy is declared before the loan closes, the courts may tie up the property in the bankruptcy, requiring the investor to try to collect through the bankruptcy proceedings.

With proper research and due diligence the investor can mitigate these risks by understanding the laws surrounding pre-foreclosures in their target market.

Foreclosure. This is when the bank seizes the property (and the deed) and tries to recoup its money through an auction. Most counties hold foreclosure auctions at the courthouse. This investment is risky, because the investor is often not allowed to inspect the home prior to the auction. The auction list is provided and the investor can do research on public records, as well as driving by the property, but are usually unable to fully inspect the home. The home could have water damage, termites, structural damage or other serious issues that cannot be discovered without a proper home inspection.

As with any auction, funds are generally paid that day, although some counties give the investor a window of time (i.e. 10 to 30 days) to pay. If the property is still occupied it may be necessary to evict the previous homeowner, though generally the homes are empty. That being said, angry homeowners have been known to cause damage to homes they are leaving. From taking all the appliances and cabinets, to putting holes in the walls, there are plenty of horror stories that have surfaced from foreclosures gone poorly. Part of the reason the prices for these homes are so low is because they will nearly always need repairs before it can be sold or used.

Post-foreclosure. This stage involves the purchase of real estate that was not sold at a foreclosure auction. These properties are also called REOs or bank-owned properties. Often, beginners start with post-foreclosure investments since these properties are often listed with local real estate agents and can be found in MLS listings. Working closely with an agent who specializes in post-foreclosures can also be very advantageous.

Post-foreclosures typically provide the lowest risk and the lowest profit margins in the foreclosure niche. You can inspect the property and, though the home or business will most likely be sold as is, there is time to evaluate the property condition and to assess the cost of needed repairs.

How Do You Begin Investing in Foreclosures?

First, you must establish the goals for the property. Will the property be a rehab, a quick sale, or will the property be used as rental property? Depending on your answer, each scenario requires a different strategy.

Rehabbing foreclosed homes requires an active market. If there are a number of foreclosed homes in the neighborhood, or within a few miles of the property, then it may be difficult to fix up the property and resell the home. Beyond the neighborhood, what is the general real estate market for the zip code and the city where the home is located? These factors can help to determine if the home is a good investment.

Typically the goal for a rehabbed home is to repair and sell it quickly. This means the initial purchase price of the property needs to be low enough, when combined with the cost of repairs, to not exceed what the home will sell for in the local market. In growing markets, money can be made quickly through rehabbing a foreclosure and reselling the home.

Savvy investors look at down markets much differently than the average person. They see an opportunity to get in on the ground floor when the prices are low and will reap the benefits as the markets turn back around (often in part to the rehabber improving the quality of the neighborhoods).

Take Gail for example, who lives in one of the country's hardest-hit real estate markets – Detroit. Some might say you'd be crazy to invest in real estate in the area, but Gail disagrees. "It's the best business to be in right now," she says. Considering the fact that Gail netted a 118-percent return on investment in the first deal she completed with her IRA, it is hard to argue with her positive attitude. At the time of her investment, the area's foreclosure sales had increased significantly compared to the previous year and Gail jumped in by purchasing a home in need of serious repair for $17,000. Gail had to invest an additional $15,000 from her IRA to rehab the property, but her efforts were well worth her time. Just a short time later, Gail was able to sell the property for $70,000, all tax-deferred, and nearly doubled the value of her IRA in her very first self-directed deal. Not a bad investment for a foreclosed home in hard-hit Detroit.

Renting a rehabbed foreclosure property does not typically require too strong of a real estate market for success. Instead, rental property requires a strong demand for homes to rent. How long are rentals listed before being filled? What is the demand and the rental rates, in relation to the carrying costs of the home? These questions will help to determine if the property will be better suited for a rental investment than a rehab investment. Certain neighborhoods may have a slower appreciation, but rent extremely well. Remember that the rental investment is more about cash flow than fast appreciation. Consider areas that have a high propensity for transient young professionals who are looking for places to stay as they transition into or between careers. Is your property near a place with many places of employment or a local university? It is equally important to consider the demographics of the areas where you seek to invest as it is to consider the economic and market conditions.

A renter generally won't care for a home as much as if they were the owner; therefore it may make sense for you to use less expensive materials with the anticipation of new upgrades as tenants turn over. It is important to remain within the market for the home when selecting improvements and repairs. Does it make sense to add a state-of-the-art kitchen and outdoor patio to a property in a low-income neighborhood? Most renters or homeowners do not wish to stand out from the rest of the neighborhood so it is important to look holistically at the area before embarking on your renovations.

What are the Benefits of Foreclosure Investing?

Depending on the strategy, foreclosures can provide quick profits to your portfolio or can provide residual monthly income. This provides many opportunities for investors with different goals. It is also possible to do a little of both and create a balanced approach to your real estate investing.

High rates of return may be obtained due to the fact that foreclosed homes are purchased at a substantial discount. Making wise purchases is essential to making money. When investors make an emotional decision or become attached to a home, like one might with a personal residence, it can result in less than advantageous purchases from an investment perspective. By letting the financial numbers guide the decision making, good investments can result in profitable returns for your portfolio. Remember this is an investment for your retirement, not your dream home, so it is important to treat it with an unbiased and profit-focused mindset.

Regardless of the market, there will always be homes that go into foreclosure. While down real estate markets may increase competition for foreclosed homes, bargains can always be found if you are patient and diligent.

An Investment for their Children

Husband and wife duo, Richard and Lorraine from Virginia, earned themselves the Equity Trust 2011 Self-Directed Investor of the Year award with their activity in the foreclosure market a few years ago.

Richard does Information Technology work for the state of Virginia and Lorraine moved from her role as Chief Nursing Officer in a local hospital to a less demanding role after the couple adopted four children from the Virginia Emergency Families for Children organization.

The newest family members came from difficult backgrounds. Upon entering his new home, their one son was ecstatic because he never had a bed before (he had formerly lived and slept in abandoned cars).

Richard and Lorraine were committed to providing a bright future for their children and wanted to provide them the financial security they could lean on, even after the couple was no longer around to help.

The couple has always been diligent at saving money, even agreeing to live on Richard's income so that Lorraine's could be stowed away in savings. Unfortunately they lost close to 25 percent of their retirement portfolio in the stock market and they weren't happy with the answers they were getting from their financial advisors.

"They kept telling us the market will recover, you'll get it back," recalls Lorraine. "Meanwhile, they were still taking their 3-percent fee." She remembers asking their advisor why they kept losing money and was shocked at the response: "They said, 'oh no, you're losing money. We're not.' That was when we knew we needed to find an alternative."

The couple was then introduced to the concept of self-directed IRAs and saw the success others were having self-directing their retirement funds and wanted the same. They asked their financial advisor but "none of the major banks knew about 'self-directed' accounts, so we weren't sure it was real."

It was real, and Richard and Lorraine soon opened their self-directed IRAs with Equity Trust and were on their way. Richard expanded on their decision to self-direct when he said, "If I'm going to lose money, it's going to be my doing."

Their decision to enter the foreclosure market was due in large part to their eldest son, Joe, who had recently moved to Lehigh Acres, Florida. Lorraine remembers receiving a call from Joe, "Mom – you won't believe it," he said, "houses are being sold at a quarter of the value down here."

Richard and Lorraine started searching and eventually connected with a real estate agent in the Lehigh Acres area. They found a home that had previously sold for $215,400 but, due to the market conditions, was available for $80,500. "You can't build a house for that kind of money," Richard says.

They purchased the home with a partnership of 50 percent cash and 50 percent from the self-directed IRA. The couple then invested another $2,000 of improvements into the home (50 percent paid from cash and 50 percent paid from the IRA) and worked with their real estate agent until they found a tenant.

The type of tenants the couple has is important to them. "We don't consider this business; it's people helping people," the couple says. Lorraine and Richard soon found a mother who also happened to have adopted children. The family lost their home to foreclosure, and then in another stroke of bad luck, the home they were renting was foreclosed upon and they were on the street *again*.

Richard and Lorraine were able to step in and provide much-needed stability to the family, offering a 5-year lease. They now receive $1,000 per month in rent, $500 returned to the IRA tax-deferred and the other half returned to the cash portion of the investment. After taxes and the expense of their property manager, they receive $9,000 each year in profit. In addition to the rental income, Richard says they've received a 21-percent year-over-year return in value on the home as it has appreciated.

Self-directed IRAs have enabled Richard and Lorraine to grow their retirement, help families in need, and provide the security they desired for their children. They now own four homes in their IRAs, one for each of their children, and routinely eat dinner with their tenants who have grown to become friends as well. Each of the homes are producing monthly rental income while also each increasing in value by approximately 25 percent since they were first purchased.

Perhaps most importantly, each of the couple's adopted children now have their "own house." They are ecstatic when they go and visit their investment properties and are proud to know that each home is earmarked for their financial security someday. What they might not realize yet is that their parents have established a firm financial future on their behalf and are teaching them valuable life lessons about saving and planning for the future.

Chapter 11: Investing in Commercial Real Estate

Commercial real estate contains a number of elements that are much different than residential real estate. Many investors begin investing in real estate with single-family homes because that is what's familiar to them. Once they begin to see the profits that can be made on the residential side they begin to look for other opportunities and soon discover the benefits that may be obtained through commercial real estate. Commercial real estate provides scalability. Scaling the profits across multiple units or through larger deals, and spreading costs across the larger volume are two benefits of commercial real estate.

What is Commercial Real Estate?

As investors consider the move from single-family homes they typically think of multi-family homes such as apartments and condominiums. Yet the commercial real estate industry includes so much more – such as strip malls, hotels and motels, shopping centers, mobile home parks, industrial buildings, office buildings, airplane hangars and independent commercial buildings.

One of the key differences between residential and commercial real estate is the size of the deal. Residential real estate typically ranges between $20,000 to $500,000 properties. In commercial real estate the numbers can range from several hundred thousand dollars to millions of dollars or more. As a result, the transactions are handled quite differently than a single-family home.

Commercial real estate not only involves more money than residential homes, it will likely take six months or longer to put a deal together so patience is required.

Commercial real estate requires more money down than an individual home so identifying sources of financing is one of the many factors to consider. Banks and lenders will look at cash flow (the amount of income the property is currently generating) to forecast the income it may generate in the future. Additionally, the location and economic development in the area are two factors used to estimate the property value.

These are all factors that need to be taken into consideration when evaluating if this type of investment is suitable for you. Residential home investors look at loan-to-value ratio, rehab costs and the costs of acquiring a renter. Depending on the goals for the property, the numbers used in commercial real estate often change. Net operating income and cap rates become more important than buying a property below value.

Partnerships

Buying your own personal home is difficult enough to finance. Obtaining financing for multi-million-dollar deals is generally not accomplished by one individual. Partnerships are often the key to success and the bridge to increased wealth in commercial real estate. Partners can come in several different forms. It may be a partner or group of partners that provide financial backing. They may provide credit backing to help secure a loan by traditional means. They may provide expertise finding properties, renovating or upgrading, finding tenants or other needs of the investment. Even political connections are important, as the investor will want to stay up-to-date with changes in zoning, updates of roads, mass transportation, surrounding business development, and other government decisions that impact the real estate investment.

One of the biggest keys to success in commercial real estate is to have solid partners. Strategic partnerships and alliances will help to create opportunities and close deals. Commercial real estate investments, unlike single-family homes, are mostly sold before they are ever officially listed. It can be beneficial to create a partnership with a commercial real estate agent to stay abreast of properties coming up for sale or to help find a tenant.

Another key partnership could be with another investor, private lending group, or other source of financing. Commercial deals involve large amounts of money. There are much larger down payments required, higher due-diligence costs, and often it can be difficult to get traditional bank lending. Having established relationships for down payments, renovation costs and complete financing can be a tremendous advantage. Finding financing in advance of an offer helps ensure a deal will be completed and can put you in a much better position to negotiate.

What are the Benefits of Commercial Real Estate?

Higher profit potential than with residential real estate. The bigger the deal, the higher the potential profit can be. Generally, when investing in a rental, the tenant will stay for a couple of years. Business tenants of a commercial property tend to stay longer, often for the duration of the business. This means there is lower tenant turnover, which can lead to more predictable profits. This steady cash flow is what can convert commercial real estate transactions into very profitable retirement investments.

Lower operating costs. Many residential tenants do not care for the property like a homeowner or commercial business tenant. This may also be true if the commercial investment involves apartments or other residential housing. If this is the case, upgrades and repairs between tenants are often needed and is an additional cost to factor into your investment analysis.

The commercial property owner is generally responsible for the outside of the building (the face) and the parking lot. Most other costs are covered by the tenants. Commercial property business tenants will often complete upgrades and take care of the location because the business is providing the livelihood of the owner and its employees and they must maintain a professional location for their business. These upgrade costs are generally paid for by the tenant. This reduces ongoing costs for the commercial property investor. Add steady rent and appreciation to the equation and it is easy to see why commercial real estate can be such an attractive investment.

Residual income. The commercial property may often pay for itself through the steady monthly rental income from the tenants. Even with the cost of financing and a management company to collect the rent and maintain the property, commercial investors can receive enough from one small strip mall to cover retirement costs. Once the mortgage has been paid off, the income can grow even further.

Not every commercial real estate deal requires millions of dollars or complicated ownership structures. Multi-family homes such as apartment buildings are similar to single-family homes, but multiple doors can often equate to multiple streams of income from the same building.

Housing the Homeless

In the life span of retirement planning, John from Indiana is a relative youngster, but he's likely years ahead of many older retirement investors when it comes to building a financial future. At 31 years old, he's showing how much an investor without decades of self-directed investment experience under his belt can accomplish.

Upon graduating from college, John bought a duplex, renting out half of it to pay the mortgage. That's when he realized the income potential that buy-and-hold real estate investing offered. It wasn't until a few years later he learned that he could use his Roth IRA to invest in real estate and watch his profits grow tax-free.

John recently completed the purchase of a partially occupied 12-unit apartment complex in Indianapolis, which was acquired from a city surplus sale for just $3,500 because the apartment was carrying delinquent taxes. It took almost two years to quiet the title of the property before he was able to clear it of any other liens and close with his Roth IRA as the sole owner.

Fortunately, John was able to manage the property and earn income during the process because he was granted the deed to the property at the outset of the deal, long before the legal process concluded. This helped to offset the $10,000 his Roth IRA would pay in attorney fees to quiet the title and make the transaction.

He also reinvested the $2,500 of monthly rental income he was receiving from the partially occupied building to improve the property and increase the value of the structure. He hired contractors to update the paint, carpets, and updated the 15-year-old furnace throughout the building and, through improvements in the plumbing, reduced the water bill from $800 to around $230 per month.

Eleven of the building's 12 units are now occupied by low-income tenants, with steady rental income of $3,000 to $4,000 (after expenses) flowing back into his account each month tax-free. Additionally, the property is now worth between $275,000 and $300,000, and with the income, he says he'll be in the black on the deal within a couple of years. John estimates the investment is netting him a 200-percent or more profit after all his legal costs.

Even more exciting, John works with the Homeless Initiative Program, a non-profit in Indianapolis that pulls people out of the shelters and helps them get back on their feet. Through the program,

John has been able to house 10-12 formerly homeless Americans and also works with an organization that has placed three homeless Veterans in his unit, with two more in the process.

"Everything I do has got to have a mission and purpose," he says. "To make money and help people, especially these vets, excites me."

John attributes his success to networking and a commitment to bettering his financial future. Since his apartment building purchase, he has acquired a second apartment building using private funding. "I'm pretty excited with what I have been able to do in the past 24-plus months and what I've got in the works for the next few years," John says.

While John doesn't believe every deal he does will be as profitable as the first apartment complex, the experience has inspired and energized him. "I'm looking at buying an apartment building a year based on the cash flow from these deals!" he says, adding, "If you find something that you enjoy doing and makes you money, then keep doing it."

What Are The Risks of Commercial Real Estate?

Liquidity risk. Commercial real estate is not likely to be a property that will be flipped. It is typically considered a long-term investment. A commercial property can take several years to sell because it is more difficult to find a buyer able to operate in the space and obtain the financing needed. As a result, the deposits needed to secure the real estate can be tied up for years. The good news is that if the property is filled the operating income should help cover the operating costs and provide a steady income stream for the investor. However, investors face the risk that the tenant leaves and there is no income while the property sits vacant in search of a new tenant. When it does come time to sell the property any appreciation will be added to the value of the land and building, potentially resulting in a profit from the appreciation as well as the income received during ownership.

Economic risk. Commercial real estate can be significantly impacted by economic risk. Cities have different growth patterns and a market that is hot today, may not be hot tomorrow. When looking at illiquid long-term investments, a change in economic development can be toxic. Everyone has seen empty strip malls that owners are unable to occupy. This is why finding a low-priced property is not necessarily the best option for commercial investments. Finding property in emerging markets where tenants are anxious to be is the best way to maximize returns. Yet, over a 10- or 20-year period the area's growth may change. Local government decisions can change road patterns, zoning laws, or even add or change public transportation options that impact the direction of that growth. Unforeseen factors such as changes in traffic patterns may affect the likelihood that a new business will want to move in to this location which is why it is important to consult with people who are familiar with the area and can speak to the future of economic growth and governmental changes in the location.

Higher carrying costs. If a recession hits, it may be necessary to carry some of the costs of the real estate during these times. As business cycles fluctuate, and the economy cycles, all of these factors will impact the ability to acquire tenants. There is also the possibility you must evict nonpaying tenants who were hit hard during a recession. All of this takes time and money. It is necessary to have a financial reserve that can get the investor through these times. Some investors accomplish this by putting money away each month in anticipation that the markets will not always be in their favor.

Higher upfront costs. Commercial real estate requires money to purchase and develop. Financial partners, whether obtained through a bank or private funding, will want the investor to have skin in the game. Having financial resources is essential for commercial investing. It's not all about using other people's money, though that is certainly a major factor in getting deals completed.

Profits, Taxes and IRS Rules

When property is purchased within an IRA or other tax-advantaged account the income, along with appreciation, can be realized in a tax-deferred or tax-free manner depending on the account that is utilized. A long-term investment and long-term rental income from the investments can amount to savings up to 40 percent. When you consider the higher rates that are charged to commercial tenants, and the longer term of their stay, the ability to save up to 40 percent in taxes per rent check becomes even more powerful. In addition, investing with a self-directed retirement account opens another financing option from the estimated $24.9 trillion held in IRAs, 401(k)s, and other qualified plans across the country[21]. This is another avenue to help with the investment financing, which is so critical in commercial real estate investing.

Commercial Real Estate Overview

Commercial real estate provides the opportunity to use the same skills acquired in residential real estate investing with a greater profit potential. It is possible to begin with smaller commercial ventures and work your way up to large multi-million-dollar properties. In general they are more passive investments and can provide larger profits than residential properties. Managing 50 rental units in an apartment complex is generally more profitable and less costly than managing 50 single-family homes located in various places across a city or region.

For those who understand and love the real estate market, moving to commercial real estate may be a good investment option. For those just getting started, having adequate funds, good partners and starting small can also provide opportunity.

> **Webinar: Investing in Commercial Real Estate with your Self-Directed IRA**
>
> Equity University welcomes Roger St. Pierre, Senior Vice President at First Western Federal Savings Bank, for a 40-minute webinar presentation about multi-unit and commercial real estate investing. Roger will break down the ways investors can cash in on different strategies, based on his decades of experience with commercial and larger real estate investors. Set up or log in to your user account to watch it now:
>
> https://equityuniversity.customerhub.net/commercial

Chapter 12: Investing in Tax Liens

Real estate property taxes are generally determined by the county in which the property is located and are due to the county each year. The revenue the county generates from collecting property taxes helps to fund the expenses of operating the county government. This can include fire and police services, road construction, educational expenses, parks and recreational maintenance, and many other services the county provides.

When property owners neglect to pay their property taxes the county has difficulty meeting their financial obligations. As a result, 29 states, the District of Columbia, Puerto Rico, and the Virgin Islands issue tax liens and hold tax-lien sales. Tax-lien sales are used to fund the government, while property owners are given additional time to pay the back taxes owed.

What are Tax Liens and Tax-Lien Certificates?

When taxes become delinquent, the county will put a lien on the property. The advantage of a tax lien is that it supersedes all other liens on the property. If there is a mortgage lien, a mechanics lien, or even an IRS lien, the tax lien will take first lien position on the property. This means if the property is sold or foreclosed upon the tax lien will be repaid before any other liens.

When the county decides to sell a tax lien, it will often issue a tax-lien certificate to the investor. This certificate gives the investor the right to receive the value of the tax lien in addition to any penalties and interest that is owed by the taxpayer. It does not give the investor the right to enter the property or obtain the property during the redemption period. The details of the lien will be outlined in the tax-lien certificate – such as how much is owed, the interest rate, how long the redemption period lasts, and if there are any penalties associated with the lien. If the property owner does not repay any back taxes, interest, and penalties owed before the redemption period set by the state expires, the investor has the right to foreclose on the property.

Another Equity Trust client whose name is also John from Indiana recently discovered the impressive returns that tax liens can bring to his self-directed IRA. The former CPA picked up a vacant lot for $5,000 using funds from his self-directed IRA at his first tax-lien sale.

"I ended up getting the deed to that property a year later and sold it for $20,000," John shares. "I was hooked."

John is one of a growing number of investors becoming aware of the advantages of this self-directed investment option. Generally, counties auction the tax liens they hold against properties, leaving those who acquire the liens to collect payments and interest from the property owner or, like John, end up with the deed to the property.

Tax liens are an attractive option for many types of investors because of the variety of price points. Even investors with smaller portfolios can find liens that work for them and multiply their assets in a short amount of time.

"It's happened for me time and time again," John says. "I ended up with a house I paid $25,000 for at the tax-lien sale. I put another $25,000 into it and sold it for $130,000. I netted $120,000 at the sale. So I had a $50,000 investment, it took a year and a half, and I turned another $70,000 gain."

Those profits seem like mere pennies compared to a transaction he completed involving a tax lien on a public company's property. After he won a local court hearing, the company made him a generous settlement offer. After investing the initial $15,000 and another $10,000 in legal fees into the deal, John ended up with a settlement price of $450,000.

"With that one property alone, when I think about how many years it would take me to make contributions to an IRA to put the equivalent of $425,000 additional into my account…it's just mind-boggling."

John could talk all day about the fabulous tax lien deals that are building up his retirement fund, and he couldn't be happier with his reversal of fortune. After losing close to 50 percent of his IRA in the catastrophic stock market collapse in 1987 known as Black Friday, John isn't about to place his future in the hands of unknown factors again.

"With all the things going on in the stock market, which you have absolutely no control over, at least with the IRA and dealing with property and so forth, I'm able to control and be hands-on," he says. "If something bad happens, it's my doing – not Greece, or Japan, or an earthquake."

What are the Benefits of Tax-Lien Investing?

Secured collateral. Tax liens offer one of the more secure forms of collateral available in the alternative space. The tax lien is secured by the property. It obtains the first lien position, meaning that if for any reason the property owner does not pay the lien, the investor will have the first rights to the property in the event of foreclosure. In essence, the worst-case scenario is you will end up with the property that you bid on (assuming you win the bid). This is why selecting a tax-lien property that you feel comfortable "getting stuck with" is so important when conducting your due diligence.

High interest rates. Many property owners of tax-lien properties will eventually pay off the lien during the redemption period. This can provide a relatively safe investment for investors seeking higher rates of returns on their investments. Interest rates can range from 5 percent to 36 percent, depending on the state or the county where the tax lien is purchased.[23] Additional penalties may also apply and may add to the return. In a competitive auction it is possible the interest rate is bid down or the price of the tax lien is bid up. Obviously this can impact the overall return of the investment. As property owners pay their delinquent taxes, the investor will receive a check for the tax lien's face value plus interest and penalties.

Some tax-lien investors are able to work with the property owners to reduce the taxes that are owed or the interest being charged since the investor was able to acquire the property at a substantial discount from the county at the auction. This creates a situation where the property owner can benefit from reduced taxes owed and can remain in their property, the investor benefits from the interest payments that are made, and the county benefits because they were able to recoup a portion of the taxes that were owed so they can continue to fund their financial obligations.

Lower initial investment. When people think of real estate investing, they often think large amounts of money are needed to participate. Tax liens can be an exception to this rule. The taxes owed on a property are generally small in comparison to the property's overall value. Tax rates vary widely from state to state and county to county. Even if the taxpayer has not paid in two or three years, you might be able to invest a few thousand dollars and win a tax lien. In smaller counties with fewer services, liens can be obtained for a few hundred dollars. This enables small-dollar investors the opportunity to get involved in the market of tax liens.

What are the Risks of Tax-Lien Investing?

An important consideration in tax-lien investing is the property's value. While some tax-lien sales are now completed online there is no substitute for physically seeing the property, especially if you are just starting out as a tax-lien investor. If you begin investing closer to home you will know the area, be able to drive by the property before the sale and get an estimate on what the property is worth. The

---

[23] Cussen, M. P. (2013, June 13). Investing in Property Tax Liens. Retrieved from http://www.investopedia.com/articles/investing/061313/investing-property-tax-liens.asp

higher the value, compared to the lien amount, the better. Try to find local investors or others familiar with the area to paint a more complete picture of the properties at the tax-lien auction.

Watch for properties that have sustained significant damage. Past events such as fires and floods will impact the value of the property and may cause the property to be worth less than the taxes due. Another area of concern is neighborhoods that are being abandoned. Consider why the neighborhood is being abandoned and why the owner no longer wants the property or is willing to refrain from paying taxes and accept foreclosure. If this is the case it may be in an area that will be difficult to rent or sell should you end up owning the parcel.

Other concerns and risks may include the owner filing bankruptcy, tax liens that are sold incorrectly, if the lien only includes improvements to the property (and not the land), special assessments, EPA sites (with potential environmental hazards), and common property or land-locked property.

Another important note: if you purchase a tax lien it is imperative that you keep up with the property taxes and other expenses. If there is a two- or three-year redemption period and the property owner is not paying the taxes and interest, you will be required to pay each year until the redemption period has expired. This is especially important if your IRA owns the property since your IRA will need to have enough funds available to carry the property until the lien redeems or expires. You should also make sure there is clean title to the property and you have performed your due diligence before making an investment.

When Does the Investor Own the Property?

While getting a high rate of interest is the primary strategy for some investors, there are others who are focused on the percentage of liens that do not catch up with their taxes, in hopes of gaining the physical property at an extreme discount. Each county has different laws regarding tax liens. All tax liens have a redemption period during which the property owner has the ability to catch up the back taxes, including interest and penalties, in order to maintain the property.

Once the redemption period has expired, the tax-lien certificate holder has the ability to foreclose on the property to obtain the deed. A tax deed is issued, allowing the tax-certificate holder to obtain rights to the property. Generally they will gain the property without any liens or encumbrances.

There is a period of time between when the redemption period has expired and the tax-lien certificate holder must foreclose on the property. If this timeframe passes and the investor does not foreclose on the property, the tax-lien certificate can become worthless. For this reason, only starting in a few counties is a way to learn the system before branching out to tax lien investing on a larger scale.

Profits, Taxes and IRS Rules

The interest earnings gained from tax liens are taxed as ordinary income if not purchased within a tax-advantaged account. Ordinary income is the taxes paid at the highest tax bracket and is determined by your combined overall income.

The county will require a W-9 to be completed when you purchase a tax lien. This provides the information needed for the county to report the interest paid to the IRS. If the tax lien is purchased in a Traditional IRA, the interest paid will be received tax-deferred, and if it is being purchased by a Roth IRA, then the interest will be received tax-free. If you purchase a lien with an 18-percent interest payment for 36 months, you're investing in 36 months of tax-free or tax-deferred profits that can grow within the account. Even more importantly, if you purchase a tax lien within a self-directed IRA, the value of the property when the lien is sold is sheltered within the tax advantages of your account.

As we mentioned earlier, when Brad from Indiana purchased a lien on a property for just over $800 and held the property for two years, he needed approximately $5,000 of additional funding from his Roth IRA to clear title to the property (paying for attorney fees and other administrative costs). When he sold the property to a commercial developer for $97,500 Brad received approximately $90,000 back into his Roth IRA, *tax-free*. Assuming a 25-percent tax bracket, Brad saved around $22,500 in taxes by using a self-directed Roth IRA. That's more than $20,000 that he can now use to reinvest in other properties or get to his retirement dream.

Tax Lien Overview

Tax-lien certificates can provide investors with higher rates of interest than CDs, money markets, bonds and other interest bearing accounts. The risk is low in the respect that the investment is secured by real estate and property owners can often pay the tax lien off, with interest, before the redemption period expires.

The collateral helps to make tax liens a relatively safe investment. Generally, redemption periods range from a few months to a few years. This means that the investor's funds will be tied up for that period of time. They also run the risk of the investment being paid off quickly, resulting in a lower return on the investment as less interest is accrued during the condensed period of time. Buying a portfolio of several tax liens is one way to mitigate this risk, as new tax liens will replace the ones that are paid off.

As with all investments, it is important to understand the market. Speak with county office personnel and learn about the procedures and rules within the county you are interested in purchasing tax liens. They are a good resource since each county operates their auctions differently.

2-Part Webinar Series: Discover the Investment Potential in Tax Liens and Tax Deeds

Join Equity University for a webinar with experienced tax-lien investor, Dustin Hahn, as he reveals how investors are taking advantage of this tactic, all while boosting their retirement savings and reducing their taxes. The first webinar went so well that Dustin rejoined Equity University for a second webinar. Set up or log in to your user account to watch them both:

https://equityuniversity.customerhub.net/liens

Richard Desich, Sr.

Chapter 13: Investing in Raw Land

Raw land is any land that is in its natural state. In our vast country finding raw land is not difficult, but finding land that will be a good investment is an entirely different story. The good news is that land has some intrinsic value and therefore may be a wise investment. There are factors that can make land a bad purchase and others that could bring fast and profitable returns.

What Factors to Consider?

Land can be used for many purposes and the function it will be used for in the future will greatly impact the value of the land. Location cannot be underestimated when it comes to the purchase of land, as the location is crucial to its value. The other thing to consider when evaluating land is zoning or use. Both current and future uses, as well as the speed of appreciation for the parcel, are major factors in determining the value. For these reasons, knowing the purpose of the land, along with understanding its location, will be key factors in evaluating whether or not it may be a good investment.

There are many uses for land and a savvy investor considers all forms of profit potential for the investment. For example, Greg is a client from Pennsylvania who used his Roth IRA to purchase a 239-acre farm with three houses on it, as well as the mineral rights. A total of

180 acres of the land were tillable and could be farmed, while the remaining 59 acres were wooded.

Greg set up an LLC with his partners to purchase the property and utilized a non-recourse loan to help finance the acquisition. Greg's team put 20 percent of the purchase price down and paid $1,900 per acre, or $454,100.

Greg began to profit from his investment in a variety of ways. First, he and his partners selectively timbered the property and earned $63,000. Then, they sold one of the three houses on the property and rented the other two for $750 and $850 per month, respectively.

Additionally, they are earning $18,000 per year in rent for the 180 tillable acres on the property. Last but not least, Greg is eager to begin earning royalty checks tax-free back into his Roth IRA from the gas well that is currently being drilled on the property.

All told, Greg's Roth IRA is benefiting from four different profit-generators on his single parcel of land for an approximate ROI of 109 percent, tax-free. His investment is a great example of the potential raw land has in a self-directed IRA and hopefully provides some insight into the various ways you can profit from raw land investments.

Where is the Land Located? How Will the Land be Used?

Land is typically purchased with one of the following end results in mind: as a long-term holding, for use or development, or as a speculative investment.

Long-term holdings are similar to rental properties in the sense of the buy-and-hold approach. Raw land is a form of real estate that, like the previous chapters discussed for rehabs, rentals, and commercial property, holds intrinsic value. Raw land investors who purchase long-term holdings understand the variety of uses for the parcel – build and develop, rent/lease, farm, mining, and beyond. They understand they can sub-divide the land to create multiple potential sources of income from a single lot. Raw land investors using a buy-

and-hold approach are also anticipating the parcel to appreciate in value during the time it is held.

The majority of raw land investments are longer-term investments and the buy-and-hold approach can be combined with the next two methods we discuss. Long-term holdings do not necessarily have to be speculative in nature. Greg's parcel of land is intended for long-term use, but he did not depend on future development. Instead he found a parcel of land that had profit-potential in its current state.

Purchase for use or development means buying a lot of land and then either developing it directly, preparing the land to be sold to a developer, or repurposing the land to create cash flow. All of these methods generally will require more time and resources than simply buying a piece of land and holding it until demand increases to the point money can be made on the sale.

This type of investment is more strategic. Perhaps the land is zoned for single-family homes and the buyer believes they can have the land rezoned for business or commercial use. Rezoning can open the door to development that is currently unavailable.

Another option is to purchase a parcel of land and add water, sewer, and electric utilities to make it more appealing to a developer. It is important to understand the costs associated with these types of investments, as they can become cost prohibitive if the land is not located close to current sources of utilities.

Another common use for land is purchasing a larger lot that can be prepared for development and then subdivided. This enables the investor to sell several smaller lots with more profit potential than the single lot purchased initially. Investors also look for alternate uses of the land, like we shared in Greg's case study. If the land is currently wooded acres, an investor can purchase the land and then sell the timber. Understanding what kind of trees are on the property and what the timber is worth is important when evaluating these investments.

Raw land can also be converted to farmland. You don't need to become a farmer, though, as many small farms are leased to individuals or groups who will work the land and split the profits gained from the crop or pay a monthly lease to the land owner. There are many crops that can be grown on small acreage and with the popularity of farm-to-table sustainability it is not difficult to find restaurants willing to purchase crops, especially those that are grown organically. Organically grown crops can produce a premium price over those crops on which pesticides are used. Developing a farm or other alternative use for the parcel can result in land with a higher value. This can make it easier to sell, especially if cash flow has been established.

Farming also extends to animals. Raising animals such as pigs or chickens does not require a large plot of land. Repurposing the land to raise livestock can produce annual income for the land owner, without the work, if a partnership is developed with a family or group who is interested in working the land.

Planting a Seed for Retirement

Kurt, a Minnesota resident with experience investing in Iowa farmland outside of his IRA, recently planted a parcel of land into his retirement account and has watched it flourish into quite a nest egg. He has utilized raw land to create a steady stream of passive income, tax-deferred back into his account.

A few years ago Kurt purchased 40 acres of farmland in Iowa for $1,750 per acre and utilized a non-recourse loan to help finance the purchase. He has earned a little over 6 percent of profit each year from the cash rent, but the investment's real gain is in the property's appreciation. In just one year the land appreciated to $2,700 per acre and he already received an offer to purchase the property at $2,650 per acre.

"So if you add in appreciation, the investment would have a return on investment of close to 60 percent in one year...I'll take that any day!" he says.

Kurt plans to hold onto the property for a while and earn income by renting it out. He's had no problem finding farmers who want to occupy the land.

"Actually," he says, "There's quite a demand for agriculture/renting. I guess weather can have an effect if you have a prolonged period of drought, but in a state like Iowa, the demand is so high, there's kind of a long list of renters available."

He also knew that crop prices would more than likely increase, which also increases the value of the land.

"As corn and soybeans prices skyrocketed, so did the value of the land. Farmland in a self-directed IRA is a powerful vehicle," he says. "This 40-acre parcel in Iowa was undervalued, and I bought it at the right price."

In addition to nearly doubling the value of his investment, Kurt is securing a tax-deferred income stream that he can use in retirement.

Kurt notes you don't have to enter the game as a farmland expert to make this type of investment, but like any type of investment, expect to take time to research the potential opportunities and be prepared to fill out some paperwork to get the deal off the ground. After that, he says, the required effort decreases significantly.

"I've hardly had to do much at all the last few months," he says. "You get your cash rent checks from the farmer who rents the grounds, that goes directly to Equity Trust, and it's all kind of taken care of from there. There's very little computer time or paperwork that you have to get into."

Furthermore, I hope you see a theme continue to emerge from the self-directed IRA investments I've mentioned in this book. Kurt's IRA enables local farmers to make a living while also providing a benefit to his own retirement. Self-directed IRA investments benefit more than the investor.

Speculation is another common investment strategy for raw land and may include land that is located in the path of future economic growth. This might include land outside a growing city or anticipating new road development. In this case, purchasing the appropriate parcel of land before the road is built could be a profitable investment. Looking at the patterns of economic development will provide clues as to what future demand for the land may be.

Since speculation often includes land that is ahead of the economic development curve, it may require the land be held for many years before development catches up to the location. Developers might be interested in lots with utility hook-ups and plan to develop the land into a residential or commercial community. These larger projects can increase the value of surrounding land. Even if you are not the developer, there is investment opportunity to be had. It is possible to attend local hearings and zoning meetings, or look up county records (most of this information is open to the public), to help determine where development may occur. A small-dollar investor can review where communities are scheduled to be built and then look for surrounding land that is for sale.

This speculation can provide larger profits than the other two land strategies; however it is also considered the most risky. Many times development starts, then something happens that changes the course of the project. Projects often take several years to complete and developers have been known to run out of money due to unforeseen circumstances. Changes in the economy or in the circumstances that initially made the land such a great investment can also derail a speculative land investment. This might result in buying land that does not appreciate as much as anticipated. The closer the project is to fruition, the less risky the investment is, but the cost of the land will likely be higher.

When looking at these three land purchase strategies, the importance of location and zoning becomes clear. Location determines the current and future demand for the land, while zoning determines the use of the land. Economic development can increase the land's value and take a moderately well-located lot and change it to a highly-desirable lot. Zoning can change the lands use and enable the owner to be more creative in what the land can be used for or to whom the land can be sold.

Equity Trust client Jim from Florida went from successfully owning and operating 10 coffee shops to making an $80,000 profit in 30 days when he made the switch to raw-land investing with his self-directed IRA.

While he loved his business, Jim mentions, "I worked an awful lot of hours for a little bit of money." Although he was always interested in real estate, he didn't take the plunge until a few years ago. Jim's Roth IRA entered a partnership with a fellow investor and located a piece of raw land in Florida they believed could be profitable if properly rezoned. Partnering their IRAs, they were able to purchase the property for $1.08 million and within 30 days were able to complete a zoning change that made the land more favorable to sell.

Days later, they sold the property for $1.85 million and realized about $770,000 of tax-free profits between the two Roth IRAs. Due to the percent ownership of his Roth IRA, Jim netted around $77,000 of tax-free profits towards his retirement. Jim recalls, "I think it's a fantastic opportunity that a lot of people just don't know about. Knowing how to raise money is the key." Now, Jim is able to relax more than he ever could as a business owner and even takes the time to stop, relax, and enjoy a cup of his very own coffee.

What are the Benefits of Investing in Land?

Acquiring land is generally thought of as a long-term investment. Even if only moderate growth occurs in the area, land can often increase in value over time. There is also the chance that economic growth can dramatically increase the land's value.

If the land is located where economic growth is obvious it will be more difficult to secure a low price for the land, as most investors will also see it as a solid investment. This will increase the demand and thus the price. Finding land that is in less obvious locations can provide the greatest potential for returns, though it may take more time and research to achieve.

Thinking outside the box is important for raw land investments. This might include investing in property around a less popular lake, where the surrounding area began encouraging more development. Getting in early can reap great rewards. Another example might be buying land on a golf course in an up-and-coming community. As the demand for homes around the golf course increases, the land values could soar.

What are the Risks of Investing in Land?

A few factors that cause land to depreciate are environmental hazards and community decline. If land is purchased in an area where there is an economic decline, or becomes a crime-ridden area, property values will plummet along with the price of the land. If the land is in an area where an environmental hazard is located, or even on the land itself, it will significantly impact the value of the land. This may also include a nuclear plant located nearby, a major highway running too close to the property, or unsealed gas tanks underground on the property. All of these situations could result in a decline in value. Investigative homework on the lot that is for sale, and also the surrounding community, may help reduce the chances of investing in a property that will have complications down the road.

The most common risk to consider when investing in land is that it is an illiquid asset, which means it is more difficult to convert into cash. Real estate as an asset class is considered to be illiquid and raw land is the most illiquid of all real estate. Consequently, the money invested in raw land should be earmarked as a long-term investment. Monthly income should not be anticipated unless the development strategy will provide an income stream. For the most part, land is initially an expense rather than an income-producing property. While you own the land you will have to maintain and manage it until you find a suitable buyer. Knowing what the land will be used for and researching the proposed use carefully will reduce the risk of purchasing an undesirable parcel.

It is imperative that you stay on top of taxes and any maintenance costs while owning the land. Generally, taxes are the main expense of owning land, but if the taxes are not paid the county can sell the property to collect the taxes owed. Additionally, if the land is located within a community or development, there may be assessments or association dues that need to be maintained as well.

Profits, Taxes and IRS Rules

Finding the right parcel in the best location is mostly about seeing what others do not see and anticipating growth that is not obvious. Understanding the zoning process and following city and county development could give you a tremendous advantage in the selection of raw land. As most of this information is public, getting involved in the community in which you wish to invest is perhaps the best strategy for maximizing profits on land purchases.

Land held in a Roth IRA will grow tax-free, regardless of how long the property is held. This allows you to make the most profitable decision without having to consider the tax consequences of a sale. Since land acquisition often costs money during the time the raw land is held, it is necessary to have enough cash in the account to cover expenses like taxes and assessments. While these change from year to year, they are fairly predictable expenses. If the investor wishes to develop the land, cost considerations must be evaluated to ensure there is enough in the account to develop the land and still make a profit.

Land owned in a Traditional IRA will offer tax-deferred savings. The funds will be taxed as ordinary income upon withdrawal from the account. For this reason many land investors seek to convert the deferred tax investment accounts to a Roth IRA, providing longer-term tax-free benefits.

Outside of an IRA, land is taxed based on how long the property is held. As a long-term investment it is possible to reduce the taxable amount to the capital gains rate. Seeking advice from a trusted advisor is recommended when selecting which vehicle to use in raw land investments.

Raw Land Overview

Investing in raw land will require research, networking, sound strategy, and creative thinking. If you're willing to put in the work, raw land can provide another avenue to grow your retirement savings.

Audio: Finding Wealth in Raw Land

Two investors, one of whom is an Equity Trust client, take 40 minutes to discuss how they've utilized self-directed IRAs to invest in raw land. They walk you through real transactions they've completed and discuss some risks and rewards of investing in raw land. Set up or log in to your user account to listen here:

https://equityuniversity.customerhub.net/land

Audio: "How I've Profited from Land Contracts"

Equity Trust client and experienced real estate investor/educator, Vena Jones-Cox, discusses land contracts and how she's found success. She shares real deals she's completed in this energetic audio presentation. Set up or log in to your user account to listen here:

https://equityuniversity.customerhub.net/land-contract

Webinar: How Natural Resources Can Fuel Your Retirement

Interest in natural resources is growing, and new accessibility to the markets allows more investors to take advantage of the profit potential. Do you know how to get in on the action? Join Equity University and an industry expert guest presenter in an exclusive webinar to reveal how new opportunities in the natural resources industry translate to the everyday investor. Set up or log in to your user account to watch it now:

https://equityuniversity.customerhub.net/fuel

Chapter 14: Investing in Notes, Mortgages and Deeds of Trust

Nearly everyone understands the concept of debt, some probably more so than they would like. Most everyone has experience borrowing money in some capacity. Whether you have purchased a car or a home, carry a credit card, taken out a student loan, or all of the above, these are all forms of debt.

As with any debt, there is a borrower and a lender. The borrower is generally the individual and the lender is generally the bank. Banks have made millions of dollars over the years as lenders. Now, individuals can put themselves in the lender's seat and benefit from investment returns similar to the profits banks have experienced for years.

A variety of regulatory developments and the consolidation among banks has left fewer, and larger, lending institutions for individuals to turn towards. As it has become more difficult to obtain financing, some investors have turned toward the democratization of capital and realized self-directed IRA and other retirement money can be utilized as a source of financing, providing capital to those seeking funds and profit potential to the investor.

Understanding the Basics of Lending

As we've showcased earlier in the book, some investors have used their self-directed retirement accounts to issue loans or to purchase existing loans. They are able to receive the loan and interest payments tax-free or tax-deferred back into their retirement account as another option to build retirement wealth. When it comes to lending or borrowing money there are two basic types of loans: secured loans and unsecured loans. You may also have heard the term note, which is a document defining the terms and conditions of the loan.

Unsecured loans are also called signature loans. This would be equivalent to a credit card or a student loan. The loan is backed by the full faith and credit of the person taking out the loan. Borrowers like signature loans because they are fast and easy to manage. From a lender's perspective, these loans carry higher risk. If the borrower does not to repay the loan, the lender has no real way of collecting the borrowed amount, thus increasing risk.

Unsecured loans are heavily based on credit. While borrowers get heartburn thinking about managing credit and maintaining a high credit score, this is a very important aspect of the process for lenders. Credit scores monitor how well we pay our bills and provide the lender a written track record of how responsible we are. Therefore the higher the credit score, the more responsible the borrower generally is in paying off their debt, the lower the risk, and the lower interest rate that is offered. This helps the lender assess risk and mitigate the risk of default with an accompanying interest rate that reflects that risk.

Credit is very important when loaning money, especially with riskier unsecured loans. While this is true for any investment, performing due diligence and doing your homework on the borrower becomes even more important for unsecured loans. Unsecured loans are generally discouraged from a risk perspective, but in certain circumstances may be appropriate.

Secured loans are also called collateralized loans. This means that the loan is backed by a form of collateral, or something of value that can be seized in the event the borrower defaults on the loan. An example of a secured loan would include a car loan. Credit is still a factor when assessing secured loans but the collateral is as important as the credit. If the borrower chooses not to make payments on the loan, or goes into default, the lender has the opportunity to get repaid for the loan by taking possession of the collateral. In the car business this is called repossession, more commonly referred to as a repo. In the real estate business it is called a foreclosure.

Secured loans have a lower risk of non-payment because the borrower will lose something important to him, such as the collateral of his home or car. As a result, the default rate is often lower so the interest rate is also lower to reflect the reduced risk. Investors prefer secured loans because they can receive a nice return on their investment but also have a way to recoup their investment if the borrower fails to make payments on time.

There are two basic types of secured loans: recourse loans and non-recourse loans. As a lender, understanding the difference is increasingly important. It is also critical to understand the difference as a self-directed IRA investor since IRAs can only receive non-recourse loans.

Non-recourse loans. IRAs cannot guarantee or be used as collateral for a loan. Therefore, any loan made to an IRA must be non-recourse, meaning the lender's sole source of recovery in the event of default is the property serving as collateral for the loan. If the IRA cannot repay the non-recourse loan, the non-recourse lender can take title to the property as recourse for the default, but cannot access the IRA or other personal funds. In essence, the only collateral of a non-recourse loan is asset that is being financed – no other recourse is available. The lender can seize the collateral but cannot seek out the borrower for any further compensation, even if the collateral does not cover the full value of the defaulted amount. The collateral of the loan and the loan-to-value ratio become especially important in non-recourse loans. If the value of the asset declines or the default results in fees and late charges that exceed the value of the asset, the lender can only use the re-sale of the asset to recoup the amount of their loan. Home mortgages are frequently non-recourse loans.

If your IRA received a non-recourse loan for the purpose of purchasing an asset, there is also the possibility of triggering something called UBIT, which stands for Unrelated Business Income Tax. UBIT will be discussed further in a later chapter. For now, keep in mind that although this tax may be owed on a normally tax-advantaged investment it doesn't mean you've broken any rules. It is simply the cost of doing business when receiving non-recourse financing to your IRA.

Recourse loans give the lender more power and access to the borrower's other assets in order to be repaid, should the borrower default on the loan. In this case, if the sale of the collateral does not fully pay off the loan, the lender can seek recourse on additional assets. Car loans are commonly recourse loans. If the insurance company does not completely pay off a wrecked car, the borrower is still often responsible for the balance of the loan.

It is also important to understand liens and lien positions when evaluating a loan. When a buyer obtains a loan for a home, the lender goes to the courthouse and files a lien on the collateral that was used to secure the loan. With a vehicle, the lien is filed with the DMV and corresponding insurance company. A lien is a legal way to announce that the lender has a claim on the property. As a lender the lien process secures the collateral, and if the process is not completely properly, the lender will essentially have an unsecured loan and a higher risk.

Liens are rated by position. There is generally only one lien in a vehicle loan because a car is a depreciating asset, meaning it loses value over time. However, homes can often have more than one lien; therefore the lien position determines who gets paid first in the event of a foreclosure.

For example, let's say a property in Florida was purchased for $200,000. The initial loan was for $180,000. Then, the homeowner went to another bank and secured a home improvement loan that was for $50,000. Now the homeowner has $230,000 in debt on the home. Let's say a recession hits, the home declines in value, and to make the scenario worse, the homeowner loses his job and can no longer make the payments. Bank 1 has a lien on the home for

$180,000 and Bank 2 has a lien for $50,000. If the home sells for $200,000, then Bank 1 receives $180,000 (as the first position lien holder) and Bank 2 only receives $20,000 (as the second position lien holder). Since most mortgages are non-recourse loans, Bank 2 would take a $30,000 loss on the loan.

As a lender it is critical to understand the lien position and how to protect that position. In general, liens are prioritized by the date the lien is filed at the courthouse. The two exceptions are tax liens and IRS liens. If the property taxes are not paid, the county will place a lien on the home (tax liens are another popular investment strategy covered in a previous chapter). Property tax liens will always be in the first lien position and will take precedent over a mortgage or any other lien. For this reason mortgage holders require taxes to be paid in a timely manner and encourage an escrow account, where money is placed each month to ensure the lender pays the taxes. IRS liens for back taxes are another type that takes priority over a mortgage.

As you can see, determining lien position and researching an investment opportunity for undisclosed liens or encumbrances is an important part of the due diligence process.

Loan-to-value (LTV) ratio has a major impact on risk in secured investments. This is the value of the asset compared to the value of the loan. In real estate, the LTV ratio considers what the property can be sold for compared to the amount that is borrowed. For example if the home appraises for $200,000 and the loan is for $160,000, there is an 80-percent loan-to-value ratio. The loan is 80 percent of the value of the property. The lower the loan-to-value ratio, the lower the risk the lender has of not being repaid because they will be able to sell the asset to pay the loan off in full, or very nearly in full.

What are the Benefits of Investing in Notes?

Along with real estate, note investing is one of the more popular alternative investment options self-directed IRA investors have utilized to grow their retirement. Some investors use their self-directed IRA to serve as the lender and issue promissory notes for agreed-upon rates of return. Others purchase existing notes (mortgages) with the hope they can provide a source of passive income to their retirement. Like any investment, there are benefits and risks associated with this asset class that must be carefully considered.

Residual income. Acting as a lender can provide the investor with steady monthly income and more predictable returns. You can determine how much is needed in income each month and then invest in notes, mortgages, or deeds of trust that can provide the level of income you desire. As with all loans, the terms are established upfront. You will typically know the interest rate, the amount and timing of the payments, and the duration or term of the loan. This can provide reliable and ongoing income for the investor without the work required with other residual channels, such as rental property.

Passive investment. You can gain the benefits of a real estate investment, without the hassles of finding tenants, collecting rent or making repairs. You can lend the money and be paid a rate of interest each month in a more passive role. Recall Matt's loan to the car dealership or Roger's loan that helped fund the acquisition of an educational and recreation facility that we described earlier. They utilized their self-directed IRAs to finance two different opportunities and received passive income tax-free or tax-deferred into their accounts.

May not require large amounts of money. When thinking of mortgages, we think a large amount of money is needed to get in the game. Mortgage notes make it possible to invest partially in a mortgage. This allows a number of investors to fund a single loan. Investments can also be made on seasoned loans with shorter terms. The advantage is creating a diversified portfolio of notes that does not rely on one individual borrower for repayment. This way, if a borrower is slow to pay, there are other notes that can help keep the returns stable. Due to this benefit, structuring your note portfolio with short- and long-term notes may be a wise investment strategy.

What are the Risks of Investing in Notes and Mortgages?

Non-payment risk. There is the risk that the borrower or borrowers will stop making payments. To mitigate this risk, many investors choose to deal exclusively in secured notes, which offer a repayment option if the borrower defaults. However, it often requires a time-consuming process of foreclosure and may tie up your funds. Thus it is important that the collateral is acceptable to you in case it ever gets to that point.

Early payment risk. Most loans today do not have an early payment penalty. This means that the investor may be counting on a 30-year loan with steady payments, but the loan may be paid off in five or 10 years. You may think this is a good thing because you did not lose any money in the deal, but the profit in note investing often comes from the residual income derived from the interest and principal payments, which you lose out on when the loan is paid off early. Plus, the investor would need to find a new investment at the market rate to grow their portfolio as originally planned. This can create uncertainty in the residual income and may cause an unwanted hiccup in your financial planning.

Interest rate risk. As with any long-term investment, interest rate risk is a concern. This is the risk that the loan will be locked into a low rate. If the interest rates rise, you are still paid the fixed interest rate for as long as the property owner maintains the loan. You may find yourself looking enviously at comparable investments with much higher interest rates. However, if the rates go down, the payments are locked in at the higher rate, though the property owner may choose to refinance the loan with another lender, thus paying the loan off early.

Decline in value. One should also consider the risk that the real estate will decline in value. If the property owner destroys the property, there is a fire or other natural disaster, or the location declines significantly in value; it is possible for the real estate to decline below the amount of the note. Requiring insurance may be a way to mitigate this risk. Many investors start by verifying the location of the property and determining the local real estate climate, and then require property insurance. A third way to mitigate this risk is to seek investments with a lower loan-to-value ratio, therefore ensuring that a decline will not significantly impact the ability to sell the home, if needed, to pay off the loan.

Notes and Mortgages Overview

Notes and mortgages are usually secured by real estate and can help to reduce the risk. This gives you the opportunity to invest in real estate without the legwork of finding and managing properties. It can also provide steady residual income if you're looking for ongoing payments. As loans are paid off, new investments can be made to ensure adequate cash flow.

It is common for investors to purchase seasoned loans, meaning loans that have a payment track record. This enables investors to get a feel for the borrower's payment history, thus reducing the overall risk. These investments are considered long-term because the notes may be difficult to sell on the secondary market and the borrower cannot be compelled to pay the loan off early in the event the investor needs the funds. Therefore it is best to invest in mortgage notes for the cash flow, recognizing that the principal investment may be tied up for the term of the loan.

Webinar: Self-Directed IRA Note Investing

Discover an investment alternative that doesn't require a large amount of capital but has the potential for huge returns. Best of all, the opportunities are easier to find than you might think. Join Equity University and successful note buyer, Eddie Speed, in a webinar as he reveals how to create profits by investing in notes with your IRA. Set up or log in to your user account to watch it now:

https://equityuniversity.customerhub.net/notes

Chapter 15: Investing in Probate

Probate is the legal process that takes place after someone has passed away. This can be a very sensitive time for the loved ones who lost their family member. After a person's death, property within the estate is often sold so debts can be paid and the estate can be settled. This can result in motivated sellers and can create tremendous opportunity for investors to buy property at a discount. Successful probate investors, however, are those who never lose sight of the people who are affected by the loss and who are able to help the family through this difficult period in their life.

How Does Probate Investing Work?

When someone who owns property passes away their estate typically must go through probate. During this process, an executor manages the estate and must make decisions about what to do with any assets left in the estate. Any debts of the deceased must be paid along with any taxes and legal fees that are incurred. Once the estate is settled, the heirs of the estate will receive their inheritance.

This process can be complicated and lengthy, even under the best of circumstances. The death of a loved one can be overwhelming to the executor and close family members. Most executors will handle only one estate in their lifetime, making this complicated process even more difficult as the executor tries to learn the system. Investment in probate creates an opportunity for the investor to help the executor and the heirs through the process in an emotionally sensitive way. You often hear to take emotion out of financial decision-making. But, while it is important to make an informed decision based on the facts, it is critical to success in probate investing to be sensitive to the family.

Probate can involve real estate, classic cars, jewelry, antiques, artwork and other assets that are often sold below market value. If investing with a self-directed IRA, it is important to verify that any investment made is not a prohibited transaction according to the Internal Revenue Code.

Once the probate process begins the information becomes part of public record. This will include the items listed in the estate, providing information for investors to approach the executor of the estate to discuss their wishes. Information about probate accounts and estates can be found through probate attorneys, newspaper announcements, and at local government offices. One of the challenges with probate investing is finding accurate information. Although it is public information that can be found through the above mentioned sources, it is not readily available online. The challenge of obtaining reliable information is the very thing that creates a less competitive market than many other real estate investment options. Only those who are aware of this as an investment option and who are motivated to find the resources will be sitting at the negotiating table. Networking and connecting with knowledgeable people is important for every investment type, but especially for probate investing.

What are the Benefits of Probate Investing?

Competitive prices for quality homes. Probate investing opportunities are the result of a death, often of someone who owns a home. The person who has passed away may have been ill for a time or may have passed suddenly. It is also possible that the home has been vacant for a period of time if the person was in an assisted living or nursing home and the family did not sell the home during that time.

Still, the condition of the homes will vary. Generally they are not abused, but may be in need of an update. Often an investor can purchase a home for 50 percent of its value, replace the carpet, paint the walls, and resell the home for market value. It is important to inspect the property carefully as there may be deeper and more expensive issues such as outdated electrical systems, mold, and the need for HVAC repair or replacements.

Probate and estate accounts might include the primary residence, a second home, or commercial property that must be sold. This creates a variety of opportunities for an investor to help the family by purchasing the real estate they no longer wish to keep.

Motivated sellers. Quite often, the adult children of the deceased already have a home of their own and are not interested in keeping and maintaining another home. Each state has different rules regarding probate and most provide a specific time when any taxes due must be paid. This can create a situation where a home must be sold to pay county, state, or federal taxes depending on the size of the estate.

For the most part, heirs are interested in obtaining the proceeds of the estate settlement rather than keeping the home or other assets, even if they are valuable. This high level of motivation presents a situation where they may be willing to part with the home for below market value in exchange for liquidity and the ability to cash out the estate. If they have jobs and families of their own, spending the time and money necessary to get a home prepared to sell is often more than they are willing or able to do.

Large inventory with less competition. There are approximately 6,100 people who turn 65 each day and that trend will likely hold steady as the Baby Boomer generation continues to reach retirement age[1]. This is increasing the demand for healthcare and other adult services. Some of those services include inheritance, estate and probate services.

There is an old adage that states, "The only certainties in life are death and taxes." Self-directed IRA investors who invest in probate seek to benefit from both of those certainties. They understand there will be a continual need to settle the estates of the deceased and they utilize their tax-free or tax-deferred retirement accounts to assist in the process.

Investment choice of rehab or rental. Depending on the location of the home, probate homes can be used to either rehab and resell or rehab and rent. This category can fit well with either portfolio strategy and could provide tremendous opportunity for a real estate investor.

What are the Risks of Probate Investing?

Time-consuming. One of the factors that has kept demand for probate investing at bay is the lack of automation and consistency. Since each state has different probate laws it can be difficult to step into probate investing in an unfamiliar area. This can also be an advantage to the investor who becomes an expert in a local market. Larger cities have hundreds of estates that go into probate each month. Not all will be valuable or have real estate opportunities, but specializing in a market can allow the investor to build relationships with probate attorneys and learn the system in their particular county. This can reduce the time needed to find and act upon opportunities. Additionally, the process of probate can take several months, if not longer, and requires patience and the ability to tie up funds in a deal that may take time to close.

Longer time to close a deal. When a home is bought at a foreclosure auction, the time from purchase to possession is often quite short. Working with a grieving family usually takes more time and patience to close the deal. They may be overwhelmed and having a difficult time going through all of the personal property of their loved one. There may be multiple family members that offer conflicting opinions as to what to do with the estate. There are also a variety of legal issues that need to be taken care of throughout the process. The longer it takes to work through these concerns, the longer the delay before the deal closes.

Deals that require more handholding. Rather than an investment where money is exchanged directly for a deed, probate real estate may require more time from the investor. If the executor is stuck getting rid of furniture and other personal possessions, offering resources such as local charities or organizations can help to take these items off their hands and may be needed to move the process along. Settling an estate is more than selling property and donating clothes. There is an emotional component to everything and it must be respected.

Dealing with the family. Every family has its own set of dynamics and grief will exasperate these dynamics. So while most of the investor's dealings will be with the executor, often all of the heirs must agree to sell the property and agree with the price. This can take time and negotiation since each heir may have different expectations and differing family dynamics may complicate the proceedings.

Probate Overview

Probate is a little-known investment strategy that can provide self-directed IRA investors another opportunity to build their retirement wealth. The sellers are typically highly motivated and, quite frankly, grateful to have someone who understands their situation and the system that can help them liquidate their inherited assets. Selling a home is often the longest process in the probate cycle and any delays can defer money that the heirs will receive. As a result, the executor and the heirs are often willing to sell the property under market value to settle the estate in a timely manner.

Though it may take time and effort to identify opportunities for probate investing, this lack of easily accessible information is what reduces the competition among investors. This is a great opportunity to help settle an estate faster and benefit your retirement at the same time. If you have the time and energy to work with grieving families, probate investing could be a very lucrative investment option.

Audio: Profiting from Probate Properties

Did you know there are opportunities available in vacant probate properties in the United States today? Would you believe almost none of them are listed for sale? The best part is many must be sold now. Join a veteran probate investor in this 50-minute audio session as he pulls back the curtain and exposes all the opportunities found in probate real estate. Set up or log in to your user account to listen now:

https://equityuniversity.customerhub.net/probate

Chapter 16: Investing in Real Estate Options

Options, in the traditional sense, involve predicting the movement of the market, index or specific stock. In the alternative space, real estate options have been utilized by some investors to grow their self-directed IRAs. This chapter will focus primarily on options in the context of real estate.

What are Options and How Do They Work?

Real estate options are similar to stock options in the sense you have the right, but not the obligation, to purchase a property at a future date for a predetermined price. This allows the investor to put a small amount of money as consideration, control the property, and identify an exit strategy. If you choose not to exercise the option, the only thing you could lose is the nominal amount of consideration money you put down. Typically option consideration money ranges from a few hundred to a few thousand dollars. Options are popular for investors who do not have a lot of money to start or those who are interested in a property, but would like more time to perform due diligence or decide an exit strategy.

Stan from Ohio put an option on a property for $100 using his daughter's CESA account. The contract gave the CESA the right, but not the obligation, to acquire the property within 60 days. Stan identified an exit strategy and assigned the option to a rehabber, providing a $5,000 profit to his daughter's education savings account. The rehabber exercised his option and acquired the property to begin his rehab project. This strategy enabled Stan to grow his daughter's education savings from $100 to $5,000 in just 60 days, tax-free.

Think of an option as the opportunity (the option) to make a purchase. Let's say you find a designer car and are interested in buying, but it's selling for $100,000 and you need time to put together the financing. You work with the owner and decide to pay $500 for the option to purchase the car within 60 days at the $100,000 price. The owner is willing to accept $500, and the prospect of a customer, to hold the listing price. If you investigate over the 60-day period and find the car is not a great deal and has a history of breaking down, you can choose not to buy the car. In this instance, you are only out $500.

On the other hand, let's say a famous actor begins driving this car in a hit new movie and there is suddenly a high demand for this particular model, driving the value up to $200,000. In this example, since the option was purchased in advance, you maintain the right to purchase the car for the initial $100,000 or sell the option to another car shopper for a profit. Since the car is now worth $200,000 you may be able to sell your option on the vehicle for $50,000. The person purchasing your option can now purchase the vehicle for a total of $150,000 (the $50,000 they paid you and the original $100,000 purchase price when the option is exercised), which is still a bargain on the value. In this example you would walk away with $50,000 on a $500 investment. An option provides the buyer with the right to exercise the option, but not the obligation to do so.

Options are generally short-term investments that evaluate market movement over a specific period of time. It can be a few days or a few months.

Mother-Son Success Story

Equity Trust client, Aisha of Maryland, is reaping the benefits from purchasing an option on a rental property with her self-directed IRA. She's doubled the value of her account in less than two years and is anticipating further rewards when the option expires.

Aisha had a Thrift Savings Plan with $5,000 that she earned from her service in the military and as a civilian government employee. She was involved with the Baltimore Real Estate Investors Association (REIA) and interested in real estate investing, but she didn't think she could afford real estate with a self-directed IRA.

Then her mentor at the REIA taught her about real estate options.

In February 2013, after moving her retirement savings to a self-directed IRA, she purchased an option on a rental property in Memphis, Tennessee. The option allowed her to buy the property after the two-year contract ended. Aisha and the seller extended the option agreement in February 2015 and Aisha's IRA will purchase the property at the end of its term. She has been happy with the investment because the property was easy to acquire and she was able to charge rent that made sense for the area while maintaining the property.

In the first 22 months that she's owned the option on this property, Aisha's IRA has increased in value by $5,000 from the initial $5,000 – a return on investment of around 50 percent per year.

While the return on investment she's already achieved and the potential for returns in the future will give her IRA a significant boost, Aisha is most excited about the impact this experience will have on others.

"The amazing experience I had with my IRA deal inspired me to help my son use the profits from his entrepreneurial ventures to open a self-directed Roth IRA with Equity Trust and buy his first rental property via option at the age of 10! I am looking forward to both of us earning double-digit ROIs on our rentals purchased via option," she says.

Note: Those who hear about her son investing in real estate don't believe it's possible because a child can't legally own a property. In fact, it is possible for her son to invest in real estate because it is actually his IRA that is purchasing the property. As long as a child has earned income, he or she can open and contribute to an IRA. In her son's case, the earned income that started his account came from selling his music CD, children's book and T-shirts. Later, we'll discuss creative ways our clients have provided their children earned income and made them a part of their self-directed investing.

"Not only am I learning how to maximize the benefits of an IRA," Aisha says, "I am also teaching my son to do the same thing. Hopefully, he will in turn teach his children to do the same."

Aisha's passion for teaching others how to take control of their own financial future doesn't stop with her son. She runs an educational non-profit for children ages 10-18 from low-to-moderate income families. Her programs provide financial literacy education and encourage entrepreneurial skills that teach the children about business ownership and investing in real estate. Students are introduced to self-directed investing and taught how to save their part-time earned income in an IRA. They are taught the power of compound interest and encouraged to get a jumpstart on their retirement savings.

She says she hopes to change a common mindset about personal finance and open more people's eyes about their retirement-saving options: "People focus on what they *can't* do, not what they *can* do."

What are the Benefits of Real Estate Options?

Low initial investment needed. One of the most attractive things about investing in real estate options is the small-dollar investment needed to get started. This enables you to mitigate the amount of money needed, and the risk, while learning the industry.

Liquidity and shorter investment-holding periods. Options can be bought and sold in a matter of days, which is a quick turnaround in the real estate industry. Options also allow you to walk away from a deal if things change, with nothing lost other than the option consideration. The liquidity of real estate options provides more freedom and flexibility than the majority of real estate opportunities.

Large profit potential. Real estate options provide an opportunity to profit quickly but often with less volatility than the stock or currency markets. Since options generally require a small initial investment, there is an opportunity to significantly profit when you sell the option to another investor. Like the example we shared earlier, Stan optioned a property for $100 and in just 60 days was able to turn that into $5,000.

What are the Risks of Option Investing?

Losing the entire investment quickly. If you decide not to exercise the option, and do not find a third-party interested in purchasing your option before the option expires, you lose the entire option consideration. While this is the risk option investors are taking and it is not typically a large amount of money, it is important to remember this risk when evaluating investment opportunities. Investors must be willing and able to lose their consideration money if the option does not go as planned.

Active investing. These investment opportunities are not for a passive investor or an investor who is more comfortable with a buy-and-hold strategy. Investors should want to be actively involved in the markets and determined to continually source deals. Networking, marketing, and advertising are three components that can help make option investing a success. Investors who are connected in the industry have a better chance of finding potential suitors for the properties they option.

Options Investing Overview

Real estate options are one method for investors interested in real estate to get started. Since they typically require less money than an individual piece of real estate, real estate options are a potential small-dollar opportunity for those just starting a retirement account.

Richard Desich, Sr.

Chapter 17: Investing in Precious Metals

Precious metals investing can include a number of different metals such as gold, silver, platinum and palladium. These metals are listed among the larger investment category of commodities. In addition to precious metals, commodities include other products in their primary form such as oil and gas, wheat, corn, coffee, or other food products.

How Does Precious Metals Investing Work?

Precious metals have caught the attention of investors for centuries. Gold and silver have historically been a status symbol of wealth and success. If the Gold Rush taught us anything, it was that speculators will go to great lengths to find gold and other precious metals. The most common types of precious metals include gold, silver, platinum, and palladium; which, if they have the prescribed purity ratio, are investments that are allowed within a self-directed IRA.

An investment in metals will be either physical or paper. A physical investment includes investing in a metal, such as gold bullion or gold bullion certificates. A paper investment includes ETFs, stocks, and mutual funds that focus on precious metals, futures, and options.

Precious metals are sold on mercantile worldwide exchanges, such as the New York Mercantile Exchange (NYMEX). Markets are open 24 hours a day, providing exchange opportunities anywhere on the globe. Metals are measured in troy ounces and the price is generally listed in contract lots of 100 troy ounces.

Physical Precious Metal Investments

Bullion is a popular option for those who worry about economic collapse. Historically, few assets hold their value when an economy collapses. Physical paper dollars or currency coins can become worthless. The two investments that frequently hold value during an economic crisis or government collapse are land and precious metal bullion. Think bars of gold. While the United States has enjoyed several centuries of stable government, after watching the world news you soon realize other countries are not as fortunate. As a result, physical possession of gold bullion is a popular investment choice among investors who are concerned about government instability and seek assets with intrinsic value. In order to hold gold, silver, platinum, or palladium bars in a self-directed IRA the metals must be produced by accredited manufacturers and must meet minimum fineness requirements.

In addition to physical bullion, certain coins can also be held within an IRA. They must hold an intrinsic value and not be deemed a collectible. For a more extensive list of permissible precious metals and more information, please use the following chart:

Permissible Precious Metals Include:				Unacceptable Precious Metals Include:
Gold	Silver	Platinum	Palladium	Austrian 100, 20 and 10 Corona
American Eagle coins*	America The Beautiful coins	American Eagle coins*	Bars and rounds as referenced below**	Belgian 20 Franc
Australian Kangaroo/ Nugget coins	American Eagle coins*	Australian Koala coins		British Britannia
Austrian Philharmonic coins	Australian Kookaburra and Koala coins	Australian Platypus coins		Chilean 100 Peso
British Britannia coins (.9999+)	Austrian Philharmonic coins	Canadian Maple Leaf coins		Colombian 5 Peso British Sovereign
Canadian Maple Leaf coins	Canadian Maple Leaf coins	Isle of Man Noble coins		Dutch 10 Guilder
Chinese Panda coins	Mexican Libertad coins	Bars and rounds as referenced below**		French 20 Franc
U.S. Buffalo Gold Uncirculated coins (no Proofs)	Bars and rounds as referenced below**			German Mark
Mexican Libertad coins (.999+)				Hungarian 100 Korona
Bars and rounds as referenced below**				Italian 20 Lira
				Mexican 50, 20, 10, 5, 2 ½, and 2 Peso
				Rare or Collectible Coins*
*Coins, including the American Eagle, that have undergone "certification" (also known as "slabbed" coins) are not acceptable in IRAs at this time.				South African Krugerrand
**Bars and rounds produced by manufacturers accredited by Nymex/Comex, LME, LBMA, LPPM, TOCOM, NYSE/Liffe/CBOT, and ISO-9000 or a national mint. The minimum finenesses for bars are: • Gold .995+ • Silver .999+ • Platinum .9995+ • Palladium .9995+				Swiss 20 Franc

A risk of physical bullion or coins is that they are highly illiquid. Selling bars of metal is much more difficult than selling paper. Another risk is theft. Whenever you take physical possession of an item, you become responsible for its security. Theft is often a concern, and storage methods should be determined prior to investing in physical bullion.

Certificates for bullion. If you want the physical bullion but do not want to store it, there is the option to invest in certificates. You own the physical bullion but do not have to take physical possession of the metal because an independent company will store it. Companies that store bullion and issue certificates are located throughout the world. This enables the investor to have the physical metals held in a stable country, which may be different from the one in which the investor lives.

Investors should consider a custodian that partners with a high-security storage facility. Look for a facility with a proven track record of quickly facilitating the purchase and sale of physical metals and one that is licensed by major commodity exchanges.

While certificates are more liquid than physical bullion it is questionable how much they would be worth in the event of a government collapse. Having the international option for holding could help to mitigate this risk, however.

Paper Precious Metal Investments

The precious metals markets are volatile and complex. We recommend that you work with your advisor or a qualified financial professional when considering any of the potential investment options discussed.

Exchange-Traded Funds (ETFs). ETFs allow an investor to invest in a specific precious-metal fund or a collection of precious metals. There are funds that are focused solely on one metal while others are a blend of different types. These funds can be actively managed or indexed. An actively managed fund will have higher fees due to the fact that the fund manager is making trading decisions on a daily basis with the assistance of other managers and researchers. An index-traded fund will benchmark a specific index and mirror that index. As a result, there is less active trading and the fees are generally lower. Index funds have a goal to match the underlying index performance. Actively managed accounts have a goal to beat the index performance. Looking at performance and comparing it to the underlying fees is the best way to decide which funds may be advantageous to your portfolio.

Stocks and mutual funds. It is possible to invest in precious metals without having a precious metal holding. There are many companies that are directly related to the industry and their stocks or mutual funds will reflect the market adjustments found in the precious metals industry. For example, mining companies can be a great investment for precious metals investors. Instead of investing in a specific gold fund, the investment is in the company's mining operations and their ability to obtain and sell the metals they are mining. These funds or stocks can have a lower level of volatility than the specific metal funds, while still related to the industry.

Futures and options. One of the most common way commodities are traded is through futures and options. This investment hedges against the markets and bets on the direction the commodities will go. Precious metals are a very volatile industry, meaning money can be made in predicting the direction of the markets. It is not unusual for the price of gold to fluctuate by 50 percent in less than a year's time. This high level of volatility provides many opportunities for gains, as well as losses, through options trading.

What are the Benefits of Precious Metal Investing?

Hedge against inflation. One of the benefits of precious metals investing is that it is a hedge against inflation. The fluctuation seen in these markets is not closely tied to the economy and not closely tied to the stock and bond market. This provides an extra level of diversification for an investor's portfolio.

High demand that outpaces supply. While it can be said that precious metals are loosely tied to supply and demand, the reality is there is a high demand for precious metals, keeping the markets moving forward. The mainstay for gold is jewelry and ornamentation and has been the case for thousands of years. Emerging markets can provide an increase in demand as these economies gain more disposable income and success is demonstrated by obtaining goods such as gold jewelry. Buying gold in the form of jewelry is a way to announce one's economic success. Gold is also used in the electronics industry and other industrial applications, along with other precious metals. Silver is widely used in electronics while platinum is used in catalytic converters to reduce emissions. These applications increase demand beyond ornamentation and are creating more opportunities for investors. When you consider silver is included in nearly every smart phone and microchip, it is clear why demand is on the rise.

Gold	The original precious metal, gold, has been critical to the success of royal dynasties and individuals for millennia.	With more demand for gold than supply, gold prices tend to rise on uncertainty concerning the strength of the U.S. dollar and macro-economic concerns.
Silver	With its electrical conductivity, silver is used in industry, electronics, and jewelry.	Like gold, there is more demand for silver than supply.
Platinum	One of the rarest metals on earth, platinum is used in emission control devices and dentistry.	Fifteen times rarer than gold, platinum is expected to increase in value.
Palladium	A byproduct of platinum and nickel, palladium is mainly used to manufacture catalytic converters and ceramic capacitors for electronics.	Increasing demand for goods containing palladium is expected to increase sharply – especially as India and China expand their consumer bases.

Intrinsic value. Gold and other metals have physical value as well as market value. This means that no matter what happens to the market, the metal itself has properties that are considered useful and valuable. This value is universal and worldwide, providing an investment opportunity that will hold intrinsic value regardless of how the markets are performing.

Liquidity. Purchasing precious metals in the paper form is a highly liquid asset, while metals in the physical form are considered highly illiquid. As an investor, evaluating your need for accessible income will help to direct which option will best suit your portfolio and liquidity needs.

What are the Risks of Precious Metal Investing?

Volatility is the number one risk. The markets fluctuate substantially – and quickly. Paper gains and losses will occur frequently over short periods of time. However, these paper gains or losses are not realized until the investment is sold. Due to the high level of volatility, having other assets that can be liquidated in the event of a financial need is essential to the buy low/sell high strategy.

International market volatility. With mines for various precious metals located throughout the world, political instability in other countries will impact the supply and demand for various metals.

These factors impact both the volatility and the price structure. For example, South Africa produces much of the world's gold. In recent years, political unrest has resulted in significant drops in gold production. As the world supply is impacted so is the price. When researching precious metal investing, looking beyond the metal itself and understanding the markets and the countries involved will help you to make better investment decisions.

Profits, Taxes and IRS Rules

When you review the IRS rules for prohibited transactions in a self-directed IRA you may notice precious metals are on the list. The exceptions include the precious metals we've reviewed such as gold, silver, platinum and palladium. These can be held in the physical form in an IRA if they meet minimum fineness requirements, or in certificate form, mutual funds, ETFs or options.

The volatility of the precious metal market creates significant gains and losses. These gains will be taxed at the highest rate of ordinary income if the investment is held for less than a year. When you are looking at a potential 50-percent profit in one year, losing 40 percent of that to taxes is tough to swallow. By placing the investment in a tax-advantaged account, you receive all potential gains, either tax-free or tax-deferred.

Precious Metals Overview

Investing in gold is the granddaddy of precious metal investing. Today there are several other investment options which can surpass the value of gold as their demand increases through industrial uses. These precious metals have high value because they are in demand and, as a natural resource, have limited supply. Understanding this market can provide another diversification strategy for your retirement portfolio.

Audio: Precious Metals Investing Panel

A panel of three experienced investors and industry experts discuss investing in precious metals, metals ETFs, and how it may help you grow your self-directed IRA in this 40-minute audio session. Set up or log in to your user account to listen below:

https://equityuniversity.customerhub.net/metals

Chapter 18: Investing in Private Equity, LLCs and REITs

This chapter covers a wide range of investment options. These investments involve the use of private funds to support businesses and investment opportunities that are not widely published. Helping local businesses you're familiar with or finding markets where you have expertise is a recipe for success. This is a chance to truly personalize an investment portfolio by investing in industries where you have advanced knowledge and a passion to support business growth.

What are the Investment Options?

Private equity involves investing directly into private companies. This might include funding new technology, research and development, or expanding the company's working capital. Providing investment dollars to advance technology that might lead to a new drug or health discovery that can change the industry is an example of private-equity investing. It can also be on a smaller scale, where funding helps a small business grow and expand their market, inventory, or product line. Exchanging funding for company equity can be risky, but when it is successful there may be a significant amount of money to be made.

LLCs and business ownership can involve a silent partner investment, where the investor's role is only to provide capital, or it can involve ownership interest which involves a more hands-on approach to the business. The backbone of our society is an entrepreneurial spirit and the growth of small business owners. You may have experience in a particular market and can serve as a consultant in addition to providing funds needed for business growth. This investment can come in the form of an equity exchange, lending money with an agreed rate of return, or a combination of the two.

Real Estate Investment Trusts (REITs). These are real estate backed investments where investors purchase shares, rather than physically owning the real estate. For investors who love the idea of real estate but do not wish to invest the time in developing a physical real estate portfolio, REITs offer an excellent alternative. REITs hold property in a fund and then shares are sold to investors to fund the investments. REITs can focus on various real estate markets. Some might only hold commercial property, where others may focus on residential markets. Some funds are region specific, while others cover a wider geographic area. REITs provide the benefits of real estate investing but diversify the risk by investing in a fund that may hold properties spread across several markets, industries, and investment types. REITs also allow the investor to participate in a more passive role.

How Does it Work?

There are many private-equity firms that specialize in these types of investments. The downside is that it takes large amounts of cash to meet the firm's minimum investment requirements. For the average investor the principles are the same, though the method of finding opportunities may vary.

The idea behind business investments is to provide an influx of cash, in exchange for an agreed return, that enables the business to improve and increase in value. An example you may be familiar with is the popular television show *Shark Tank*. A private business investment may be a distressed company with an opportunity to improve or a successful business that is looking to expand.

Identifying why the company is distressed or how your investment will be used to grow the business is a critical step in the due diligence process. Is the company in need of help due to a bad economy, mismanagement, or rapid growth that has created a cash flow or inventory problem? Each of these issues requires a different solution. You must determine if you have the knowledge and resources needed to turn the company around and earn a profit.

These factors can make private-equity investing more personal. Although millionaires who place money with a private equity firm typically eliminate the personalization and focus solely on the expected returns. On the smaller scale, taking a personal interest in the business helps to make wiser decisions about what the investor has to offer the company's growth.

Fueled by misfortune, Chicago-area resident Seth discovered that you don't need to be rich to find ways to secure your financial future. Seth worked as a sanitation worker until he broke his back a few years ago. Even after multiple surgeries, he physically couldn't do the same type of work. After learning about self-directed IRAs, he used the $13,000 in his pension plan and opened a Roth IRA. The account sat without activity for a few years because Seth didn't think there was much he could do with his savings.

After attending an Equity University educational workshop, Seth discovered that he could loan money from his Roth IRA. This allowed him to put his retirement savings to work, even with the smaller account balance. In the past, Seth lent $4,000 to a business acquaintance for a real estate deal and did well, but it was with his taxable income. So when the same investor approached him about securing a loan to expand his trucking company, Seth felt ready to make his first self-directed IRA investment.

Seth's IRA loaned the investor's business $10,000 after reviewing the business plan and agreeing to the 20-percent interest offer. Based on their past transaction Seth felt safe with the agreement. "After he paid me back from the original deal, he had proved himself to me," Seth says.

Seth receives monthly payments on his loan deposited back into his Roth IRA, tax-free, for a 20-percent ROI. When the loan is repaid in full, Seth's original $10,000 will grow to $12,000 in his tax-free account.

When Seth hears of someone being hesitant to complete their first self-directed IRA deal, he responds by telling them that you have to be willing to take action, but to take an educated, strategic risk. "You don't want to just be throwing money out there," he says.

The self-directed deal has opened Seth's eyes and made him excited to discover more opportunities.

"I was only looking at real estate and stock market investments when I found out I could invest in private companies and make a steady return," he says. "This has led me to look for more companies considering expansion, where I might be able to get a piece or earn favorable returns."

The size of the loan also expanded Seth's awareness of the prospect of small-dollar opportunities, in businesses and elsewhere.

"Sometimes a real estate investment might only need $2,000 to $4,000 for closing costs, light rehab work or just to get a deal done. You may not only get a piece of that deal and get your principal back, but you can get monthly cash flow as well," he says. "It's exciting that there are a lot of different possibilities out there."

What are the Benefits of Investing in Businesses?

Expertise. Business investing provides an opportunity to add a level of expertise to an investment. What do you know the best? Often there are businesses in these industries where the right investment could bring the business to the next level. As the business grows, so does the value of the company, and in exchange the investment returns.

Potential high rates of return. When an investor understands the industry and how it works, he or she can use this expertise to make wise investment decisions. Some industries are cyclical and an investment to help weather a downturn has the potential to provide higher returns during the busy periods. Other businesses need an influx of cash while technology is developed and products patented. Once the product launches, the company value increases significantly and the investors receive the benefit.

Research can mitigate risk. The risk of private equity funding and investing in businesses can be mitigated with solid research. Solid research, planning and business savvy can make it easier to control value fluctuations. Businesses, especially small businesses, are able to adjust their business strategies and innovate to improve profitability. Downturns are not set in stone as long as corrections are made in a timely manner. This benefit gives investors better control over their investment returns than many other investment opportunities.

What are the Risks of Investing in Businesses?

Capital risk. It is possible to lose your entire investment if the business fails. For this reason, identifying why the company is underperforming and understanding the needed solutions is critical to mitigating this risk. Similarly, if you are investing in a start-up business it is important to do your research so that you feel confident that the business, and your investment, will find success down the road.

Additional capital needs. Private-equity and business investments often need more than one influx of cash. Additional funds may be needed down the road to get the company in a place where it has significantly increased in value. An investor needs to be prepared to meet these needs.

Long-term horizon. Companies generally take time to increase profitability. This long-term investment should be balanced with the needs of the investor's portfolio. It may take several years with no gains, to achieve any type of return.

Economic risk. The success of businesses can be dependent upon market conditions. When the economy is strong, a poorly run company can still find success. When the economy contracts it tends to weed out the weaker companies with less cash to withstand slower sales. Good management and efficient operations can help offset this to some degree. Long-term recessions and economic downturns can weaken even well-managed companies. It is not always possible to predict the economic development or decline of a specific area or unforeseen developments in the industry. This can result in a loss of money or lower returns than anticipated.

Private Equity, LLCs, Business Ownership and REITS Overview

The opportunity to invest in industries where the investor has expertise and passion is a great way to use money earmarked for retirement. The challenge is many business transactions are not as standard as purchasing a piece of real estate or buying a stock. There is more complexity concerning prohibited transactions, disqualified persons or entities, Unrelated Business Income Tax and other IRS rules and regulations that we'll review later. Therefore, it is important to have a tax consultant or attorney available to answer questions to ensure the rules are followed and the tax-advantages of your account are maintained.

Audio: Private Equity Investing

This 37-minute audio session will delve into the types of private entities that you can invest in with your IRA and how to research potential investments before committing. Set up or log in to your user account to listen now:

https://equityuniversity.customerhub.net/equity

Audio: The Wide World of REITs 101

What do you actually know about REITs? This 50-minute audio session will share details on REITs and explore this asset class as an investment option. Set up or log in to your user account to listen now:

https://equityuniversity.customerhub.net/reits

Chapter 19: Not Enough Money Yet? – How to Get Started Anyway

The previous chapters have discussed some common alternative investment options that can be held in a self-directed IRA. As investors review the exciting investment opportunities that are available, one of the most common concerns is having enough money to pursue the opportunities they have found. For those who want to get started immediately but do not have funds available, there are still opportunities that can help build a nest egg for retirement.

Here we will showcase several tactics that can take the excuse "I don't have enough money" and throw it out the window. Think back to the beginning of this book when we discussed the democratization of capital. An exciting aspect of self-directed investing is the ability to leverage the democratization of capital and finance deals through a variety of methods. Self-directed IRA investments can be financed with a loan from a financial institution or from a private investor's personal or retirement money. Additionally, self-directed IRA transactions can be conducted with multiple investors (or even multiple retirement accounts) in the deal. Many investors give up on self-directed investment opportunities because they don't think they have enough money to get started. If self-directed investing seems right for you, this chapter can help you get started on the path to financial freedom, even if your account balance isn't where you'd like it to be today.

We won't have a chance to delve into all the specifics of raising money for self-directed IRA investments, but the important takeaway is that it can be done and investors should not give up on an opportunity simply due to the amount of money currently in the account.

Debt Financing

One of the primary ways investors can finance deals without having the full purchase amount in their IRA is with debt financing. Essentially, the investor receives a loan for a specified amount to make their investment and agrees to repay the lender (either an individual or financial institution) a specified return for the use of the funds. Financing inside of an IRA is very different than outside of one so it is important to understand the differences in lending procedures.

One of the biggest challenges with self-directed IRA real estate investments is that large cash purchases can significantly limit investment opportunities. Just as most homeowners did not pay cash for their primary residence, many investors do not have the cash within their IRA to purchase homes outright. The ability to leverage debt allows the IRA owner to increase their investment holdings without having to sell the homes and recoup cash for the next investment. Some investors still utilize debt financing even when they have enough money available in their IRA. They prefer to purchase multiple properties with debt financing as opposed to one property owned outright by the IRA to increase their profit potential or have multiple sources of income.

When purchasing a personal residence, you typically go to the bank and take out a loan with your home as collateral. Banks generally want a loan that is personally guaranteed by the borrower in addition to the collateral. This ensures that if the payments are not made, the home can be foreclosed on, and the bank can sell the property to recoup their money. If the sale of the home does not produce enough to cover the loan amount, the bank has the option to seek other assets the homeowner may have to repay the loan in full.

However, self-directed IRAs require non-recourse loans since your IRA (or your personal money) cannot serve as collateral for the loan. The only recourse is the investment that is being financed. Non-recourse loans indicate the loan does not have a personal guarantor.

Since the investment property is the only collateral and only option for recourse in the event of default, many lenders do not offer loans for property within a self-directed IRA. Fortunately there are a select few who specialize in non-recourse loans so this option is still available to self-directed IRA investors.

Non-recourse loans do not have to originate from a financial institution either. Any loan made to a self-directed IRA must be non-recourse, but the lender can also be a private investor or another retirement account. The following story about Emerich, a client from Ohio, demonstrates the objection of "not having enough money" can be overcome by something as simple as a loan from your neighbor.

Solving a First Deal Financing Dilemma

Emerich is a member of his local Real Estate Investment Association (REIA) and had heard Equity University speak about self-directed IRA investing in the past, so he was familiar with the concept. As a real estate investor for the last 20 years he was also well-versed on the investing side. He knew he wanted to open a self-directed IRA so he could use his real estate investing knowledge to build for his retirement. But how could he combine the two and get started when his IRA was underfunded and did not have enough to make a deal?

Emerich was stuck. He didn't think there was any way for him to get the funding he needed in his IRA, aside from maxing out his annual contributions (which can often take several years until the account grows to the requisite balance).

Then, at one of his local real estate club meetings he learned that an IRA could utilize a non-recourse loan to purchase a property. "This was the green light I had been waiting for," he recalls. "As soon as I learned I could invest with debt financing when my IRA couldn't purchase outright, I was ready to go."

Emerich opened a Roth IRA to do his first deal, which was funded with $10,000 from an existing retirement plan. Knowing there were few real estate opportunities available for only $10,000, he enlisted the help of his neighbor as the non-recourse lender.

Emerich purchased his first property in his Roth IRA for $15,000. Emerich used $10,000 from his Roth IRA and $5,000 came from his neighbor in a non-recourse loan. He was able to purchase the four-unit property at a discount because a member of his network was getting older, could no longer keep up with the property and wanted it off his hands.

Three of the four units were already occupied with long-term tenants so it was cash-flowing from day one. Additionally, Emerich already had a buyer lined up who he worked with in the past and was purchasing an assortment of properties in the area.

Three months after the purchase Emerich was able to sell the property for $55,000. After his IRA paid any expenses, taxes (UBIT), and fees associated with the maintenance or sale of the property, plus repaying the $5,000 non-recourse loan to his neighbor, Emerich deposited approximately $40,000 back into his Roth IRA, tax-free.

As Emerich states, "I was able to quadruple my account within three months with my first real estate deal in my IRA. I think that is awesome!"

Emerich wants his experience to be a lesson to other investors. "You don't need as much money in your account as you think," he says. "Go out and talk to people and find people who are willing to lend money. Just go for it, make the offers. You can't find the deals unless you make the offers. You'll come up with the money if the deal is right."

Now that Emerich has grown his retirement savings and solved the "I don't have enough money to do my first deal" dilemma, he's spreading the good news he found about non-recourse loans to other investors in his network and is continuing to invest for his retirement. He recently provided a hard money loan from his Roth IRA to another investor and is currently working on the purchase of another property with another non-recourse loan from the same neighbor who originally kick-started his first Roth IRA deal.

In a true self-directed investing circle of life, Emerich has gone from the investor whose Roth IRA needed a non-recourse loan to make his first deal to the investor who is providing loans from his Roth IRA so others can complete their deals, while still earning money for his retirement.

Emerich's story demonstrates that investors hoping to make their first self-directed IRA investment shouldn't be discouraged by the amount of money currently available in their account. If you know the options available, and are interested in an opportunity, there are ways to make it happen.

Webinar: How to Purchase Real Estate in an IRA with a Loan

If you've found a great opportunity for your IRA, but lack the capital necessary to complete the deal, this webinar is for you. Matt Allen – Vice President of the IRA Lending Division of North American Savings Bank joins Equity University to discuss how to obtain a loan in your IRA – the correct way. Set up or log in to your user account to watch it today:

https://equityuniversity.customerhub.net/non-recourse

When debt financing is utilized in self-directed IRA investments, investors must be aware of a potential tax implication called Unrelated Business Income Tax.

Unrelated Business Income Tax (UBIT), Unrelated Business Taxable Income (UBTI) and Unrelated Debt Financed Income (UDFI)

These three acronyms relate to tax implications within an otherwise tax-advantaged account or entity. Unrelated Business Income Tax/Taxable Income (UBIT/UBTI) is a provision added to the Internal Revenue Code by Congress in the Revenue Act of 1950 to eliminate an unfair competitive advantage enjoyed by exempt organizations and entities over their taxpaying counterparts in the non-exempt world. This provision was later amended to also include IRAs and other tax-advantaged retirement accounts.

UBTI and UBIT are often used interchangeably. UBTI represents the type of income that is taxable; UBIT is the actual tax that is owed based on the UBTI received within the tax-advantaged account or entity.

The result of the Revenue Act of 1950 (and its subsequent application to entities such as IRAs) is that certain investments owned within a retirement account (such as a Roth IRA, Traditional IRA, SIMPLE IRA, SEP IRA, or other tax-advantaged entity) must consider UBIT depending on the investment choices.

As it pertains to retirement accounts, UBIT investments typically fall into the category of debt-financed real estate/other property and investments in "flow-through entities" such as Limited Partnerships, Limited Liability Companies, and similar entities that are involved in an unrelated business/operating company.

As always, it is important to check with a qualified tax professional, attorney, CPA or financial planner to determine if your investments will be subject to UBIT.

Unrelated Debt-Financed Income (UDFI) is a term primarily used in the context of IRA investments with income that is derived from debt-financed real estate or other property. The UDFI is subject to Unrelated Business Income Tax (UBIT) and is the scenario we will discuss in this chapter.

When first exposed to the idea Unrelated Business Income Tax may be owed on IRA investments, most people are confused. One of the primary benefits of IRAs is the tax-free or tax-deferred savings, so when confronted with UBIT many ask why and wonder if it is a double taxation.

When you begin to delve deeper into the subject of UDFI, however, you learn that you are paying tax on the portion that was financed with another person's (or institution's) money, not your IRA's money. The debt-financed portion, or more specifically the income derived from this portion, did not come from a tax-advantaged entity and thus is not exempt from taxes and is subject to UBIT. If you had identified another investor who wanted to pay for the financed portion with an IRA then you could regain the tax benefits and would likely avoid UBIT. But since you financed a portion of the investment with money from a non-tax-advantaged source, it is subject to tax. While this may appear complicated, the result is generally a very small tax when compared to the profit generated from the investment. It is simply a cost of doing business.

The key is to understand that the investment profits will be prorated based on the portion of the real estate that was paid from the IRA and the portion that was secured with a non-recourse loan. Debt-financed income is calculated in direct proportion to the percentage of the real estate or business that is leveraged by debt. This is the income that is subject to UBIT. The percentage that was paid in cash from the IRA is generally not subject to UBIT.

Taxes are calculated similar to how taxes on real estate outside of an IRA are calculated. The income from the property is offset by the expenses and depreciation as it would be if the account was not within the IRA. If the depreciation creates a loss, that loss may be carried forward to write off against possible future gains. This is a lesser-known upside to UBTI. While the tax consequences may be small, filing the proper paperwork with the IRS each year is essential to maintaining the tax-advantaged treatment of the account. Equity Trust is one of a few self-directed IRA custodians that offers a service to prepare the Federal Form 990-T, state returns, and other supporting schedules for clients impacted by UBIT.

Let's look at two examples of what UBIT may look like:

UBIT on Annual Income: Let's say you purchase a property for $100,000. $50,000 came from your IRA and $50,000 was financed with a non-recourse loan. This property generates a net profit of $500 per month, or $6,000 annually. For simplicity's sake, let's say this is the net profit, after factoring in depreciation and other expenses, which you are able to deduct prior to paying the tax on the UDFI. Since you financed 50 percent of your initial purchase with a non-recourse loan, 50 percent of your net income is considered UDFI and is subject to UBIT. Half of the annual net income is $3,000 but the IRS grants a specific deduction on the first $1,000 of net income from UBTI sources. For net unrelated business taxable income greater than $1,000 UBIT is owed and is taxed at the trust rates. In this example, after the $1,000 specific deduction only $2,000 will be filed as Unrelated Business Taxable Income (UBTI). This amount is taxed at 15 percent, according to the 2015 trust tax rate schedule. The IRA in this example will have to pay $300 in UBIT this year, but the property will still net $5,700 back into your IRA's favorable tax environment.

UBIT on the Sale of a Property: Once again, let's say you purchase a property for $100,000. $50,000 came from your IRA and $50,000 was debt financed with a non-recourse loan. After a year or two, you locate a buyer and your IRA sells the property for $150,000. To keep the numbers simple, let's say you have a net profit of $50,000 on the sale after repaying the loan. 50 percent of your $50,000 profit is subject to UBIT because you financed half of the purchase with a non-recourse loan. After receiving the specific deduction of $1,000, a total of $24,000 will be subject to UBIT. $24,000 will be assessed $7,861.80 in UBIT according to the IRS tax rate schedules for estates and trusts. This amount will be paid in UBIT and filed using the Form 990-T. The remaining $16,138.20 will re-join the $25,000 of the profit not subject to UBIT back into your IRA's tax-advantaged environment. After it is all said and done, your IRA will have netted $41,138.20 and an 82-percent ROI on your IRA's initial investment of $50,000.

Paying tax on a portion of the profits is better than not having the financing to make the profits possible in the first place. Starting out with financing options can help to build the account to a level where financing is no longer necessary.

Let Us Focus on UBIT so You Can Focus on Success

At UBIT Professional LLC, an affiliate of Equity Trust Company, our goal is to take the "complicated" out of the UBIT equation. Whether it is learning through the extensive information we provide, or having UBIT Professional prepare the required Form 990-T, our goal is to focus on UBIT so you can focus on your success. Learn more today by visiting our website:

http://www.ubitprofessional.com/

Raising Capital Using Retirement Plans

It's conceivable to use your self-directed IRA and other retirement plans to fund your deals. As discussed, recent estimates place over $7.6 trillion within IRAs across the country and over $24.9 trillion of total retirement assets.[21] These funds could be used to invest in a variety of alternative investments, such as real estate, private equity, start-up businesses, notes, and more. Often the first step is to make others aware of the possibilities of their own retirement plans – the ability for them to be in control and to invest in alternatives to the market.

A case study from our files illustrates how one of our clients, Bill an investor/rehabber, raised capital for an investment he couldn't fund on his own. A few years ago Bill ran out of money for additional investments. He was in a hot market and he didn't want to miss out. What he did next changed his life. He found a great house that he could buy for $25,000, all cash. It needed about $5,000 in repairs. Bill went to some friends and relatives and borrowed money from their IRAs to purchase the house. He paid them 15 percent interest ($2,250) for the six months it took to finish the rehab and resell the house. He sold the house for $52,000. After paying back his investors, he had a net profit of $19,750! Let's look at the ledger...

Bill started with	$0		House sold	$52,000
House cost	$25,000		Loan	($30,000)
Repair	$5,000		Interest owed	($2,250)
Total amount borrowed	$30,000		Bill finishes with	$19,750

Bill's friends were so pleased with their returns that he had no trouble working with them on future deals.

A second example demonstrates how Bob, a real estate investor, raised self-directed IRA capital for an opportunity to acquire a property for $100,000.

Based on his experience and research, Bob knew this property was easily worth $150,000. Bob's friend Mary was unhappy with the low fixed-income investment restrictions with her current IRA custodian. Bob told Mary about the property he wanted to buy and, after she conducted her due diligence and felt comfortable with the investment, agreed to loan Bob $105,000 from her IRA ($100,000 for the house and $5,000 for the repairs). Bob and Mary agreed that he would pay her IRA back in one year with 10-percent interest, all due at the time of payment. After receiving Mary's IRA investment, Bob purchased the house for $100,000, put new carpet in the living room and planted flowers in the front yard. A year later, Bob sold it for $150,000, just as he thought he would. He paid Mary back the $105,000 plus the $10,500 in interest he owed her. Mary made 10% on her money, tax-advantaged in her IRA, just by letting Bob borrow funds for one year. What's even better is that Bob, as the active investor, made $34,500 on the deal and didn't need any of his own funds.

These two examples demonstrate how self-directed IRAs can position investors to benefit their retirement in either an active or more passive role. It is another tactic that can be utilized by investors who may not have enough money to invest on their own.

It is important to remember the risks associated with this money-raising strategy. Not every investor is as trustworthy as Bill and Bob were in the examples we shared and not every investment will succeed. When dealing with your own or other people's retirement funds, you need to make sure that you have thoroughly examined the investment opportunity and your business partners.

If you are raising money from other investors you have an increased responsibility to do right by your investors and ensure they are repaid according to the terms of your deal. If that means you lose money on the investment to ensure your investors are paid accordingly, that's the risk you must accept.

If you are faced with an opportunity to lend money for an investment, don't take the analysis provided by the investor at face value. Perform your own due diligence, research the opportunity and the investor raising money, and only commit to the investment if you feel comfortable it will benefit you or your portfolio.

Later, we will discuss due diligence techniques, identifying and helping to prevent fraud and other important risk management techniques.

> ### Webinar: Secrets to Private Money Lending
>
> Looking to make a self-directed investment, but don't have enough capital to get started? Do you currently have money in an IRA or 401(k) and are looking for passive investments that are outside the stock market? Have you considered private lending as a potential opportunity?
>
> Jay Conner, a private investment lender with 12 years of experience in the industry, joins Equity University's National Education Specialist for a webinar to reveal his approach. Set up or log in to your user account to watch it today:
>
> https://equityuniversity.customerhub.net/lending

Investment Partners

Utilizing investment partners is another strategy way to use your expertise to identify and invest in alternative investment opportunities without having to pay for the entire deal. Real estate can typically be purchased by an individual, a business, as joint tenants with the right of survivorship, or as tenants in common.

Since the IRA is its own entity, when the investor purchases the property in cash from the IRA the title is in the name of the custodian for the benefit of the IRA owner (i.e. *Equity Trust Company Custodian FBO Client Name or Account Number, IRA*). Remember your IRA is what holds title to the property.

When two spouses purchase a property outside of an IRA they often do so as joint tenants. This gives each owner rights to the entire property. In the event of someone's death, the partner can receive the deed to the property without going through probate.

A tenant-in-common relationship is how real estate is titled when partners are involved and is used when obtaining partners within an IRA. Tenants in common divide the interest of the property and give each partner a percentage of ownership based on an agreement by the owners before the purchase is made. This strategy of titling gives each partner a vested interest in the real estate and, when the property is sold, the proceeds will be divided by the tenants-in-common arrangement.

For example, let's say you decide to purchase a property with your Traditional IRA, your spouse's Roth IRA and your child's CESA. You structure the agreement so that 45 percent of the purchase came from your IRA, 40 percent came from your spouse's Roth and 15 percent came from the CESA. According to this titling structure 45 percent, 40 percent and 15 percent of all expenses must come from each respective account and income that is derived from rent or the sale of the property will be returned in direct proportion to the titling structure of your Traditional IRA, your spouse's Roth IRA, and your child's CESA respectively.

The tenants-in-common relationship is not exclusive to IRAs either. You can enter a tenants-in-common relationship with your IRA and a non-disqualified person's personal money if you so choose.

This allows investors to pool money from more than one account or from another's personal money to purchase property. Again, it is important to remember that when property is purchased as tenants in common within an IRA, all expenses must be shared by the percentage of ownership granted within the tenants-in-common agreement. In addition, all profits are returned to the respective IRAs according to the percentage of ownership as demonstrated in the example below.

Partnerships can be among family members or other investors who are interested in combining funds. Using the tenants-in-common structure makes it possible to combine accounts, like your IRA, your spouse's IRA, your HSA account and/or your child's IRA or CESA account. This may allow smaller accounts to grow with the support of larger accounts. It is also possible to use your IRA money and combine it with non-IRA money which allows you to add your personal funds to finance the purchase.

It is essential that all expenses and all profits are distributed exactly, based on the percentage of ownership. Failure to do so may trigger a prohibited transaction and disqualify the investment for the tax-advantaged treatment. Solid recordkeeping and the assistance of a tax professional will help ensure all activity and transactions are managed correctly.

The process of partnering as tenants in common secures funding without paying a set rate of interest. It instead uses the gains from the sale to calculate the return on investment. This is a great option for partners who wish to be actively involved in a transaction but do not have enough to purchase a property with cash, or choose to preserve cash for additional investment opportunities.

Webinar: Discover How 3 Clients Created Successful Returns Using Multiple Self-Directed IRAs

Do you miss out on potentially profitable investment opportunities because of a lack of money? Could you participate in bigger investments if you had more cash in your IRA? Those two common obstacles are not an issue for these three Equity Trust clients. Hear how they have succeeded by combining multiple accounts. Set up or log in to your user account to watch it now:

https://equityuniversity.customerhub.net/multiple-accounts

Conclusion

As you can see, you don't need an IRA with a lot of cash to begin investing. We discussed a few strategies that can provide a launching pad to get you started. These methods are not only used by beginners but also by experienced investors who wish to preserve cash and extend their portfolio faster than can be achieved by use of the funds from only one account. You should no longer be hindered by a lack of funding. If you have a passion and knowledge for your investment, can negotiate with others and are willing to take action, you can be on your way to tax-deferred or tax-free profits.

Chapter 20: What You Need to Know – Rules, Regulations and Prohibited Transactions

I hope by now you are seeing the benefits self-directed IRAs have to offer. To take advantage of the tax savings, compounding interest, and the other benefits we've touched on, you must stay compliant with the IRS rules and regulations pertaining to these accounts. The IRS does not specify what can be held inside of an IRA; instead they offer strict guidelines regarding what an IRA *cannot* invest. The IRS rules are more of an exclusive rather than inclusive list. The IRA owner takes responsibility for where funds are invested and what investments they deem appropriate for the account. The custodian follows the directions of the account owner and holds the tax status of the IRA. Therefore, you need to understand the IRS rules and prohibited transactions before investing.

Since the IRS provides a guide of *don'ts*, your opportunities are essentially only limited by your imagination, plus a few IRS specifics. This leaves a great deal of flexibility to invest in opportunities that align with your passions, experiences, and expertise.

Self-directed IRAs are treated much like a trust. The IRA is its own entity and is separate from the individual who owns the IRA. The IRA (the account) and the beneficiary (you) are two separate entities and must be kept separate with all transactions. This exclusive benefit rule states that all transactions must be made for the exclusive benefit of the IRA and not the IRA owner. IRS rules state that when it comes to a self-directed IRA investment, you and the investment must be at arm's length. In other words, you can't directly benefit from an asset owned by the IRA. The IRA entity can benefit from the transactions, but not the IRA owner. Remember, the IRA is built to provide for your future and is not intended to benefit you now. It is considered an "indirect benefit" if your IRA is engaged in transactions that, in some way, can benefit you personally. This is strictly prohibited.

Some examples of indirect benefits include:

- Personally using your IRA property – using real estate purchased through your IRA as an office, personal residence, vacation home, retirement home, etc. is not allowed.

- Receiving personal benefits from your IRA – you can't lend yourself money from your IRA. Additionally, you can't personally work on your investment property or pay yourself or a company that you own to do work on an investment owned by your IRA.

- Revenue and expenses must flow directly through the IRA – since the self-directed IRA is for retirement, it's important to remember that all expenses related to an investment are paid from the IRA and all profits are returned to the IRA.

To provide a clearer understanding of the IRS rules and regulations, let's break each topic down specifically.

Disqualified assets include tangible personal property such as collectibles. This includes artwork, rugs, antiques, metals (with the exception of the precious metals discussed earlier), gems, stamps, coins and alcoholic beverages. These are the prohibited transactions specifically listed under Title 26 of the Internal Revenue Code. Your IRA is allowed to invest in hedge funds or mutual funds that specialize in these items, but not to hold the specific items as a collection within the IRA.

Additionally, the IRA cannot invest in life insurance or S Corporations. The IRA can own businesses that are structured as a Limited Partnership (LP), LLC, C Corporation or other entities as long as a disqualified person does not own more than 50 percent of the entity.

Disqualified individuals include you as the IRA owner, your spouse, and your ascendants or descendants. This includes your parents, grandparents, and great grandparents as ascendants. It also includes your children, grandchildren, and great grandchildren (and any of their spouses) as descendants. Other disqualified individuals include those who have fiduciary responsibility over the IRA. This could include your custodian, an accountant that has power of attorney over the account, an attorney, CPA, financial advisor or other individual that has access and fiduciary responsibility over your IRA. IRS rules dictate that a self-directed IRA may not buy an investment from, sell to or otherwise be involved with any disqualified person.

Aside from these exclusions, there is a wide range of people with whom your IRA can do business. Relatives such as brothers and sisters or aunts and uncles are not disqualified. Any third party, business partner, friend, business associate and so forth are all eligible to buy or sell to and from the IRA. While transactions with non-linear relatives will not violate the disqualified person rule, if the transaction provides a benefit to a disqualified person, it will still be deemed a prohibited transaction.

In addition to disqualified persons there can also be disqualified entities. This includes any businesses that have more than 50 percent ownership by a disqualified person.

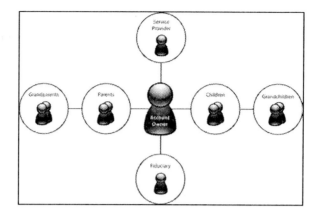

Chart of Disqualified Persons

Prohibited transactions include any improper use of your IRA by you, your beneficiary or any disqualified person. Such activity could include disqualified persons borrowing money from the IRA, lending money to the IRA, selling or buying an asset to or from the IRA, receiving unreasonable compensation for managing the account, using the account as security for a loan or buying property with the account for personal use. Essentially, a disqualified person cannot be involved in any transaction, regardless of the actual result of the transaction. If the benefit was intended, even if the investment fails, it will be deemed a prohibited transaction based upon intent. Any benefit received is viewed by the IRS as self-dealing and results in a prohibited transaction.

A few common questions regarding prohibited transactions relate to the use of the property. The account owner or any disqualified person cannot use any assets inside the IRA for their personal use. This would include a vacation home that serves as a rental property. The IRA owner cannot stay in or on the property, cannot use the property as security for a loan, and cannot receive unreasonable compensation for any transactions involved within the IRA.

If the investor chooses to rehab property within the IRA, he or she cannot complete the work (or what is considered by the IRS as sweat equity) as this is considered to offer an immediate benefit to the account holder. Work must be contracted to a non-disqualified third-party. However, it is acceptable to manage the property as long as no personal benefit is received.

Paying bills, collecting rent and directing the actions of the IRA are generally acceptable. Completing the paperwork, establishing leases, and contracting a third party for repairs also generally fall within the acceptable guidelines.

A common question arises over the ability to act as a real estate agent and be paid a commission. This would constitute as a prohibited transaction because you, as the agent and IRA owner, would receive a personal benefit from the transaction. This would be considered self-dealing. It is important to be very conservative when it comes to the self-dealing provision. For example, if your IRA purchased raw land, you would be prohibited from hunting on that land with your friends. Even a one-time hunting trip could put your entire IRA at risk.

Occasional attempts have been made to use what is termed a "straw person" to avoid prohibited transactions. The IRS considers these events a violation of the "Step Transaction Doctrine", making them prohibited transactions. Let's consider an example. If the real estate broker from the previous example wanted to receive the commission on a sale of his or her IRA property, he or she might consider adding a step where a friend acts as a "straw person" and receives the commission from the IRA before passing it on to the IRA owner. While the IRA isn't directly paying the IRA owner the commission, the Step Transaction Doctrine considers this an extra step added solely to circumvent the IRS tax code and would be deemed a prohibited transaction.

A second aspect of prohibited transactions is that the IRA owner must pay fair market value for any assets that are purchased. This is interpreted as buying an asset for the price the seller would sell to anyone in the existing market. The purpose of the rule is to prevent special treatment between a seller and the buyer. This concept is an expansion of the exclusive benefit rule. For example, while your brother or sister may not be a disqualified person, it is still imperative that you conduct any transactions at fair market value. This demonstrates that you are not receiving an undue benefit of a discounted price (due to your relationship) that would not be available in the current market.

Excess contributions receive a yearly excise tax of 6 percent. Excess contributions occur when more money is added to an IRA than is allowed. Each year the IRS publishes the contribution limits for each type of retirement account, occasionally raising the limits to account for inflation. If you contribute more than the allowable amount in a given year, you will be penalized 6 percent of the excess amount that remains in your IRA when your tax return is due.

It is important to keep in mind that the contribution limits apply to all IRAs you hold. For example, if the contribution limit for 2015 is $5,500, then the maximum you can contribute to both your Traditional IRA and Roth IRA is $5,500 (unless you are 50 or older, in which case you are eligible to set aside an additional $1,000 as a catch-up contribution). Contribution limits vary for the other account types such as the SEP IRA, SIMPLE IRA, CESA, HSA, and Traditional and Roth 401(k) and Solo 401(k).

Updated Contribution Limits

For the updated contribution limits and account specifics, please visit:

https://www.trustetc.com/contributions

Early distributions are generally penalized if they are taken before age 59½. (Distributions are also commonly referred to as withdrawals.) Your account will be assessed a 10-percent penalty and will have to pay tax on the distributed amount at the ordinary income tax rate. This includes both Traditional and Roth IRAs, along with business retirement accounts like the SEP and the SIMPLE IRA. The power of Roth IRAs is that you can withdraw funds that you have contributed to the account at any time without incurring tax, after the account has been established for five years. It is the profits and account growth that is subject to the 59½ age requirements and early distribution penalties.

CESAs require distributions to be for qualified educational purposes, rather than reaching a certain retirement age. Any distribution that is not used for a qualified education expense will be subject to a 10-percent penalty and will be taxed at the ordinary income tax rate. There are also penalties associated with the CESA account if the funds are not used by the beneficiary's 30th birthday. If the account is still funded when the beneficiary reaches the age of 30, the entire account balance will be distributed, assessed a 10-percent penalty, and taxed at the ordinary income tax rate. Fortunately, CESAs allow the investor to change beneficiaries. For example, if you have two daughters and the first one reaches the age of 29 and does not plan to utilize the last $10,000 in her CESA, you can transfer the funds and make your younger daughter the account's beneficiary. Lastly, the HSA account will incur a 10-percent penalty on any withdrawals not used for qualified health-related expenses.

Exceptions to the early withdrawal penalty for IRAs and retirement accounts include death or the permanent disability of the account owner. Other exceptions include medical expenses or medical insurance within the exception guidelines, higher education expenses, the purchase of your first home, payment of an IRS Levy or a distribution taken as an annuity in equal payments.

Required Minimum Distributions (RMDs), also called mandatory withdrawals, impact Traditional IRAs, SEP, and SIMPLE retirement accounts. At the age of 70½ the IRA owner must begin taking distributions from their accounts each year. The amount of the distribution is determined by IRS calculations and will result in penalties if a minimum distribution is not made. If all IRAs are held by the same custodian, the custodian will generally calculate the RMD for the account holder and send appropriate notifications regarding the RMD. If an investor owns IRAs held by different custodians, it is important for the account owner to communicate with each custodian to ensure the proper amounts are distributed each year. You can reference our website's RMD calculator to help determine how much you may be required to withdraw: https://www.trustetc.com/resources/tools/calculators/retire-distrib

Roth IRAs do not have mandatory withdrawals determined by age. The CESA accounts must be used for educational purposes by the

30th birthday of the beneficiary, or transferred to a new beneficiary, while following IRS guidelines.

Penalties for non-compliance can be significant. If the IRS determines a prohibited transaction has occurred, even unintentionally, your entire account will lose its qualified tax-advantaged IRA status. This triggers a distribution of those funds from the IRA, resulting in taxes and penalties. Not only does the account lose its tax-advantaged status, the funds are taxed at your ordinary income tax rate along with a 10-percent penalty. As you can see, it is critical to ensure you are conducting your self-directed IRA investments within the confines of the IRS rules and regulations.

With the flexibility self-directed IRAs provide, there is a wide range of investment transactions that can be completed without working in the gray area of the IRS code. Equity Trust strongly encourages clients to work firmly within the IRS rules and regulations so there is no question about the legitimacy of the transaction. With so few limitations it is unwise to complete transactions that may have the potential to be considered a prohibited transaction or with a disqualified person. Regardless of the investment opportunity, the risk of losing your retirement savings is never worth it.

The self-directed IRA gives account owners a great deal of discretion. While the final decision is always yours, seeking education from Equity University or calling our Senior Account Executives with questions is always encouraged. In addition, seeking counsel from your CPA, tax attorney, financial planner or accountant experienced with the IRS rules regarding self-directed IRAs is the best way to avoid penalties.

> **YouTube Video: Self-Directed IRA Rules and Regulations**
>
> A Senior ERISA attorney takes 5 minutes to discuss some of the frequently asked questions regarding self-directed IRA rules and regulations. Visit out YouTube channel to watch it today:
>
> https://youtu.be/XENmSrSfB3E

Chapter 21: Importance of Due Diligence and Your Support Team

Due diligence is the process of investigating investment opportunities and gathering information that will help to make informed decisions. This process helps investors evaluate the risks and opportunities of the deals they are interested in and can also help avoid expensive mistakes. Due diligence puts the investor in a better position to negotiate a strong deal by understanding the factors involved and what a good value might look like. Lastly, it will help reduce risks and will help the investor evaluate how much risk, and what kind of risk, is acceptable on each investment opportunity.

Self-directed IRAs are directed by you. This means that you take responsibility for both the due diligence and the quality of investments that are chosen for your portfolio. The custodian can help guide you through the investment procedures and account requirements but the final investment decisions are ultimately yours to make. Due diligence is critical to the success of your portfolio.

When Should Investors Complete Due Diligence?

There are certain times in the lifecycle of your self-directed IRA investing when due diligence is essential. The first is when the account is opened and initial goals are set. The second is each time you consider an investment opportunity. You should continue to circle back on your investments and re-conduct your due diligence to ensure everything is going according to the plan you set at the outset of the investment.

When you open your IRA, take the time to assess your goals, potential risks and review your financial and retirement plan. *Are you seeking investments that are mainly for growth or mainly for cash flow? Are you interested in long-term strategies or are you looking for investments with a shorter time horizon? What areas do you understand the best? What areas will require assistance from others?* There are many opportunities available. Identify what you want to get out of your self-directed investing, where you feel most comfortable and how this can best be accomplished.

From there, consider a few investment strategies and create goals that are specific to the investments of interest. *What are the financial benchmarks you've set for yourself and what timeframe do you anticipate needing to meet those goals?* To be effective, goals must be specific, actionable and measureable.

The process of due diligence helps you learn about the investment. Learn as much about these markets as possible, though you don't need to know *everything* before investing. It is common for investors to let the fear of the unknown take hold of them and create a situation of "paralysis by analysis," where you are not investing in fear you're missing something. This can be counterproductive.

Instead, select an area where you have basic knowledge or find a mentor who can help get you started in an investment area that interests you. Utilize Equity University and all of its educational offerings to learn more about the investment options others have used to find success. Talk to other investors. Conduct some research so you understand where to find investments and how to evaluate whether it is a sound opportunity. Once you are ready for the next step, create parameters that will help you evaluate your investments. These parameters will help determine if the investment meets your needs, minimizes risk and helps further your goals.

The second instance to perform due diligence is with each investment opportunity. Once the overall goals and investment parameters have been established, each opportunity should be tested against these guidelines. *Do they help to reach your financial goals? Do they meet the timeframe you have established for yourself? Do they fit into the "business plan?"* If these criteria are met you can feel more comfortable pursuing the opportunity.

For example, if you are interested in real estate, you should consider the current value of the property. *What's the market like? How fast are homes selling? How much needs to be invested in the home for a positive return? What is the maximum you can put into the home and still earn the return you are looking for? Will you be able to stick to that number or are there factors in the home that may cost more than you think? How is the price of the home in relation to the value of other homes in the neighborhood? Do you have a contact in the area who can give you a feel for the market?*

Are you beginning to grasp the idea of due diligence? You should play devil's advocate and ask yourself about every detail regarding your investment. Consider worst-case scenarios and try to anticipate potential issues. It is wise to enlist the help of an investor who has experience in the opportunity you are vetting. They will often be able to share their experience and knowledge to help you understand the myriad of factors to consider while performing due diligence. A thorough and diligent due diligence process at the beginning of an investment opportunity may help to reduce risks and issues that may arise once the investment has been made. If you have contingency plans in place because you prepared with a systematic review, your investments will be less likely to be derailed by factors that other investors may have glossed over.

Seasoned investors evaluate the numbers behind each investment opportunity. Setting parameters, such as a maximum value you will invest, helps take emotion out of the process. This can prevent overpaying for deals that could take more time and money to turn a profit. The due diligence process will help to test the opportunity against specific benchmarks. This process reduces risk, increases the likelihood of maximizing profits and helps make the investment process more efficient.

There should be a plan for every investment. *How will the investment be acquired, how will it be managed, and when and how will it be sold?* This should be the case whether the investment is in stock, real estate, precious metals or any type of investment. Having a complete plan of action makes it easier to determine when to buy and when to sell. If the parameters are established before the investment is made, determining success becomes more consistent and measurable.

Every investor should have two sets of plans or goals. One is a long-term plan of action to get you to retirement and beyond. The second is a specific plan of action for each investment. We've only touched on the basic concepts of due diligence but I hope it helps to paint a picture in your mind of the time and detail proper due diligence requires. Providing yourself with specific and actionable steps to complete an investment will help to measure your results and your success with each deal, as well as tracking progress toward the larger goal of retirement.

Additionally, it is imperative that you perform due diligence on any individual, company or group that is involved with your investment. It's possible to research an opportunity and determine it meets your parameters and is worth pursuing, only to lose money because a person or company offering the investment or somehow involved in the deal was unreliable or even fraudulent. This is such an important aspect of the due diligence process that it will be covered in-depth in the next chapter.

Using Strategy for Success

When strategy is added to a good opportunity, it can turn a good investment into a great investment. Structuring a deal the most efficient way can reduce risk, increase profits, and decrease the amount of time the asset must be held before it is sold for a profit.

This might include partnering with another investor, working with an investment group that can pool resources, structuring the deal a certain way, or negotiating terms that are more favorable for the investor. If you are considering a fairly risky investment option, you may consider investing with partners so that the risk is spread across several members and doesn't fall solely on your shoulders. You may ask for additional collateral than you normally would for a less risky option. If you perform your due diligence properly and think creatively, you can reduce the risk and find success. It is not always necessary to have all the money or all the resources yourself in order to take advantage of a good deal. Take the time to look at all the options, examine all the angles and work closely with those you trust and the best option for each deal will likely surface.

Establishing a Support Team for Success

Investing does not have to be a one-person activity. Too often investors feel alone in the mission to achieve a successful retirement, especially as a self-directed investor. It sometimes feels as if it is you against the markets. Will they smile on you today or not? Will the markets be up when you need the money, or down? The markets can change on a daily basis and at times it can feel overwhelming.

Self-directed IRAs provide more control over your financial future. It is possible to establish specific goals and then meet those goals with thorough due diligence and wise investment choices. One of the best ways to do this is to surround yourself with a team of people you trust and whom you can rely on for help.

You don't have to know everything. As Confucius once said, "To know what you know, and know what you do not know – this then is wisdom." Build your team with this in mind. Identify your areas of strength and areas of weakness. Then identify partners or mentors who complement your strengths and enrich your areas of weakness.

There are a few key factors to consider when looking for partnerships that will help cultivate an investment's success. First is to evaluate what you know and understand and where there are gaps in your knowledge. The team you build should fill those gaps with knowledge to create confidence that you will have the resources you need to make good decisions. The second key to building a team is that everyone must benefit. Building a team with you as the only beneficiary is shortsighted and will result in a dysfunctional team. When everyone on the team benefits, everyone has a vested interest in the success.

Team members could include a financial planner, accountant, attorney, real estate broker, title insurance company, IRA custodian, collection services agency, property management servicer, home inspector, bank lender or private lender. This list is by no means all-inclusive. Determine which investment strategies you will employ and seek team members that will provide you the knowledge and resources needed to make wise investments.

Some of your team members will benefit because you will pay for their services. Others may be more like partners. For example, if you partner with a real estate agent who helps to identify homes, pay a fair commission. Sometimes, in an effort to increase our returns, we beat people down on price. If you negotiate a very low commission that is favorable only to yourself, the real estate agent will not be motivated to go the extra step to help. Remember, everyone's work has value and the more that value is appreciated, the harder they will work on your team for your success as well as their own.

Networking is the most important thing when it comes to building a strong team. Attend local investment club meetings, join a group, and stay connected with anyone and everyone who is of interest to you and your investing. Ask trusted colleagues for recommendations of team members they utilize and attempt to build favorable relationships with them. Once you complete a few successful transactions and create a strong working relationship the process should only grow easier.

Identifying and preventing fraudulent behavior and investment scams is another critical component of the due diligence process. It is so important that it will be covered in detail in the next chapter.

Due Diligence Resources

The Retirement Industry Trust Association and its member firms, such as Equity Trust, encourage each investor to review the following materials when considering various investment opportunities. Please set up or log in to your user account to view the material, including:

RITA Check Before You Invest Due Diligence Checklist

RITA Check Before You Invest Due Diligence List of Questions

https://equityuniversity.customerhub.net/due-diligence

Richard Desich, Sr.

Chapter 22: Check Before You Invest – Identifying and Preventing Fraud and Scams

Fraudsters tend to go "where the money is" and unfortunately that means targeting Americans who are nearing or already in retirement. Fraudsters also have their sights set on the millions of Baby Boomers who have been accumulating sizeable retirement nest eggs through various retirement accounts.

Recent research has shattered the stereotype of investment fraud victims as isolated, frail and gullible. In fact, the profile of an investment fraudster's prime target, according to FINRA's (the Financial Industry Regulatory Authority) Investor Education Foundation is someone who meets the following description[24]:

- Self-reliant when it comes to making decisions

- Optimistic

- Above-average financial knowledge

- Above-average income

---

[24] FINRA Investor Education Foundation. (2014, June). Fighting Fraud 101: Smart Tips for Investors. Retrieved from http://www.saveandinvest.org/file/document/fighting-fraud-101

- College-educated

- Experienced a recent health or financial setback

- Open to listening to new ideas or sales pitches

Clearly that doesn't sound like the person most people think would succumb to fraud, but it is the profile of fraudsters' prime targets. Their profile also sounds like a description of what makes a successful self-directed IRA investor so the importance of understanding and detecting fraud grows increasingly important as you consider embarking on your self-directed investing journey.

In reality, investor fraud is a problem for every American and the greatest tool for preventing fraud is education and knowledge. In fact, SEC Chairman Mary Schapiro remarked at the FINRA Investor Education Foundation Conference that, "an informed and skeptical investor is the best defense against fraud."

Equity Trust Company knows the threat of fraud is a real concern for self-directed IRA investors. Our clients are free to invest in anything permitted by the IRS to be held in an IRA. With that great freedom to explore exciting investment options comes the potential for con artists and fraud schemes to attempt to take advantage of an unsuspecting investor. We want to see our clients grow their investments to create a lasting legacy, not lining the pockets of scam artists.

Equity Trust, in conjunction with the Retirement Industry Trust Association (RITA), has compiled governmental and industry resources to help you, the self-directed investor, in making your investment decisions.

Identifying Scams and Fraudulent Investments

Ask yourself a few questions about the potential investment: *Is it too good to be true?* or *Can I easily explain what the investment is and how it works?* The ability to identify fraud sets you on the right track to review a potential investment with your personal financial team and see if it's the real deal or if someone is trying to con you.

Equity Trust Company knows the sad truth is fraudulent investments, Ponzi schemes, and scams can look legitimate and even come from a trusted source. Listed below are some of the most common signs of a fraudulent investment or scam.

- **Did you find the investment or did the investment find you?** Be cautions if you receive unsolicited, unexpected calls, emails, mail, or even visits from strangers or an unfamiliar company. This can be a tipoff of a fraudulent investment or scam.

- **Does the deal sound just too good to be true?** If the person pitching the investment promises low or no risk, assures quick, high rates of return or states the investment is guaranteed – be skeptical. We all want to believe we found a good opportunity but there comes a time when good crosses over to *too good*. Even the best investments come with the possibility of loss and a fair degree of risk.

- **Did you feel bullied, harassed, or intimidated by the salesperson or investment promoter to agree to the investment?** There is no reason to tolerate high pressure sales tactics, especially when it concerns investing. Take it as a warning sign if the sales person is pushing a prospective investor to sign up immediately or trying to talk them out of taking time to think it over and research the deal. Equity Trust Company urges our clients to keep their guard up, do their due diligence and be prepared to walk away if an investment starts to smell like a scam, fraud, or scheme. Legitimate investment promoters understand the desire to get a second opinion.

- **Can you explain, in your own words, what the investment is and how it works?** People trying to commit fraud or run a scam will seek out people who may be less sophisticated or inexperienced. Using fancy terms, elaborate or complicated concepts or trying to make a person feel stupid or guilty for asking questions or requesting documentation such as a prospectus are all red flags for fraud.

- **Does the investment sound like a conspiracy theory?** Legitimate investments don't rely on "special secrets of the rich," "inside information 'they' don't want the public to know," or use rhetoric regarding how the U.S. Government is keeping the 'little guy' from being rich.

- **Does this investment require all or the majority of your life savings or are you being pressed to take out a loan or to cash-in your IRA?** Legitimate investment advisors advise their clients to diversify their investment holdings and suggest investments that meet their clients' tolerance for risk.

- **Can you verify who the investment promoter is?** Be wary of any investment that cannot be verified through the Securities and Exchange Commission (SEC), the state securities regulator, the National Association of Securities Dealers (NASD) registration process or other methods of verification.

- **Are you able to verify where your funds are and how they are being used in the investment?** Equity Trust Company stresses caution with any investments offered from overseas or international locations or schemes that hide funds in tax shelters, trusts, or offshore accounts.

- **Did you have any trouble cashing out or experience delays getting your money if you want out of the investment?** Fraud such as Ponzi schemes, pyramid schemes, and other fraudulent investments rely on other victims' funds to cover the amount of payouts to earlier investors.

What Schemes and Scams Should Investors Look Out For?

While it seems like thieves and con artists are coming up with new schemes every day, committing acts of fraud are as old as time.

As the owner of a self-directed IRA, all of the investments in your account(s) will come from your own discovery and direction. We know there is always risk when it comes to investing, but education is one of the best ways to manage those risks.

When it comes to fraud, bad things can and do happen to even the most careful, cautious, or conservative person. Below is a list of common types of fraud, though it is not all-inclusive.

Ponzi Schemes. This well-known fraud scheme was named after Charles Ponzi, who became famous for using the technique. In essence, investors earn returns based on the money from new investors. The earlier investors are getting regular returns and everything seems fine, except the scheme relies on a constant stream of new investors before it inevitably collapses. The organizer relies on attracting new investors to make promised payments; but funds are usually used for personal gain instead of engaging in any investment opportunities.

Pyramid Schemes. Another well-known type of fraud is the pyramid scheme. It sounds very similar to a Ponzi scheme, as a Ponzi scheme can be a type of pyramid scheme. However, pyramid schemes are not always illegal, while Ponzi schemes are certainly always outside the law.

A pyramid scheme works by convincing people to invest into a distributorship or franchise. The promoter may say the product is the next big thing and tells the prospective investor they are getting in on the ground floor of something amazing. In reality, the focus is less on the product the franchise sells and more on how to recruit other investors.

Ultimately, no product has been sold, no investment has been made, and no service has been provided. It becomes mathematically impossible for everyone buying in to see a profit.

Advance Fee Schemes. An advance fee scheme can be presented as various opportunities, all requesting an upfront fee. The victim pays money with the expectation he or she will receive something of greater value but ends up with nothing or practically nothing in return.

There's really no limit to how varied these scams can be. Potential investments include: the sale of products or services, contracts, loans, or found money (gifts). The victim is asked to pay a contract fee, a finder's fee, or provide money for some other reason in advance, sometimes also signing a contract stating they will pay the advanced fee in exchange for accepting the investment, loan, or other item of value. This contract may be legally binding unless the victim is able to prove the "finder" or "promoter" never intended to provide the item of value.

Affinity Fraud. Affinity fraud occurs when an individual exploits the connection and trust within a group to promote a fake investment opportunity. This type of scheme may involve elements of a pyramid or Ponzi scheme while specifically targeting members of an identifiable group. Religious groups, ethnic groups within a community, individuals connected through military or professional affiliations and groups united by a specific cause or demographic are just a few examples of the types of groups these con artists will prey upon. They may directly approach the group or focus on convincing the leader of the group to buy into the fake investment, taking advantage of that person's respect and position to access the members. One of the biggest challenges this type of fraud brings is the victimized group may prefer to 'work out the matter on their own' instead of reaching out to law enforcement or regulators for help.

The Securities and Exchange Commission (SEC) issued an Investor Alert and an Investor Bulletin on the dangers of affinity fraud.

Letter of Credit Fraud. A letter of credit is not something that can be purchased as an investment. The fraud perpetrators are taking something used to ensure there will be payment for goods shipped and trying to manipulate it for fraudulent purposes. Letters of credit are issued by banks and most commonly used for international trade. The letter of credit states that the receiving entity has the funds to pay for the shipment and the shipping entity provides proof the goods are en route.

This becomes fraud when the entity shipping the goods provides documentation stating the goods have shipped in order to collect payment, but has no intention of sending items or sends items of far less quality.

Prime Bank Note Fraud. Like other shady investment schemes, fraud perpetrators offer a deal that promises remarkably high yields in a very short time frame. This scam uses "bank guarantees" to be purchased at a discount and guarantee a high return. They will state these guarantees are coming from "prime banks" of the world and is why the return is so high with almost no risk. In reality, the fraudster is trying to get the victim to send his or her money to a foreign bank where it will be laundered or make its way to an account belonging to the con artist.

This type of fraud is also called a bank guarantee, which is a legitimate financial instrument for international trade, similar to a "letter of credit" used by U.S. banks.

For more information regarding fraud topics please visit, https://www.fbi.gov/scams-safety/fraud.

How to Protect Yourself from Fraud and Scams

With many different fraud schemes out there, it is important for you to be aware and educated to protect your investments. As the owner of a self-directed IRA, your knowledge and expertise is your first line of defense against fraudulent investments.

To protect against fraud and scams investors need to perform due diligence on every investment, as we've discussed. Review potential investments with your personal financial team to see if the gains and losses seem natural before you invest. This is one way to minimize your chances of becoming a victim to a scheme. You should also verify the standing and legitimacy of the company or person seeking your investment dollars before committing.

Salespeople promoting legitimate investments know a prospective investor will have serious questions to ask and will readily provide the information you seek. If you feel like questions aren't welcome or respected this should cause concern.

The same is true when making sure the answers you receive actually answer your questions. Are you able to verify the claims made about the patent or trademark, or the salesperson's qualifications and licensing?

If you asked for financial documents or proof of ownership for the collateral securing the note, did you receive it without a fight or delay? What was their reaction when you told them you needed your attorney, accountant, or financial advisor to review the investment?

Knowing your exit strategy in advance of a sales call or investment offering makes it easier to leave the conversation, even if the pressure starts to rise. Practice saying "No." Simply tell the person, "I am sorry, I am not interested. Thank you." Or tell anyone who pressures you, "I never make investing decisions without first consulting with my _____. I will contact you if I am still interested." If the person is not interested in working with you to provide more information or is not respecting your wishes to consult with your support team, this should raise a red flag.

In addition to the due diligence practices we've already discussed, be aware of the following while performing due diligence to avoid being the victim of a fraud scheme or scam:

- **Have you heard of this person or company before?** If not, take the time to learn more. Visit their location, research their standing with the Better Business Bureau and check to make sure they are registered to do the type of business they are offering.

- **Do you understand what you are agreeing to with this investment?** Consider having a competent attorney review the investment.

- **Do you understand how this investment can gain or lose funds for you?** Fraud perpetrators often make the details of an investment as complex as possible. Never feel intimidated to ask questions or bring in a qualified third party to help you understand a deal.

- **Does this type of investment exist?** Check with the International Chamber of Commerce (ICC), Securities and Exchange Commission (SEC), and other governing bodies to see if there are any fraud warnings that match what was offered to you.

- **Is the only information you have on this person or entity the information they provide you?** Do your own independent research. Make sure you can verify their claims and identities from other, reliable sources. Be skeptical.

- **Does the pattern of gains and losses look natural for this type of investment?** Again, having a qualified third party to assist you in investigating and understanding the information you find can be invaluable. Ponzi schemes, for example, are known for having eerily consistent and especially high returns before the whole thing collapses. Equity Trust Company knows ups and downs are part of investing. Make sure the information makes sense and decide if it seems too good to be true.

Resources Available to Help Protect Against Fraud

The following additional resources contain advice and tips on how to identify investment fraud and scams.

- Investor.gov – Brought to you by The SEC's Office of Investor Education and Advocacy, Investor.gov is your online resource to help you invest wisely and avoid fraud. Their investing basics section outlines types of fraud/scams, how to avoid them and also provides examples.

- NASAA.org – The North American Securities Administrators Association (NASAA) is the oldest international organization devoted to investor protection and offers many tips to help spot and avoid investment fraud.

- FINRA.org – The Financial Industry Regulatory Authority (FINRA) is the largest independent regulator for all securities firms doing business in the United States. One of the organization's main goals is to protect the investing public.

- SaveAndInvest.org – A project of the FINRA Investor Education Foundation is a free, unbiased resource site dedicated to your financial health. SaveandInvest.org offers advice for <u>protecting your money</u> and tools to help identify if you're at risk or if an investment may be a scam.

- o The FINRA Investor Education Foundation also encourages you to check with them before you invest, either by visiting their website or calling 888-295-7422.

- <u>AARP.org</u> – An organization dedicated to the well-being of Americans over age 50, has many resources to help protect seniors against fraud.

- <u>RITA</u> – The Retirement Industry Trust Association (RITA) is a professional trade association for the self-directed retirement plan industry. RITA provides resources to help prevent fraud aimed at seniors.

- <u>SEC.org</u> – U.S. Securities and Exchange Commission provides information on reporting a Ponzi scheme, pyramid scheme, high-yield investment program, fraudulent offering or other potential fraud or violation.

- <u>IRS.gov</u> – The Internal Revenue Service (IRS) lists consumer alerts for tax scams, phony tax arguments and identity theft scams.

- <u>InvestorProtection.org</u> – Investor Protection Trust (IPT) is a nonprofit organization devoted to investor education. Their primary mission is to provide independent, objective information needed by consumers to make informed investment decisions.

You may also utilize the following resources to check a specific investment offering or for more information about:

- **A broker or firm** – FINRA BrokerCheck

  - o <u>www.finra.org/brokercheck</u>

  - o 800-289-9999

- **An investment advisor** – SEC Public Disclosure Database

- o Available through BrokerCheck or www.adviserinfo.sec.gov

- **A broker, investment adviser or investment** – North American Securities Administrators Association

    - o www.nasaa.org
    - o 202-737-0900

- **An insurance agent** – National Association of Insurance Commissioners

    - o www.naic.org
    - o 866-470-6242

- **A commodities/futures/foreign exchange dealer** – National Futures Association BASIC Check

    - o www.nfa.futures.org/basicnet
    - o 800-621-3570

- **An investment** – SEC EDGAR Database

    - o www.sec.gov/edgar.shtml or www.investor.gov

- **To take your name off solicitation lists:**

    - o Telemarketing Calls – www.donotcall.gov or call toll-free 888-382-1222

    - o Direct Mail and Email Offers – www.dmachoice.org

    - o Credit Card Offers – www.optoutprescreen.com or call toll-free 888-567-8688

    - o Online Cookie Collecting – www.networkadvertising.org

What to Do if You Suspect Fraud? – Reporting Fraud, Scams, and Ponzi Schemes

If you believe you have been defrauded or treated unfairly – or if you suspect that someone you know has been taken by a scam – be sure to send a written complaint to a securities regulator. According to the

FINRA Investor Education Foundation, here's where you can turn for help:

FINRA Complaints and Tips
9509 Key West Avenue
Rockville, MD 20850
Fax: 866-397-3290
www.finra.org/complaint
www.finra.org/fileatip

U.S. Securities and Exchange Commission (SEC) Office of Investor Education and Advocacy
100 F Street, NE
Washington, DC 20549-0213
Phone: 800-732-0330
Fax: 202-772-9295
Email: enforcement@sec.gov
www.sec.gov/complaint.shtml

State Securities Regulator
North American Securities Administrators Association
Phone: 202-737-0900
Email: cyberfraud@nasaa.org
www.nasaa.org
Contact Your Local Regulator

U.S. Commodity Futures Trading Commission (CFTC)
Office of Cooperative Enforcement
1155 21st Street, NW
Washington, DC 20581
Phone: 866-366-2382
www.cftc.gov/tiporcomplaint

Federal Bureau of Investigation (FBI)
https://www.fbi.gov or contact your local office

Better Business Bureau (BBB)
http://www.bbb.org/

You may also contact your local District Attorney's Consumer Protection Unit or, if mail was used as part of the investment fraud process, your local Postal Inspectors Office.

Conclusion

The unfortunate reality is that for all the good that can come from self-directed IRA investors (as we've discussed throughout the book), there will always be people who resort to dishonest means for financial gain. We urge you to take due diligence very seriously and to reach out to CPAs, financial advisors, attorneys and other trusted individuals from your personal history to create a team of trusted support. Along with your knowledge and personal expertise, and the resources and best practices covered in the last two chapters, your team can help you find and review opportunities to make sound investment choices.

FINRA Save and Invest Fraud Prevention Resources

Fighting Fraud 101: Smart Tips for Investors is a 14-page pamphlet that discusses fraud prevention and protection.

http://www.saveandinvest.org/file/document/fighting-fraud-101

Additionally, the FINRA Investor Education Foundation created a one-hour documentary titled, *Trick$ of the Trade: Outsmarting Investment Fraud* that shows you how to stop fraudsters from taking your money. It reviews how to recognize fraud, tricks and tactics used by fraudsters, shares real-life fraud stories and provides tools to help protect yourself.

You can order a FREE DVD copy from FINRA by calling 866-973-4672 or online at:
http://74.121.201.86/FinraSAINew/

Richard Desich, Sr.

Chapter 23: It's Time to Cash In! – Taking Distributions

When retirement finally arrives it is time to begin living off the investments that you've cultivated over the years. Sometimes it is difficult to move from the accumulation stage to the distribution stage because you have become accustomed to saving. But when the income stops, having a substantial nest egg to rely on for monthly bills and expenses is why you've worked your account.

The best approach is to organize a plan when it is time to begin taking distributions. Consider all sources of income, what funds need to be available for distribution, and whether distributions will be received monthly, quarterly, or annually. Then, schedule distributions based on your anticipated retirement budget. It is a good idea to have investments that continue to work for you during retirement rather than sitting as cash waiting for a designated distribution date.

Many investors find success by changing their investment strategy rather than liquidating a significant portion of their investment portfolio. There are options for lending, tax lien investments, and rental property which can provide monthly cash flow options while the funds remain invested. These strategies can help your retirement funds last longer and create a legacy for your family, in addition to ensuring that you do not outlive your money.

Distribution Rules

Prior to 59½, any distribution made from an IRA is considered an early withdrawal and may be subject to taxes and penalties. There is a finite list of exceptions. If any of the following exceptions are met, the funds will not incur the 10-percent penalty, although taxes may be incurred depending on the type of account. For a complete explanation of exceptions see IRS Publication 590.

Exceptions include:

- Death or permanent disability of the account holder. Distributions can be made to the beneficiary of the account.

- Continuous payments that are made based on the life expectancy of the account owner for at least five years, or until the account owner reaches 59½. This exception essentially establishes an annuity for the account holder with equal and periodic payments that are made at least annually.

- Payments made under a Qualified Domestic Relations Order. This exception allows for retirement accounts to be settled and divided in the event of a divorce.

- Withdrawals for payments of medical care or the cost of insurance. For medical care, the medical expenses must be in an amount that is greater than the allowable medical expense deduction. The exception for insurance payments can cover expenses for insurance during periods of unemployment.

- Qualified educational expenses for CESA accounts.

- To buy, build, or rebuild a first home

- Distribution due to an IRS levy

- Distributions after the age of 59½

As you've learned, there are two basic types of retirement accounts. The first is the tax-deferred account such as a Traditional IRA, SEP

IRA, SIMPLE IRA or Traditional 401(k). The second account type is a Roth account, which is available as an IRA, 401(k) or Solo 401(k).

Traditional IRAs and similar tax-deferred accounts receive funds that are tax deductible at the time of the contribution. They grow tax-deferred and incur taxes, at the rate of ordinary income, when distributions are taken. Roth IRAs do not receive a tax deduction at the time the contributions are made but they grow tax-free and no taxes are due at the time of distribution.

Distribution Rules for Tax-Deferred Accounts

The taxes are incurred at the time of withdrawal when taking distributions from traditional accounts. As this creates a change in your tax situation, it is best is consult with your accountant or tax advisor regarding distributions. They will be able to consider all sources of income and advise a tax strategy that can keep the taxes to a minimum, while providing the income necessary to meet your retirement needs.

The other important consideration with tax-deferred accounts is at the age 70½, a Required Minimum Distribution (RMD) is required. At this point, even if the funds are not needed, distributions must be taken from the account each year based on the account balance. The IRS has a distribution formula that is used to determine how much must be withdrawn each year.

If the IRA holder has more than one IRA, the RMD can be taken from any of the accounts. This becomes important if some accounts have more liquid assets than others. The full RMD may be taken from one account, rather than having to liquidate an illiquid asset (such as real estate) held in another account. To accomplish this, the IRA owner must communicate with the IRA custodians so that the correct amount is distributed. If the full required distribution is not withdrawn, it may result in a 50-percent excise tax on the amount of RMD that was not taken.

Another step that must be completed each year is an assessment of the account value. When investments are in non-traditional investments there may not be an obvious threshold, such as a monthly account statement, that establishes a value for the account. Therefore, it is up to the account holder to determine the value of the account. Equity Trust can provide guidance as to which evaluation methods are acceptable to the IRS when establishing a value of investment holdings.

Distribution Rules for Roth Accounts

Roth accounts are established with after-tax contributions; therefore they have the benefit of tax-free growth. The advantage is seen during the distribution phase. Many investors find that they can balance withdrawals from the Roth tax-free account and the tax-deferred accounts to minimize the taxes owed. A tax advisor is the best resource for establishing what options are most advantageous for your personal tax circumstances.

Roth account contributions can be withdrawn at any time with no tax consequences and without an early withdrawal penalty, regardless of age. However, withdrawing the money before retirement does not give the account the opportunity to grow over time, as it would if the funds remained in the account. If no exception exists, all profits that were earned must remain in the account until the owner is 59½ or they will be subject to early withdrawal penalties.

Another important feature of the Roth IRA is that it requires a five-year seasoning period, regardless of age. This means that if an investor opens an account at the age of 60, the account owner must wait until age 65 to withdraw any gains without penalty.

A key advantage to the Roth IRA is that the funds will grow tax-free. Another is that there are no age limits on contributions or required minimum distributions, like there are for the Traditional IRA and other tax–deferred accounts. With a Traditional IRA, no contributions can be made after the age of 70½ and withdrawals must begin at this time. With the Roth, neither one of these restrictions apply.

Establishing Adequate Income

Retirement is when all your hard work and financial planning comes to fruition. It is time to set a retirement budget and determine where the income will come from. Meeting with a financial advisor can provide guidance during this decision making process and tax advisors, accountants and other retirement planners are also great resources. The process starts with determining your monthly cash flow needs, then reviewing your sources of income. You will need to determine when to take Social Security payments and what strategies can be used to maximize those payments. Social Security will likely provide the starting point for your income stream.

Evaluating other income streams outside of the retirement accounts might help to fill the gaps in your income needs. If you have passive income, such as a pension, interest payments, dividend income, CD income, or rental income, this will increase your cash flow. You should consider any income not inside your retirement accounts, but is paid in regular intervals. At this point you will have a clearer picture of how much money is coming in to replace your working income.

You may have a 401(k) from a former employer that can be rolled over into an IRA. As you plan, evaluate your total investment portfolio, how much can comfortably be withdrawn, and how long your money will last under the current investment structure. You shouldn't hold back in your planning and strategizing when it comes to withdrawals. The same diligence and care that was used in finding great investments should also be employed here.

Consider spreading distributions over both tax-deferred and tax-free accounts. This may help to minimize taxes. Establish a strategy that will preserve the investments and extend them as long as possible, while providing the income needs for your retirement. Often retirees can establish a strategy that will allow the bulk of the retirement funds to continue to grow, while liquidating some funds to use on the fun stuff you laid out for yourself at the beginning of this book.

It is also important to consider potential unexpected expenses such as healthcare costs, home repairs, travel expenses, and new hobbies that you might now have time to enjoy.

Planning for the distribution phase of retirement should be a meticulous but exciting process. Hopefully, you've been able to grow your portfolio over the years and, seeing the retirement you've dreamed of lay in front of you, can now enjoy the fruits of your labor with a confident and well-thought-out strategy.

Retirement Calculators

RMD Calculator – Determining how much you are required to withdraw is an important issue in retirement planning. Use this calculator to determine your Required Minimum Distributions:
https://www.trustetc.com/resources/tools/calculators/retir e-distrib

RMD and Stretch IRA Calculator – Use this calculator to help determine how you can stretch your payments for as long as possible:
https://www.trustetc.com/resources/tools/calculators/stret ch-ira

Retirement Planner with Retirement Earnings Calculator – Do you know what it takes to work towards a secure retirement? View your retirement savings balance and your withdrawals for each year until the end of your retirement. Social security is calculated on a sliding scale based on your income:
https://www.trustetc.com/resources/tools/calculators/retir ement-plan

Retirement Shortfall Calculator – One of the biggest risks to a comfortable retirement is running out of money too soon. This calculator helps you determine your projected shortfall or surplus at retirement and can also see how long your current retirement savings will last:
https://www.trustetc.com/resources/tools/calculators/retir e-short

---

Chapter 24: Building and Keeping Wealth for Generations to Come

Investing and building wealth are two phrases that are related, but are actually quite different. Investing generally focuses on a specific investment that will produce a certain rate of return, with the hope that through a series of savvy investments we can build wealth. Building wealth is a longer-term strategy and implies an abundance of valuable resources and riches. Successful investing does not necessarily equate to wealth. Many successful investors have squandered their earnings because they lost sight of the importance of building wealth. Wealth building requires a sophisticated and strategic management of your investments, your savings, your taxes and your estate as a whole.

Building Wealth

Saving and investing is not the same thing. The process of saving sets money aside. It represents living within your means and storing extra money for unexpected expenses or future goals. Investing is the act of taking those savings and putting them in an investment vehicle that is thoughtful and with the hope you'll grow your savings. As investment gains are realized, and compounded, wealth is built.

Building wealth implies a long-term vision that is accomplished through wise investments. Wealth is generally not gained through lottery winnings or get-rich-quick schemes, but is obtained through prudent investments. The first step to building wealth is to earn more than you spend. Setting money aside each month will help create savings. From there, an investment strategy can be developed to build wealth.

Letting investments work for you and then re-investing the gains will allow you to take advantage of compound interest. This is the most powerful way to build wealth. For example, if you invest in a real estate property, rehab the unit and then resell it, you may have gains from this investment. Taking the profit, adding it to the initial investment and doing it again can result in additional growth. This process of repeating success allows wealth to build upon itself.

Investing within an IRA provides incentive to leave the contributions and the profits within the account to compound tax-free or tax-deferred. For example, having a rental property outside of an IRA makes it much easier to spend the rental income rather than re-investing it into additional properties that could bring additional returns and further compound growth.

Essentially the key component of wealth building is the verb in the phrase – *build*. Building wealth requires an active focus and strategic actions to ensure wealth continues to build. Think of it this way – saving implies a finite amount of money that continues to dwindle as the savings are used whereas wealth building implies continued growth that compounds and continues to work for you, even as you begin to live off what you've accumulated. Thus, the goal should be on wealth building as opposed to simply saving.

Keeping Wealth through Retirement

When it's time to retire there are important questions regarding how the money will be distributed. Aging presents many unknown factors that must be considered. No one knows how long you will live and how healthy you will be. Good financial planning that begins in your twenties, thirties, forties or even fifties can help provide solutions to account for unknown contingencies. It is much easier to acquire products such as life insurance, long-term care or disability insurance at a younger age. These steps can help prepare for life's unexpected events that may happen during your retirement, without using funds that are earmarked for living expenses or enjoyment.

The other aspect of maintaining wealth and extending it is to invest in instruments that create cash flow. Cash flowing investments leave the core investment intact. They create a passive income stream that can be enjoyed during retirement, while the principal investment is untouched. This strategy can help preserve income so even if you live to be 120 and are the oldest person alive, there can still be funds to pay for your living expenses and care. The other thing this strategy does is provide the opportunity to leave a legacy to your family.

Legacy Planning

Legacy planning can provide money to pay for your grandchildren's college expenses, leave retirement nest eggs for your children, or provide the ability to leave funds to a favorite charity, school, or other organization.

> ### Video: Legacy IRA Investing
>
> Join us for a 15-minute segment from an Investor Insights webinar that discusses several strategies you can implement to potentially begin building wealth for your entire family. Set up or log in to your user account to watch it below:
>
> https://equityuniversity.customerhub.net/legacy

Well-thought-out legacy planning can provide structure and guidance to your heirs that cannot be obtained through an inheritance. Unfortunately, 70 percent of the average inheritance is spent by the end of the second generation and 90 percent has evaporated by the end of the third generation.[25] This means all the hard work and wealth building can be gone in a very short time if planning is not a part of the legacy and estate plan.

Asset Protection

One of the most significant protections that assets within an IRA receive is the protection from bankruptcy proceedings. Investments in IRAs and 401(k)s are protected from creditors and are not considered as an asset in the event of bankruptcy. It is important to note that IRAs inherited from someone other than a spouse do not enjoy this high level of protection. The rules around protection from creditors, lawsuits, and judgments outside of bankruptcy vary depending on the state you live.

Webinar: Understanding Asset Protection

Equity University is joined by Lee Phillips, an Attorney and nationally recognized author and speaker in the area of asset protection, for this 25-minute webinar about asset protection and how it relates to an IRA. Lee has held licenses in real estate, mortgage brokering, securities and life insurance, as well as a Registered Investment Advisor. Lee is nationally recognized in the fields of business structuring, asset protection, financial planning and estate planning. Set up or log in to your user account to watch the webinar:

https://equityuniversity.customerhub.net/asset-protection

Estate Planning

No one likes to think about their mortality, but a lack of planning can leave your loved ones with a financial mess and substantially

---

[25] Sullivan, M. & Parmar, N. (2013, March 8). Lost Inheritance: Studies show Americans blow through family fortunes and remarkable rate. With trillions being passed on, can today's baby boomers break the cycle?. Retrieved from http://online.wsj.com/articles/SB10001424127887324662404578334663271139552

increases the cost of settling your estate. Who really wants all their hard-earned money to be enjoyed by attorneys instead of family members? And who wants to put their family through a turbulent probate process when they should be supporting one another?

It is a common misconception that estate planning is only for the wealthy. In general, everyone should have a basic estate plan. This plan should include a will, a power of attorney, and a living will or health care proxy. These documents provide basic instructions for loved ones in the event you die or are incapacitated. There are three basic ways for your assets to be transferred on your death: the will, which is the standard method; the living trust, which offers some advantages over a will; and beneficiary designations, for assets such as life insurance and IRAs.

Another big misconception about estate planning is that trusts are only for the wealthy. A trust essentially allows you to put conditions on the inheritance. The primary difference between a will and a living trust is assets placed in your living trust, except in rare circumstances, avoid probate at your death. Because probate is time-consuming, potentially expensive and public, avoiding probate is a common estate planning goal. Trusts can be a very useful tool for many estates, regardless of size. The money earmarked for the estate will be placed into a trust and then distributed according to instructions you provided. This can prevent young children from obtaining a large inheritance that they do not have the skills to manage. It can prevent others from taking advantage of the person inheriting money and it can protect handicapped children and provide for their well-being.

Meeting with an estate planner, attorney or financial planner is the best way to get started. Take an inventory of your assets and think about how you want them distributed. Then, set a plan that will allow your hard-earned money to be directed in the way that you are most comfortable. The three fundamental questions you should ask yourself when considering your estate are: *Who should inherit my assets? Which assets should they inherit?* and *When and how should they inherit the assets?*

Beneficiaries

Beneficiaries might include spouses, children or grandchildren as well as charitable organizations, universities and other organizations to which families leave money. The manner in which you leave an inheritance to a beneficiary is extremely important.

Every account should have a beneficiary. This should include IRAs, 401(k)s, insurance policies, CDs and every account that offers the option to name a beneficiary. If your estate includes a trust, the attorney who established the estate plan will direct you on how to name the beneficiary so that the funds will end up as you intended. Although it is wise to revisit your estate plan throughout your life, it is especially important to do so when major life changes occur.

Personal or family changes such as marriages, divorces, births, adoptions and deaths can all lead to the need for estate plan modifications. An increase in income and net worth is another time to revisit your estate plan because what may have been appropriate when your income and net worth were lower may no longer be effective today. Anytime you move geographically, such as from one state to another, you should review your estate plan since laws vary by state and can affect your estate plan. Finally, new health-related conditions may require an update to your estate plan. A child may develop special needs due to physical or mental limitations or a surviving spouse's ability to earn a living may change because of a disability.

Other areas that require thoughtful planning and potential insurance options include business ownership and real estate. Since these are not easily liquidated, arranging for their transfer is an important part of estate planning. This will ensure that the business and real estate can be operated by the heirs, if desired, rather than sold. Often investors will purchase life insurance to cover expenses involved in the estate settlement and enable the business to continue operations without interruption. Having transfer instructions and legacy planning helps ease this process.

Building Wealth for Children and Grandchildren

Every family is unique and many want to leave their children a legacy. This legacy is more than just money – it should include a legacy of financial responsibility and planning. Our society does not provide the financial education of our children as well as it should. It falls on families and parents to impart their knowledge to their children and educate them on how to build their own wealth.

Some of this can occur through conversation, but one of the most powerful ways to impart a financial education on children is through direct experience. As a result, some investors find that involving their children, and even their grandchildren, in their investments or self-directed IRA holdings is a great way to teach them how to build their own wealth.

One strategy that can be employed is to create Roth IRAs for children and grandchildren. Most people are unaware that children can have a retirement plan, but it is possible as long as they have earned income. Putting children to work doing research online, stuffing envelopes or otherwise helping the business can provide them with income that, in turn, can be invested in an IRA. Using your children's photos to advertise for your business and paying them royalties is another way to provide earned income and contribute to their retirement or educational accounts. This enables a family to fund a Roth IRA that can be used to pay for future educational expenses or left to grow tax-free until the child needs it. This strategy can offer tax-free income for their entire life, along with the financial skills necessary for success.

<u>Investing…Family Style</u>

Unsatisfied with some of her past retirement saving strategies, Equity Trust client, Jan, has been helping her daughter take control of her own financial situation for several years now. So far, so good: Jan predicts that if her daughter Brittany stays on pace, she will retire a multi-millionaire.

Jan has been successful buying, fixing up and selling high-end real estate in the suburbs of St. Louis and Los Angeles for decades, but she admitted that she made some bad choices when it came to her retirement saving strategy. She heard about self-directed IRAs decades ago, but it wasn't until 2008 – when she lost an unsettling amount of money in the stock market – that she decided to seriously research them.

"I decided it was time to take control of my IRA...I converted everything (in my retirement account) to a Roth IRA when the account balance was at its lowest."

Jan focused her investments in the area in which she has more than 25 years experience. "My business is real estate, so I understand it very well," she says. "My expertise is in renovating houses — finding properties, hiring contractors, making decisions and selling properties."

Ever since she can remember, Brittany has enjoyed helping her mom with the business. That interest only grew when she was 13 and Jan and her husband Gary gave Brittany a check for the work she'd done for her mom.

Brittany recalls her first thought was, "This is a lot of money...I'm going to go shopping!" That's probably what a lot of teens would have done. But when her parents introduced her to another option, Brittany realized a new level of excitement. With the help of her parents, Brittany opened a Roth IRA and partnered the money in it with her parents' accounts to buy two houses.

Brittany smiled, saying, "I enjoy being able to go see homes, help out with contractors and give opinions on things; it's a great learning experience...it's what I want to do when I'm older."

Brittany began learning to budget her money when she was in fifth grade. "Before the budget, my mom and I would go into a store and it was a game to see if I could get her to buy things for me," she says. This helped Brittany develop her negotiation skills, but little else. Now her mom works as her consultant and Brittany makes all the decisions and enters her transactions in a phone app to track her income and expenses.

Whether children are in fifth grade or in college, investing isn't out of the question, Jan says.

"People think later in life, 'it's too late for me.' If they have teenage kids or even a one-year-old, you could get them into IRA investing," Jan says, adding, "For example, you could put their picture on your website and give them a $5,000 fee for the photo to deposit in their IRA at age one. It makes perfect sense to get them started early."

Jan says that some of her investments achieve returns as high as 40 percent and knows that with the power of compound interest, Brittany's early start will have a huge impact on her financial future. "Even if she only makes half that (40 percent), a 20-percent return, she'll have oodles of millions of dollars by the time she is able to start withdrawing funds at age 59½," Jan says. "It's fun to run the numbers with her and inspire her in that way."

Since, they've made investing a family project. Here's one example of the effect Brittany's small role in an investment can have on her financial future.

In February 2013 the family used their Roth IRAs to buy and renovate a single-family home in St. Louis County.

- IRA funding source: Gary's IRA (65 percent), Jan's IRA (30 percent), and Brittany's IRA (5 percent).

- Purchase price: $132,500

- Sale price in July 2013: $349,000

- Profit after all expenses (renovation, commission, property taxes, utility and other expenses): $80,000 tax-free profit back into the IRAs

- Bottom line for Brittany's account: Her contribution was $9,800, or 5 percent. A 5-percent portion of the total $80,000 profit was $4,000. Her IRA increased in value by 40 percent from February to July, taking her balance from $9,800 to $13,800.

Time is Brittany's most powerful ally, especially when it comes to the compound interest she's earning tax-free in her account. By involving her in the investment process early, Gary and Jan are setting their daughter up for a lifetime of financial success – both with the ROI on her investments and the ROI on the knowledge she's gained along the way.

Video: Investing, Family Style

One Equity Trust client, along with two parent/daughter client duos, share how anyone can advance the principles of wealth building to their children and future generations in a 44-minute video presentation. They detail how they've decided to not only involve their children in their investing, but how their children are learning to take the reins for their own financial future. Set up or log in to your user account to watch it now:

https://equityuniversity.customerhub.net/family

Chapter 25: Getting Started – Selecting a Custodian

Now that you have seen the advantages of investing with a self-directed IRA, you must choose a custodian before you get started. As self-directed IRAs are becoming more popular, many companies are beginning to offer IRA custodial or administrative services. According to the IRS code, a custodian must be a bank, credit union, savings and loan company, or a company that is licensed and regulated by the IRS to act as an IRA custodian. This regulatory oversight is meant to protect investors. Essentially, a non-bank custodian must go through much of the same regulatory oversight that a bank does to ensure customers' money and assets are safe and handled properly.

Differences between a Custodian and an Administrator

A self-directed IRA custodian is regulated. Administrators do not have the same regulatory oversight and, as a result, they cannot hold assets and most cannot issue funds to the investor. Their focus is in the marketing and promotion of self-directed IRAs. They can provide basic administrative services, such as statements, but must partner with a custodian for all other services. This extra layer can cause delays in the funding of projects and the accounts do not offer the same level of security as a self-directed IRA custodian's account.

A self-directed IRA custodian is able to hold titles to assets and issue funds via check or wire transfer to fund investment opportunities as directed by the investor. Custodians are subject to regulatory oversight and are required to conduct both internal and external audits to ensure the soundness of their business practice. All of these checks and balances provide a safety net for the investor and ensure that the accounts are maintained appropriately.

Important Considerations and Questions When Choosing a Custodian

By definition, the self-directed IRA custodian must act as a passive custodian to a self-directed IRA. This means a custodian cannot offer investment advice, tax advice or otherwise make recommendations to investors as to how they should invest their funds. The self-directed IRA is exactly that: self-directed by the owner of the IRA.

Yet a custodian can provide a wealth of educational and procedural knowledge and experience that can simplify the process for investors. It can provide education about investment options and provide valuable resources to assist investors with their decision-making processes.

A few questions to ask a custodian when evaluating where to open an account include:

- What kind of transactions can you handle? How flexible are you with unique transactions?

- Can you hold title for the assets I want to invest in, in the state where the asset is located?

- What is the typical turnaround time for executing investment instructions?

- How experienced is your staff? Your administrators?

- What training do you offer your staff?

- Do you offer ongoing education to investors?

- How long have you been in business?

- Is your company involved in current, pending, or ongoing litigation?

- Where do you go for tough questions?

- Can you provide automatic sweeps?

- How are the fees structured?

- Can I access the account online? Make account changes and submit orders online?

- Is the company audited? Internally or by a third party? How often?

Selecting a custodian is a very important decision. Investors should look at the whole package a custodian is offering to determine which company will be the best fit for the investments they have in mind.

We are a very fee-conscious society and it is easy to make decisions based solely on fees. Every custodian will charge fees because they must be able to operate their business and complete all of the regulatory requirements mandated by the IRS. When you compare fees between multiple institutions, look at both annual fees and transaction fees. Are there hidden administrative costs that are included? Are you charged for every movement of the account? Some companies charge a fee every time an investment is bought or sold. Others charge an annual fee and then provide necessary services for all account transactions. Some custodians offer additional services such as UBIT 990-T filings. Evaluate the services you will need, both today and in the future. As you gain experience you may wish to invest in more sophisticated deals that require additional services. You must make sure the company meets your needs as your confidence and expertise grow.

Education may be one of the most important features a company offers. It is one thing to find a YouTube video to learn how to invest in tax liens or Forex accounts, but it is another to have confidence that the education is credible. Finding a company that provides written information, in addition to live guidance from experienced personnel, will make a large difference in your ability to execute successful investments.

The Equity Trust Difference

Experience. Equity Trust was one of the first companies in the United States dedicated to self-directed IRA custodial services. With 40 years' experience and more than 130,000 accounts from all 50 states, Equity Trust Company is a leading custodian of self-directed IRAs.

Our number one goal is to offer investors the opportunity to create tax-free growth through education, innovation and our commitment to customer service.

Investment diversity. Equity Trust offers a great deal of investment flexibility regarding which investments can be executed. In addition to permitting stocks, bonds and mutual funds, Equity Trust self-directed IRAs provide investors the ability to find creative investment opportunities that operate within the IRS guidelines. Within these guidelines there are unique opportunities for investors to gain profits from areas of interest and expertise. These investments can include real estate, tax liens, oil and gas, precious metals, options, hedge funds, private money opportunities and more.

Safety and security. Equity Trust is a custodian that meets the IRS guidelines and complies with all regulatory requirements to ensure the investors' money and assets are held appropriately. We are also subject to internal and external audits. All of these procedures are done to protect our clients' assets.

Continuing education. Equity Trust offers an extensive knowledge library that provides resources from experts across the industry. This enables customers to gain knowledge and complete appropriate due diligence for the investment they are seeking. This information is presented in an objective manner so the investor can make choices based on accurate and unbiased information.

Easy to work with. As a pioneer in the industry, Equity Trust has been able to streamline and perfect processes. This enables us to execute instructions and wire funds in a fast and efficient manner. We offer top-of-the-line online resources that provide investors with a complete array of online tools to manage their accounts. We also offer a service team that is a phone call away and can assist with any account questions.

Unbeatable value. Equity Trust offers a simple to understand fee structure. The fee schedule is all-inclusive, allowing investors to be active with their accounts without constantly paying additional fees for basic services. We also offer advanced services when they are needed for specific account features and IRS filings.

Equity Trust is focused on providing the services that are most valuable to clients. This has enabled us to gain a reputation for being a trusted company that leads the industry. It has also lead to recognition by organizations *such as The New York Times, Bloomberg, Forbes, Investor's Business Daily, Smart Money, Fortune,* and *The Wall Street Journal.*

Let us work for you.

Videos: Hear Directly from some of Equity Trust's Clients

You can hear from some of our satisfied clients as they detail how they got started with self-directed IRAs and the role Equity Trust has played in their financial future.

In this short 5-minute video, our clients will share their success stories and how Equity Trust has helped them take control of their financial future.

In this 2-minute video, Tami from Ohio, shares why she decided to open a self-directed IRA with Equity Trust and details the change it has made in her life.

In this short 1-minute video, Pat from New York, shares her self-directed IRA investing experiences.

In just 44 seconds Steve, a client from Ohio, shares how self-directed IRAs have changed the course of his retirement.

You can hear from more Equity Trust clients on our YouTube channel by using the link below:

https://youtu.be/QnnXb6kP-2s?list=PL5E7F4BF2E6424ACD

Chapter 26: Time to Take Control of Your Financial Future

The hardest step in any decision is the first step. You are stepping into the unknown and this can create a level of fear. We understand that, and with one phone call can get you started with confidence. Our experienced representatives can guide you through the account set up process and help you along the way. There are hundreds of thousands of investors who have taken their first step and never looked back. As they have watched their portfolios grow, it has enabled them to reach their financial goals much faster than they ever thought possible.

At the beginning of this book we discussed setting goals, understanding where you are financially and where you need to go. Re-examine those goals and select one investment option that you will commit to learning about.

If there is an old 401(k) from a previous employer, or an IRA currently at a bank or other financial institution, you already have the funds needed to start enabling that money to work harder for you. It does not have to be an all-or-nothing decision. Select a percentage of your existing portfolio and invest it in a self-directed option. Once you see the profits from your labors, additional investments can be added to the account over time.

If you do not have an IRA or other retirement funds already established, now is the time to get started. The longer you have for money to grow, the better and earlier retirement you can enjoy. Set a budget that allows you to pay yourself first. With the dwindling pensions and uncertainty of the Social Security system, there is no time like the present to take your retirement and put it in your own hands to secure your financial future.

It is simple to open an account and make monthly contributions to the account. Any cash funds will be held in FDIC-insured accounts until you are ready to invest. If you are just getting started, consider some of the options that do not require a lot of cash. This might include working to find opportunities and then borrowing money from other investors who do not have the time to find the deals. It can also include options like tax liens, mobile homes, or raw land, which do not require as much capital.

If you are married or have children, it is possible to increase contributions to build the accounts more quickly, providing a wider range of investment options. Combining resources can help everyone in your family gain the benefits of a safe and secure retirement. Parents and grandparents can be included in securing their financial future as well.

Whatever option suits your circumstances, the sooner you get started the faster you will begin to enjoy the benefits of self-directed IRA investing.

To your success.

Schedule Your FREE, No Obligation Retirement Consultation

If you'd like a personalized Retirement Consultation to ask questions and find out how self-directed investing could work for you, please use the following to schedule a time that works for you:

www.trustetc.com/consult

Video: How to Set up a Self-Directed IRA

In this 3-minute animated video you will learn the simple process of opening and establishing a self-directed IRA at Equity Trust. It overviews the account open and self-directed investment process in an entertaining and easy-to-understand format:

https://www.youtube.com/watch?v=bHX4P9eOdS8

Introducing the *Jumpstart to Financial Freedom* Interactive, Online Home Study Course

Equity University recently launched brand-new education designed to help self-directed investors and prospective investors understand the important aspects of self-directed IRA investing. To learn more and access the course, please visit the course's webpage:

http://bestiracourse.com/

Contact Us for More Information

Website: www.trustetc.com

Physical Address for Corporate Headquarters:

1 Equity Way
Westlake, OH 44145

Official mailing address:

P.O. Box 451340
Westlake, OH 44145

Phone: 1-888-ETC-IRAS (1-888-382-4727)

Email: help@trustetc.com

Fax: 440-366-3750

Customer Service Hours:

Monday – Friday
9:00am – 6:00pm, Eastern Standard Time

About the Author

Richard Desich, Sr. has been involved in the securities industry for over 35 years. In addition to being the Founder and Chairman of the Board of Equity Trust Company, a leading self-directed IRA custodian, he also founded Retirement Education Group. He is nationally recognized as a pre-eminent authority on commercial and residential real estate, oil and gas investing and non-traditional investing in IRAs and qualified plans.

Mr. Desich is also the author of the informative book, *Proven Wealth Building Secrets for You and Your Children* and the former host of *Accelerated Wealth Building*, a three-day intensive boot camp.

Mr. Desich has published numerous articles regarding the use of self-directed IRAs to invest in real estate, notes and mortgages, and he has spoken to thousands of investors throughout the country on these topics.

Available Resources

Equity University delivers innovative education and resources to help investors create lasting wealth. From insightful articles to step-by-step case studies to online education presentations, Equity University is the ultimate self-directed investing resource. Various resources, reports and videos were referenced throughout the book and can be found below.

Chapter	Page #	Resource	Access Link
Instructions	iv	Website: Setting up your free account	https://uz966.infusionsoft.com/app/page/ebook-resources
Foreword	xii	Video: The Equity Trust Difference	https://equityuniversity.customerhub.net/equity-trust
Introduction	xvii	Calculators: Retirement Income & Retirement Distributions	https://www.trustetc.com/resources/tools/calculators/retirement-income https://www.trustetc.com/resources/tools/calculators/retirement-distribution
Introduction	xxii	Website: U.S. Debt Clock	http://www.usdebtclock.org/

Chapter 1	pg 8	Webinar: Small-Dollar Opportunities for Self-Directed IRA Investors	https://equityuniversity.cust omerhub.net/small-dollar
Chapter 5	pg 61	Website: Updated Contribution Limits	https://www.trustetc.com/c ontributions
Chapter 5	pg 68	Calculators: Compound Interest & Investment Return	https://www.trustetc.com/r esources/tools/calculators/i nvestment-return https://www.trustetc.com/r esources/tools/calculators/ compound-interest
Chapter 6	pg 79	Website: Resource Calculator Directory	https://www.trustetc.com/r esources/tools/calculators
Chapter 7	pg 86	Infographic: How Does a SDIRA Investment Work?	https://equityuniversity.cust omerhub.net/process
Chapter 7	pg 88	YouTube Video: Self-Directed IRA Rules & Regulations	https://youtu.be/_bj_gzjuN jY

Chapter 8	pg 101	Webinar: Maximizing Your IRA with Rehab Investing	https://equityuniversity.customerhub.net/rehab1
Chapter 8	pg 101	Webinar: "How I've Turned Real Estate into Pots of Gold in my IRA"	https://equityuniversity.customerhub.net/rehab2
Chapter 9	pg 112	Audio: Real Estate Client Panel	https://equityuniversity.customerhub.net/real-estate-panel
Chapter 11	pg 128	Webinar: Investing in Commercial Real Estate with your Self-Directed IRA	https://equityuniversity.customerhub.net/commercial
Chapter 12	pg 135	2-Part Webinar Series: Discover the Investment Potential in Tax Liens and Tax Deeds	https://equityuniversity.customerhub.net/liens
Chapter 13	pg 146	Audio: Finding Wealth in Raw Land	https://equityuniversity.customerhub.net/land

Chapter 13	pg 146	Audio: "How I've Profited from Land Contracts"	https://equityuniversity.customerhub.net/land-contract
Chapter 13	pg 146	Webinar: How Natural Resources Can Fuel Your Retirement	https://equityuniversity.customerhub.net/fuel
Chapter 14	pg 154	Webinar: Self-Directed IRA Note Investing	https://equityuniversity.customerhub.net/notes
Chapter 15	pg 160	Audio: Profiting from Probate Properties	https://equityuniversity.customerhub.net/probate
Chapter 17	pg 174	Audio: Precious Metals Investing Panel	https://equityuniversity.customerhub.net/metals
Chapter 18	pg 180	Audio: Private Equity Investing	https://equityuniversity.customerhub.net/equity
Chapter 18	pg 180	Audio: The Wide World of REITs 101	https://equityuniversity.customerhub.net/reits
Chapter 19	pg 185	Webinar: How to Purchase Real Estate in an IRA with a Loan	https://equityuniversity.customerhub.net/non-recourse

Chapter 19	pg 189	Website: UBIT Professional	http://www.ubitprofessional.com/
Chapter 19	pg 191	Webinar: Secrets to Private Money Lending	https://equityuniversity.customerhub.net/lending
Chapter 19	pg 194	Webinar: Discover How 3 Clients Created Successful Returns Using Multiple Self-Directed IRAs	https://equityuniversity.customerhub.net/multiple-accounts
Chapter 20	pg 200	Website: Updated Contribution Limits	https://www.trustetc.com/contributions
Chapter 20	pg 202	Video: Self-Directed IRA Rules and Regulations from an ERISA Attorney	https://youtu.be/XENmSrSfB3E
Chapter 21	pg 209	PDFs: RITA Check Before You Invest Due Diligence Checklist and List of Questions	https://equityuniversity.customerhub.net/due-diligence

Chapter 22	pg 216	Website: SEC Investor Alert	http://www.sec.gov/investor/pubs/affinity.htm
Chapter 22	pg 216	Website: SEC Investor Bulletin	http://investor.gov/news-alerts/affinity-fraud
Chapter 22	pg 217	FBI Website: Types of Fraud and Scams	https://www.fbi.gov/scams-safety/fraud
Chapter 22	pg 219-220	Resources and Organizations to Check for Fraud	Investor.gov – http://www.investor.gov/investing-basics/avoiding-fraud NASAA.org – http://www.nasaa.org/2815/nasaa-fraud-center/ FINRA.org – http://www.finra.org/investors/protect-your-money SaveandInvest.org – http://www.saveandinvest.org/ AARP – http://www.aarp.org/money/scams-fraud/

			RITA – http://www.ritaus.org/senior-fraud-initiative
			Securities and Exchange Commission – http://www.sec.gov/complaint/tipscomplaint.shtml
			Internal Revenue Service – http://www.irs.gov/uac/Tax-Scams-Consumer-Alerts
			InvestorProtection.org – http://www.investorprotection.org/protect-yourself/
Chapter 22	pg 220-221	Website: To Check a Specific…	Broker or firm – http://www.finra.org/brokercheck
			Investment advisor – http://www.adviserinfo.sec.gov/
			A broker, investment advisor, or investment – http://www.nasaa.org/
			Insurance agent – http://www.naic.org/

			Commodities/futures/foreign exchange dealer – http://www.nfa.futures.org/basicnet An investment – http://www.sec.gov/edgar.shtml or http://www.investor.gov/
Chapter 22	pg 221	Website: To take your name off solicitation lists	http://www.donotcall.gov/ http://www.dmachoice.org/ http://www.optoutprescreen.com/ http://www.networkadvertising.org/
Chapter 22	pg 222	Website: Reporting Fraud and Scams	**FINRA Complaints and Tips** www.finra.org/complaint www.finra.org/fileatip **U.S. Securities and Exchange Commission (SEC) Office of Investor Education and Advocacy** Phone: 800-732-0330 Fax: 202-772-9295 Email: enforcement@sec.gov www.sec.gov/complaint.shtml

			State Securities Regulator North American Securities Administrators Association Phone: 202-737-0900 Email: cyberfraud@nasaa.org www.nasaa.org Contact Your Local Regulator – http://www.nasaa.org/about-us/contact-us/contact-your-regulator/ **U.S. Commodity Futures Trading Commission (CFTC)** **Office of Cooperative Enforcement** Phone: 866-366-2382 www.cftc.gov/tiporcomplaint **Federal Bureau of Investigation (FBI)** https://www.fbi.gov or contact your local office – https://www.fbi.gov/contact-us/field **Better Business Bureau (BBB)** http://www.bbb.org/

Chapter 22	pg 223	PDF and Video: FINRA Save and Invest Fraud Prevention Resources	PDF: http://www.saveandinvest.org/file/document/fighting-fraud-101 DVD: You can order a FREE DVD copy from FINRA by calling 866-973-4672 or online at: http://74.121.201.86/FinraSAINew/
Chapter 23	pg 230	Calculators: RMDs, RMD and Stretch IRA, Retirement Planner with Retirement Earnings & Retirement Shortfall	https://www.trustetc.com/resources/tools/calculators/retire-distrib https://www.trustetc.com/resources/tools/calculators/stretch-ira https://www.trustetc.com/resources/tools/calculators/retirement-plan https://www.trustetc.com/resources/tools/calculators/retire-short
Chapter 24	pg 233	Video: Legacy IRA Investing	https://equityuniversity.customerhub.net/legacy
Chapter 24	pg 234	Webinar: Understanding Asset Protection	https://equityuniversity.customerhub.net/asset-protection
Chapter 24	pg 240	Video: Investing, Family Style	https://equityuniversity.customerhub.net/family

Chapter 25	pg 246	YouTube Videos: Equity Trust Client Reviews and Experiences	Multiple Clients: https://youtu.be/_MT5EA ZTNes?list=PL5E7F4BF2E 6424ACD Tami from Ohio: https://youtu.be/AMKziV-kCxU?list=PL5E7F4BF2E6 424ACD Pat from New York: https://youtu.be/NiDSz3r NhPo?list=PL5E7F4BF2E6 424ACD Steve from Ohio: https://youtu.be/j8x0Hh81 eBE?list=PL5E7F4BF2E64 24ACD YouTube page: https://youtu.be/QnnXb6k P-2s?list=PL5E7F4BF2E6424 ACD
Chapter 26	pg 249	Schedule a FREE Retirement Consultation	https://www.trustetc.com/consult
Chapter 26	pg 249	Video: How to Set up a Self-Directed IRA	https://www.youtube.com/watch?v=bHX4P9eOdS8
Chapter 26	pg 250	Jumpstart to Financial Freedom Education Course	http://bestiracourse.com/

Richard Desich, Sr.

Footnotes/References

1. Statistics Brain. (2015, September 8). Retirement Statistics. 2015 Statistic Brain Research Institute, publishing as Statistic Brain. Retrieved from http://www.statisticbrain.com/retirement-statistics/

2. United States Social Security Administration. (July 2015). Benefits awarded – time series for all benefit types. Retrieved from http://www.ssa.gov/cgi-bin/awards.cgi

3. Moneynews. (2014, October 29). 5 Shocking Retirement Facts. Retrieved from http://www.moneynews.com/MKTNews/Retirement-Financial-Crisis/2013/07/08/id/513815/

4. DeSilver, D. (2013, October 16). 5 Facts About Social Security. Retrieved from http://www.pewresearch.org/fact-tank/2013/10/16/5-facts-about-social-security/

5. Social Security and Medicare Boards of Trustees. (2015). A Summary of the 2015 Annual Reports. Retrieved from http://www.ssa.gov/oact/trsum/

6. US Debt Clock. (2015). Retrieved from http://www.usdebtclock.org/

7. Internal Revenue Service. (2014, October 31). National Taxpayer Advocate Delivers Annual Report to Congress; Focuses on IRS Funding and Taxpayer Rights. Retrieved from http://www.irs.gov/uac/National-Taxpayer-Advocate-Delivers-Annual-Report-to-Congress;-Focuses-on-IRS-Funding-and-Taxpayer-Rights

8. HealthView Services Financial. (2015). 2015 Retirement Health Care Costs Data Report. Retrieved from https://www.hvsfinancial.com/PublicFiles/Data_Release.pdf

9. Wadsworth, G. H. (2012, June 14). Sky Rocketing College Costs. Retrieved from http://inflationdata.com/Inflation/Inflation_Articles/Education_Inflation.asp

10. Herships, S. (2014, September 16). Rising numbers of seniors are paying off student loans. Retrieved from http://www.marketplace.org/topics/wealth-poverty/rising-numbers-seniors-are-paying-student-loans

11. Shiller, R. & Standard and Poors. (2015). S&P Earnings History. MacroTrends. Retrieved from http://www.macrotrends.net/1324/s-p-500-earnings-history

12. Schaeffer's Investment Research. (2013, December 30). History Suggests Dow's Bull Run Still Has Legs. Retrieved from http://www.forbes.com/sites/greatspeculations/2013/12/30/history-suggests-dows-bull-run-still-has-legs/

13. Alternative Investment. (n.d.). In Investopedia Dictionary online. Retrieved from http://www.investopedia.com/terms/a/alternative_investment.asp

14. Morgan Stanley Wealth Management. (2014, February 6). Millionaire Investors Name Real Estate as Most Popular Alternative Asset Class by Wide Margin. Retrieved from http://www.morganstanley.com/about-us-articles/404f321a-29ad-438c-afab-ff18ceb302ac.html

15. U.S. Small Business Administration Office of Advocacy. (2014, March). Frequently Asked Questions about Small Business. Retrieved from https://www.sba.gov/sites/default/files/FAQ_March_2014_0.pdf

16. Harmon, K. (2015, June 15). Invest Local. The Huffington Post. Retrieved from http://www.huffingtonpost.com/kevin-harmon/invest-local_b_7586582.html

17. Crippen, A. (2012, February 27). Warren Buffett on CNBC: I'd Buy Up 'A Couple Hundred Thousand' Single-Family Homes If I Could. Retrieved from http://www.cnbc.com/id/46538421

18. New York University Leonard N. Stern School of Business. (2014, January 5). Annual Returns on Stock, T. Bonds and T. Bills: 1928 – Current [Data file]. Retrieved from http://pages.stern.nyu.edu/~adamodar/New_Home_Page/datafile/histretSP.html

19. Erzan, O., MacAlpine, K., & Szmolyan, N. (2012, June). The Mainstreaming of Alternative Investments: Fueling the Next Wave of Growth in Asset Management. Retrieved from http://www.mckinsey.com/insights/financial_services/how_alternative_investments_are_going_mainstream

20. Vardy, N. A. (2013, October 15). How to invest like Harvard and Yale. Retrieved from http://www.marketwatch.com/story/how-to-invest-like-harvard-and-yale-2013-10-15?page=1

21. Investment Company Institute. (2015, March 31). The U.S. Retirement Market, First Quarter 2015. Retrieved from https://www.ici.org/research/stats/retirement/ret_15_q1

22. Holden, S., Ireland, K., Leonard-Chambers, V., & Bogdan, M. (2005, February). The Individual Retirement Account at Age 30: A Retrospective. Investment Company Institute Perspective, 11. Retrieved from https://www.ici.org/pdf/per11-01.pdf

23. Cussen, M. P. (2013, June 13). Investing in Property Tax Liens. Retrieved from http://www.investopedia.com/articles/investing/061313/investing-property-tax-liens.asp

24. FINRA Investor Education Foundation. (2014, June). Fighting Fraud 101: Smart Tips for Investors. Retrieved from http://www.saveandinvest.org/file/document/fighting-fraud-101

25. Sullivan, M. & Parmar, N. (2013, March 8). Lost Inheritance: Studies show Americans blow through family fortunes and remarkable rate. With trillions being passed on, can today's baby boomers break the cycle?. Retrieved from http://online.wsj.com/articles/SB10001424127887324662404578334663271139552